The publisher gratefully acknowledges
the generous contributions to this book provided by the following:

The Grimshaw-Gudewicz Fund of the Department of Classics,
the Royce Family Fund in Teaching Excellence,
and the Program in Ancient Studies at Brown University

The Magie Fund of the Department of Classics at Princeton University

The Classical Literature Endowment Fund
of the University of California Press Foundation,
which is supported by a major gift from Joan Palevsky

Origins of Democracy in Ancient Greece

Origins of Democracy in Ancient Greece

Kurt A. Raaflaub, Josiah Ober,
and Robert W. Wallace

With chapters by
Paul Cartledge and Cynthia Farrar

UNIVERSITY OF CALIFORNIA PRESS
Berkeley   Los Angeles   London

University of California Press, one of the most distinguished
university presses in the United States, enriches lives around
the world by advancing scholarship in the humanities, social
sciences, and natural sciences. Its activities are supported by
the UC Press Foundation and by philanthropic contributions
from individuals and institutions. For more information, visit
www.ucpress.edu.

University of California Press
Berkeley and Los Angeles, California

University of California Press, Ltd.
London, England

Library of Congress Cataloging-in-Publication Data

Raaflaub, Kurt A.
      Origins of democracy in ancient Greece / Kurt A. Raaflaub,
Josiah Ober, and Robert W. Wallace ; with chapters by Paul Cartledge
and Cynthia Farrar.
      p.   cm.
   Includes bibliographical references and index.
   ISBN 978-0-520-25809-9(pbk : alk. paper)

   1. Democracy—Greece.—History—To 1500.   2. Greece—
Politics and government—To 146 B.C.   3. Democracy—Greece—
Athens—History—To 1500.   4. Athens (Greece)—Politics and
government.   I. Ober, Josiah.   II. Wallace, Robert W., 1950–
III. Title.

JC75.D36R33   2007
320.938'5-dc22   2006026246

16   15   14   13   12   11
10   9   8   7   6   5   4   3   2

CONTENTS

ABOUT THE AUTHORS

Paul Cartledge received his DPhil from Oxford in 1975. He is currently Professor of Greek History in the Faculty of Classics and Professorial Fellow of Clare College, University of Cambridge. His main interests are Greek social, political, and cultural history, Sparta's history through the ages, and the continuing significance of ancient history in our own time. He has edited or coedited several volumes, including *The Cambridge Illustrated History of Greece* (1998) and *Money, Labour, and Land: Approaches to the Economies of Ancient Greece* (2002), and recently published *Spartan Reflections* (2001); *The Greeks: A Portrait of Self and Others*, second edition (2002); *The Spartans*, second edition (2003); *Alexander the Great: The Hunt for a New Past*, revised edition (2005); and *Thermopylae: The Battle That Changed the World* (2006). He is currently writing a specialist history of Greek political thought from Homer to Plutarch.

Cynthia Farrar received her PhD from the University of Cambridge in 1984. She currently directs a project on deliberation and local governance at Yale University's Institution for Social and Policy Studies (ISPS) and teaches in the Department of Political Science. She explores and pursues strategies for energizing citizenship, particularly at the local level. Among other projects, she coordinates the Citizen Deliberations for MacNeil/Lehrer Productions' national *By the People* initiative. She is the author of *The Origins of Democratic Thinking: The Invention of Politics in Classical Athens* (1988) and articles on deliberative democracy.

Josiah Ober received his PhD from the University of Michigan in 1980. He is Mitsotakis Professor of Political Science and Classics at Stanford University. He works primarily within and between the areas of Athenian history, classical political philosophy, and democratic theory and practice. His current research focuses on problems of collective action, knowledge exchange, and human nature. His books include *Mass and Elite in Democratic Athens* (1989), *Political Dissent in Democratic Athens* (1998), *The Athenian Revolution* (1996), and *Athenian Legacies: Essays on the Politics of Going on Together* (2005).

Kurt Raaflaub received his PhD from the University of Basel in 1970. He is David Herlihy University Professor and Professor of Classics and History as well as Director of the Program in Ancient Studies at Brown University. His interests focus on archaic and classical Greek and Roman republican social, political, and intellectual history as well as comparative history of the ancient world. He has recently coedited *Democracy, Empire, and the Arts in Fifth-Century Athens* (1998) and *War and Society in the Ancient and Medieval Worlds* (1999) and published *The Discovery of Freedom in Ancient Greece* (2004). A volume of collected essays to be titled *War and Peace in the Ancient World* is in press. He is currently working on a book tentatively entitled *Early Greek Political Thought in Its Mediterranean Context*.

Robert Wallace received his PhD from Harvard University in 1984. He is Professor of Classics at Northwestern University. His main interests are in archaic and classical Greek and Roman republican history, Greek law, Greek music theory, and numismatics. He has coedited *Poet, Public, and Performance in Ancient Greece* (1997) and *Symposion 2001: Vorträge zur griechischen und hellenistischen Rechtsgeschichte* (2001) and published *The Areopagos Council to 307 B.C.* (1989) and *Reconstructing Damon: Music, Wisdom Teaching, and Politics in Democratic Athens* (forthcoming). He is currently working on a book titled *Freedom and Community in Democratic Athens*.

CHRONOLOGY OF EVENTS

478	Foundation of Delian League under leadership of Athens
472	Performance of Aeschylus's *Persians*
465	Earthquake and helot revolt at Sparta
463	Performance of Aeschylus's *Suppliants*
462/1	Reforms initiated by Ephialtes, Cimon ostracized
459–451	First Peloponnesian War between Athens and Spartan alliance
458	Performance of Aeschylus's *Oresteia,* including *Eumenides*
451/0	Pericles' citizenship law
446	Thirty Years' Peace with Sparta
443	Ostracism of Thucydides son of Melesias, Pericles' last major opponent
431–404	Second Peloponnesian War
429	Death of Pericles
413	Defeat of Athenian expeditionary force in Sicily
411	Oligarchy of the Four Hundred at Athens, followed by a moderate oligarchy of Five Thousand
410	Democracy restored
410–399	Revision of laws in Athens
404	Defeat of Athens, tyranny of the Thirty
403	Democracy restored
399	Trial and death of Socrates

ABBREVIATIONS

CAH   *Cambridge Ancient History.*
DNP   *Der Neue Pauly: Enzyklopädie der Antike.* Stuttgart, 1996–2003.
FGrH F. Jacoby, ed. *Die Fragmente der griechischen Historiker.* Berlin; Leiden, 1923–.
IC   *Inscriptiones Creticae.* Rome, 1935–1950.
IG   *Inscriptiones Graecae.* Berlin, 1873–.
LCL   Loeb Classical Library.
ML   Meiggs and Lewis 1988.
RE   *Realencyclopädie der classischen Altertumswissenschaft.* Stuttgart, 1893–1978.
SEG   *Supplementum Epigraphicum Graecum.* Amsterdam, 1923–.
Syll. Wilhelm Dittenberger, ed. *Sylloge Inscriptionum Graecarum.* 3d ed. Leipzig, 1915–1924. Repr., Hildesheim, 1960.

Chapter 1

Introduction

Kurt A. Raaflaub

Over the past thirty years or so, work on Athenian democracy has intensified and yielded most impressive results. The development and functioning of democratic institutions and of the democratic system as a whole, as well as individual aspects, such as the roles of the elite, leaders, and the masses, and democratic terminology, have been analyzed and reconstructed in detail. The sources relevant to the study of democracy have received new editions and valuable commentaries. Democracy's relation to its opponents, on the individual and collective, political and intellectual levels, its impact on religion, law, warfare, ideology, and culture, and the reactions it provoked from antiquity to our modern age have been reexamined thoroughly and comprehensively.[1] As a result, we are now able to understand Athenian democracy much better and to interpret and discuss it with more sophistication than was ever the case.

Moreover, this democracy is no longer mainly the property of specialists among classicists: it has become a matter of public interest. The year 1993 marked the 2,500th anniversary of a comprehensive set of reforms enacted in ancient Athens in 508/7 B.C.E.[2] The man whose leadership Athenian memory credited with the realization of these reforms was Cleisthenes, a member of the prominent Alcmaeonid family. Some seventy years later, Herodotus stated as a matter of fact that Cleisthenes "had instituted for the Athenians the tribes (*phulai*) and the democracy" (6.131.1). Unfortunately, the historian did not think it necessary to explain why and how tribal reform and the establishment of democracy were connected. By the late fifth and fourth centuries the Athenians sought the origins of their democracy even earlier, with Solon (a lawgiver of the early sixth century) or even

1

Theseus (one of their founder heroes: Ruschenbusch 1958; Hansen 1989d). Few scholars today are ready to take the latter seriously. But together with Solon and Ephialtes (an Athenian leader in the 460s), Cleisthenes, who was rediscovered after more than two millennia of obscurity by George Grote and thrust into great prominence by the publication of Aristotle's *Constitution of the Athenians* (*Athēnaiōn Politeia* or *Ath. Pol.*) in 1891 (Hansen 1994: 25–27), remains a prime candidate for the title "founder of Athenian democracy"—even if some near contemporaries perceived Ephialtes rather as its corruptor, and if the value of this title itself will be questioned vigorously by some of this volume's authors.

At any rate, the anniversary of Cleisthenes' reforms prompted a further increase of scholarly and popular activity focused on Athenian democracy, especially since it fell in a period that witnessed a surge of democracy around the world (represented most dramatically by the fall of the Iron Curtain in Germany and the failed push for democracy in Beijing, followed soon afterward by the disintegration of the Soviet Union and the demise of Communist rule in Eastern Europe). In 1992 an exhibition on fifth-century Greek sculpture opened at the National Gallery of Art in Washington, D.C., with the flashy title "The Greek Miracle: Classical Sculpture from the Dawn of Democracy." The exhibition's sponsors emphasized the connection between Athenian democracy and the "explosive" development of the arts, and that between ancient and modern democracy. Critics did not wait long to assault both connections, and an intensive debate ensued (Buitron-Oliver 1992; see Morris and Raaflaub 1998: 1–2). Independently, from 1988, supported by the American School of Classical Studies in Athens, Josiah Ober and Charles Hedrick spearheaded the development of a series of public programs, known as the "Democracy 2500 Project," that resulted, among other activities, in the conference "Democracy Ancient and Modern" and the exhibition "The Birth of Democracy," both of which took place in Washington, D.C., in 1993 (Ober and Hedrick 1993, 1996). Whether inspired by the same event or not, other collected volumes on democracy appeared around the same time (e.g., Eder 1995b; Sakellariou 1996). In particular, a volume Ian Morris and I edited in 1998, based on discussions in 1993 titled "Democracy 2500? Questions and Challenges," dealt critically with some of the issues brought up by democracy's anniversary. Another volume (Boedeker and Raaflaub 1998) focused on a different set of questions that had been raised not least by the "Greek Miracle" exhibition: the connection between democracy, imperial power and wealth, and the evolution of the arts in fifth-century Athens. All these activities brought Athenian democracy and the work of classical scholars studying and interpreting its many facets to the attention of a broad public and firmly entrenched ancient democracy in wider discussions of democratic theory (see, for example, recently Urbinati 2002, Rhodes 2003a, and Farrar, chapter 7 below).

By now the intensity of debates about "Democracy 2500" has calmed down, and we have gained critical distance that makes a synthesis of arguments possible and valuable. The time seems ripe to revisit some of the issues discussed ten years ago. Both because of its intrinsic importance and the progress achieved in more than thirty years of intensive research, this volume focuses on the question of how democracy really originated, where it came from.[3] In chapter 2, Robert Wallace and I collect and discuss the evidence that illustrates the roots of egalitarianism and "people's power" in archaic Greece, attesting to an elementary disposition that facilitated a development toward democracy, without, of course, making democracy necessary or inevitable. In chapters 3–5, Wallace, Josiah Ober, and I present, in critical interaction with each other, the arguments that speak for an origin of democracy in the early sixth century (prompted by the reforms of Solon), in the late sixth century (as a consequence of popular revolt and reforms attributed to Cleisthenes), and in the mid-fifth century (connected with reforms introduced by Ephialtes and Pericles). In chapters 6 and 7, Paul Cartledge and Cynthia Farrar comment on our arguments and add their own thoughts from the perspective of ancient history and political science, respectively, thus opening the door for a more general discussion among the readers of this volume. This, ultimately, is our purpose: we hope this volume will stimulate thinking and debate in a wider public and in classrooms throughout this and other countries where people place a high value on democracy and wonder about its origins. As published here, these seven chapters represent the result of much discussion among the authors, conducted in a spirit of mutual respect and constructive criticism that truly invigorates thinking, advances understanding, and stimulates the development of new ideas.[4]

ATHENIAN DEMOCRACY

The democracy that existed in Athens roughly from the middle of the fifth century was a remarkable system, unprecedented, "unparalleled in world history" (Hansen 1999: 313), exhilarating, capable of mobilizing extraordinary citizen involvement, enthusiasm, and achievement, enormously productive and at the same time potentially greatly destructive. We know this democracy best in the shape it took in the fourth century, after a comprehensive revision of laws between 410 and 399 (Hansen 1999: 162–65). By then it could be understood as a system of rather clearly defined institutions that operated according to legally determined rules, which to some extent approached a "constitution." Parts of this system (analyzed in much detail by Bleicken 1994; Hansen 1999; see also Samons 2004) are described in the second half of the Aristotelian *Ath. Pol.* (42–69). To mention only the most obvious elements, the assembly (*ekklēsia*) met at least forty times a year. For some of these meetings, items on the agenda were prescribed (44–46). The presidents of the assembly and council were selected by lot and essentially could not serve for more than one day (44). The democratic "council of 500" (*boulē*)—to be distinguished from the Areopagus council composed of former magistrates (archons) who were life-long members—was selected by lot; its five hundred members, limited to two (nonsuccessive) years of service, represented, according to a sophisticated formula, the population of numerous districts in Attica (*dēmoi*, demes, consisting of villages and sections of towns and of the city of Athens: Traill 1975, 1986). This council broadly supervised the administrative apparatus (*Ath. Pol.* 45–49), dealt with foreign policy issues, heard reports of officials, and deliberated the agenda and prepared motions for the assembly (Rhodes 1972). The latter was free to accept such motions, with or without amendment, to refer them back to the council for further deliberation, or to reject and replace them with different ones altogether (Hansen 1987). The assembly passed decrees (*psēphismata*) on specific policy issues, while laws with general validity (*nomoi*) were formulated by a board of "lawgivers" (*nomothetai*), passed in a trial-like procedure, and, if challenged, scrutinized in the people's court (Hansen 1999: chap. 7).[5]

The assembly, assisted by the *boulē* and the law courts (*dikastēria*), decided upon policies, supervised every step of their execution, and held a tight control over the officials who were in charge of realizing them. Professional personnel (whether in administration, religion, or the maintenance of public order) was minimal, mostly consisting of a few hundred state-owned slaves who served in specific functions at the disposal of various officials or as a rudimentary police force (Hunter 1994: 3). Virtually all administrative business was in the hands of numerous committees of various sizes (totalling about seven hundred members), who assisted, and in turn were supervised by, the *boulē* and various officials (Hansen 1980). (In the fifth century, hundreds of other officials served in various functions throughout the empire; *Ath. Pol.* 24.3 with Rhodes 1981: 305; Balcer 1976.) A small minority of these officials, primarily those holding major financial and military responsibility, were elected (*Ath. Pol.* 43.1, 44.4); all others were selected by lot (43.1, 47–48, 50–55.1), as were the chief magistrates (archons, in a double sortition procedure, 8.1), and the thousands of citizen judges (in modern scholarship usually called jurors), who on every court day staffed variously large juries (or, more precisely, assemblies of judges) that tried several cases simultaneously in various locations. These jurors were chosen in a sophisticated mechanical procedure (by an allotment machine, *klērōtērion*) that eliminated tampering and made bribery virtually impossible (63–66;

Boegehold 1995: 58, 230–34; Hansen 1999: chap. 8; Demont 2003). The law courts themselves were an important part of democratic life and procedures: much political business was conducted there, one might say, in a continuation of politics by different means (Hansen 1990).

Several thousand citizens thus were politically active every year and many of them quite regularly for years on end—out of a population of adult male citizens that in the fourth century comprised hardly more than 30,000 (Hansen 1999: 90–94, 313, 350). Most impressively, "over a third of all citizens over eighteen, and about two thirds of all citizens over forty" served at some point in their lives at least one year-long term in the council of 500, a very time-consuming office (249). It is thus clear that this democracy was not only "direct" in the sense that decisions were made by the assembled people, but the "directest" imaginable in the sense that the people through assembly, council, and law courts controlled the entire political process and that a fantastically large proportion of citizens was involved constantly in public business. Moreover, the system of rotation of offices (Aristotle *Politics* 1317b2–7; see already Euripides *Suppliants* 406–7) made sure that those who were not involved at a given time would be at another (if they wished to) and that the citizens through their engagement in various offices and functions achieved a high level of familiarity with the administration of their community and its policies. On top of all this, these same citizens also regularly served in their polis's infantry army or helped row its fleet, even if mercenaries played a more significant role in fourth-century warfare than they did earlier (Burckhardt 1996).

We cannot know exactly how much of all this was realized already in the fifth century. Precisely the categories of sources that in the fourth century offer by far the most information on the technical or "constitutional" details of how democracy operated are almost entirely lacking in the fifth: in particular, we do not have a fifth-century predecessor to the Aristotelian *Ath. Pol.*,[6] and court or assembly speeches were not published until toward the end of that century. Some offices or committees did not yet exist, others had different functions, the number of assembly meetings was perhaps not yet fixed at forty per year, and before the Peloponnesian War the number of adult male citizens was much larger, reaching perhaps 60,000 or more (Hansen 1988). Despite all this, however, and despite much debate about the differences between fifth- and fourth-century democracy (see the end of this chapter), there do not seem to be good reasons to assume that in the fifth century the citizens were substantially less involved in running their democracy than in the fourth. By contrast, if the reforms at the turn of the century achieved the goal of making the political process somewhat more objective, transparent, and subject to the law (see note 5), we should assume, and elite complaints would seem to confirm, that before then citizen control over this process had been even more immediate and intense.

With modifications, then, the political system described above was in place by about the mid-fifth century. When we are asking about the origins of Greek democracy, we are ultimately asking about the origins of this system. Before we pursue this question further, we need to take a brief look at the evidence on which our inquiry is based and to become aware of the opportunities it offers and the problems it poses.

EVIDENCE

The late fifth century (from the time of the Peloponnesian War) and especially the fourth are exceptionally well documented.[7] For all earlier periods, evidence is much more scarce, scattered, and, with few exceptions, late. I already mentioned the lack of a fifth-century *Ath. Pol.* and corpus of orators. With the exception of Aeschylus's and a few of Sophocles' plays, extant tragedies and comedies were performed in the last three decades of the fifth century and even later. Thucydides, an active Athenian politician, spent most of the Peloponnesian War (the subject of his *History*) in exile, apparently revising and perhaps even writing at least parts of the extant version after the war. He focused thoroughly on power politics, foreign relations, and military history and paid attention to economic, social, or religious issues and to domestic politics or constitutional or institutional developments only when they had immediate significance for the war (Gomme et al. 1945–81: 1. 1–28; Hornblower 1987). This is true even for the "Fifty Years' History" (*pentēkontaëtia*, 1.89–117), which traces the buildup of Athenian power after the Persian Wars and almost entirely ignores domestic events.

Herodotus, Thucydides' older contemporary, is our most important literary and historical source for archaic Greek history. Most likely, he wrote his *Histories* in the 430s and 420s, certainly under the influence of contemporary ideas and events, but not about these; his topic was another great war, half a century earlier, between Greeks and Persians, and earlier developments both on the Persian and the Greek side that had culminated in this war (Lateiner 1989; Bakker et al. 2002). His "cut-off date" is 479; although he provides occasional comments on later events, he certainly does not pay systematic attention to them. He talks about persons and events that are important in our present context but does so again in the framework of his overarching theme and—no less importantly—with his own interpretive purpose in mind. Moreover, the oral tradition on which he was mostly relying preserved from the seventh and sixth centuries anecdotal memory of outstanding persons and sensational events but rarely of matters of everyday life or constitutional developments (Raaflaub 1988a). Thus Herodotus knows Solon as a statesman but is interested in him as one of the archaic sages rather than as a political reformer. He describes, anecdotally, the period of Peisistratid tyranny because it explains why Athens at the time was weak and oppressed. He elaborates on Cleisthenes because he reunited Athens after a period of tyranny and factional strife and thus was responsible for Athens' rise in self-confidence and power, documented impressively in its victories of 506 and a condition for its role in the Persian Wars. Hence the fact and result, not the details, of Cleisthenes' reforms are important to Herodotus.

Cleisthenes and Ephialtes did not leave writings of their own (Anderson 2006). Some of Ephialtes' laws apparently were still accessible at the end of the fifth century: the stele on which they were inscribed was removed from the Areopagus Hill by the Thirty in 404 (*Ath. Pol.* 35.2; Rhodes 1981: 440). In the context of the oligarchic coup of 411, the proposal was made "to also seek out (or consult, *prosanazētēsai*) the ancestral laws which Cleisthenes enacted when he founded the democracy" (*Ath. Pol.* 29.3). As Mortimer Chambers (1990: 277) notes, this hardly proves that the (or some) laws of Cleisthenes were still available in 411 (see also Hignett 1952: 15, 130; *contra* Andrewes in Gomme et al. 1945–81: 5. 214–15). At any rate, none of Cleisthenes' or Ephialtes' laws are extant. Nor did Plutarch write a biography of these men (Hansen 1994: 25). By the time historical interest focused on the development of the Athenian constitution, both had long been overshadowed by Solon (Hansen 1989d), who had written a large set of laws and composed a substantial body of poetry. The former, displayed publicly on the Acropolis and later in the Prytaneion (Stroud 1979), were still available at the time of Aristotle, who wrote about them, but many of the laws cited by later authors are of dubious authenticity, and it is altogether uncertain how the specifically constitutional arrangements underlying Solon's "timocratic system" fit into this law code (de Ste. Croix 2004: 310–17). The purpose of the poetry is debated: its form (elegiac and iambic) suggests performance at elite symposia rather than in public, but public performance was assumed by later tradition and is accepted by many scholars (Raaflaub 1996c: 1038–42). We may assume that Solon expressed similar ideas in public orations (which would have been in prose and of which nothing has survived), but cannot exclude that the poetry was strictly limited to private symposia and thus may reflect an aristocratic perspective and bias (Wallace, chapter 3 below).

At any rate, the Aristotelian *Ath. Pol.* quotes large passages from the poems and refers to individual laws: these must have provided the author with the bulk of the evidence he had at his disposal to reconstruct the crisis Solon was grappling with. How much other evidence survived, and how good it was, remains disputed (Stroud 1978 offers an optimistic view; see now de Ste. Croix 2004: chap. 7). It seems clear, though, that by Aristotle's time, more than 250 years after the events, and probably much earlier, people had no clear understanding anymore of how different archaic Athens had been from the community they knew. We thus constantly need to reckon with the danger of conscious or unconscious retrojection of conditions taken for granted in later times and of interpretation of earlier evidence in the light of such later conditions.

This is even more true for post-Aristotelian sources. The fourth century featured many historians (such as Ephorus, Theopompus, and several writers of "Attic histories") whose works, though lost to us except for scattered fragments, were important and influential in their time and were used by extant later authors (such as Diodorus Siculus and Plutarch). Although they may have used some evidence that survived outside the Herodotean and Aristotelian tradition, it is hard to see what this might have been, and what we know about such "independent" traditions, for example from the earliest orators who reflect "memories" of aristocratic families, makes us cringe and despair about their historical reliability (Thomas 1989). Moreover, we have good reasons to suspect that some of these historians were remarkably uncritical in dealing with some of the evidence (such as comic jokes or philosophical polemics) they used for their purposes of historical reconstruction. Much of what later authors (such as Pausanias or Diogenes Laertius as well as ancient commentators on earlier works) tell us about Athenian history from Solon to Ephialtes and Pericles (beyond the information contained in Herodotus, Aristotle, and other archaic or classical sources) thus needs to be scrutinized critically and used with caution. This unfortunately applies to Plutarch as well, who wrote lives of Solon, Cimon, and Pericles, all with information that is potentially significant for our questions. His *Solon*, based largely on the *Ath. Pol.* and what he could learn about Solon's law code, is particularly important, but here, too, we are constantly in danger of falling prey to information of questionable authenticity (Manfredini and Piccirilli 1977).

Since we know so little overall, and since so many of these late bits of information seem highly interesting and valuable, scholars often find it hard to resist them. The wise person steers a middle course between overcredulity and hypercriticism, but this line is hard to find and even harder to maintain consistently. The decision about whether or not to accept unique but attractive pieces of late evidence is every scholar's personal responsibility and often a matter of personal judgment. To some extent all the authors of historical chapters in this volume had to grapple with these problems; others will judge whether we did so successfully.

We would expect to learn much about Athenian democracy from the inscriptions that have come to light in Athens and Attica. The habit of recording important public decrees and documents on stone began in the early fifth century (Hedrick 1999; also 1994). The number of inscriptions increased greatly in the second half of the fifth and again in the fourth century. Their subject matter ranges widely, including political decrees, laws, financial and other public accounts of officials and committees, treaties, contracts, honors bestowed on citizens and noncitizens, lists of inventories, state debtors, victors at athletic and dramatic competitions, officials, councilmen, war casualties, and much more. As Mogens Hansen observes, "over 20,000 inscriptions have been found just in Attika . . . , and several thousand of them are public documents from the golden age of democracy. For the fourth century alone we have some 500 decrees, ten laws, over 400 accounts and inventories, and fifty odd inscriptions with the names of *prytaneis*" (members of the council's executive committee) and other councillors (1999: 12). For the fourth century, indeed, these inscriptions provide all kinds of valuable information on many aspects of democracy, and they illuminate its day-to-day workings in most interesting ways. What has survived from the fifth century, however, offers more information about Athenian foreign relations and the Athenian empire than, strictly speaking, about the evolution and workings of democracy.[8] On the other hand, inscriptions dating from the archaic period, when few literary texts were produced that were directly concerned with political issues, are immensely important in illustrating the emergence and development of early legislation concerning political institutions and regulations (see also chapter 2).[9]

What survives from the archaic period, besides these inscriptions, is material evidence and poetry. The former only rarely offers insight into political contexts, and when it seems to do so, the interpretation is often uncertain and contested.[10] The latter proves unexpectedly rich in social and political information but needs to be read with careful consideration of the conventions and limitations of the genres involved.[11]

Overall, then, we have at our disposal a very substantial amount of evidence, at least some of which is of high quality. Most of it, however, is open to various interpretations. This prompts another observation on a more positive note. Our volume as a whole exhibits what is, of course, essential to every historical inquiry but is exposed relentlessly and often brutally in ancient history. Our sources are not only severely limited; they also most often do not tell a straightforward, univocal story, and they were usually not written to answer the questions we are most interested in. The historian thus has to test the quality of his sources, interpret them, and tease out of them what he seeks to find out. In this situation, the application of clear and explicit methodologies is crucial. The advantage is, as the historical chapters in this volume demonstrate, that we are able to present to the readers' critical examination the entire (or at least most of the) source base on which our arguments rest. As Cynthia Farrar suggests, "the beauty of ancient history is that the students can achieve familiarity with virtually all the sources on which the scholars rely, and match their own wits with theirs. Not for us the archivist's ability to trump other historians with a hitherto unknown bit of parchment. In ancient history, as in ancient politics, the matching of wits is all—and posing one interpretive scheme against another, offering competing ways of making sense of the very same evidence, is precisely what is on display in this volume" (personal communication). Processes of historical reconstruction in ancient history can thus be open and vulnerable to the reader's scrutiny to an unusual degree, which in turn stimulates further discussion. This we hope to have achieved. The purpose, of course, is not competition per se but reaching deeper insight and better understanding. This, too, we hope to have achieved, even if we continue to disagree on major issues.

QUESTIONS AND ISSUES

The chapters of this volume speak for themselves, and it seems superfluous to summarize them here. But I need to offer a few preliminary remarks about some larger issues underlying our venture. These concern the relationship between "Greek" and "Athenian democracy" and that between ancient and modern democracy, the definition of democracy, and the difference between "foundation" and "evolution" of democracy—or rather, that between "rupture moments" and incremental changes in the historical process that resulted in democracy.

Athenian vs. Greek Democracy

I concluded my brief sketch of the fully developed democracy in its fourth-century shape with the remark that it is the origins of this system that we are exploring when we ask about the origins of Greek democracy. Yet, no sooner said, this statement needs to be modified, for there was no one system labeled "Greek democracy." In *Politics,* based on more than 150 constitutions collected and written up in his school (*Nichomachean Ethics* 10.9, 1181b18–24), Aristotle distinguishes several types of democracy, based on qualifications required for office holding, the type of citizens who are able to attend the assembly and thus dominate in politics, and the respect enjoyed by law (Dolezal 1974; Robinson 1997: 35–44; see also Ober 1998a: chap. 6). The spectrum reaches from near oligarchy to extreme forms of democracy that are close to a "tyranny of the masses." Critics of Athenian democracy (Roberts 1994: chaps. 2–4; Ober 1998a), especially in its fifth-century version, would have placed it near the latter. As I shall argue in chapter 5 below, fifth-century Athenian democracy was unique not least because it was, both in its development and in its workings, closely linked to an empire ruled by a powerful fleet. This created special conditions that could not be replicated elsewhere. When we look at Athens in the fifth century, we should thus speak of Athenian, not of Greek, democracy.

But, whether independently or under direct or indirect Athenian influence, democracies in many shapes and forms, and mostly much more moderate and modest than Athens', became more frequent in the fifth century (Robinson forthcoming). Moreover, egalitarian forms of constitution, some of which were considered "democratic" already in antiquity and continue to be assessed as such by some modern scholars, were fairly widespread in Greece already at the end of the sixth century (O'Neil 1995; Robinson 1997). Democracy was thus also, and importantly, a Greek phenomenon. If our discussions in this volume focus more on Athens than on the rest of Greece the reason is threefold: detailed analysis of the emergence of democracy is possible only with the source material available for Athens; the Athenians were the first to identify their political system as a "democracy," and it was the Athenian model of democracy, discussed and criticized by authors who were Athenian citizens or residents or at least closely familiar with Athens, that stimulated debate and condemnation of democracy among political thinkers and leaders for centuries to come. Still, some of the ideas explored in all chapters have broader validity, and chapter 2, deliberately intended to offer some degree of balance, as well as chapter 3, has a broader scope.[12] In view of all this, the title of this volume deliberately—and, we think, correctly—emphasizes origins not of ancient Athenian or ancient Greek democracy but of democracy in ancient Greece.

Ancient vs. Modern Democracy

My brief sketch of the workings of Athenian democracy should make another point very clear: this system was radically different from just about anything we citizens of the twenty-first century know as a democracy.[13] Even the few examples of direct democracy that have survived to be studied by modern scholars (one of which is analyzed by Hansen 1983a: chap. 12) are comparable with the Athenian model only in elementary ways. The level of citizen involvement in the political process and in public administration, mentioned before, is only one of the aspects to be considered here. Exclusiveness is another—and seems to offer an easy opportunity for devastating criticism. After all, women were excluded from the political realm (although they played communally significant roles in other areas, such as religion; Dillon 2002), and so, of course, were foreigners and slaves. The democratic citizen body was composed of only the adult male citizens; that is, it represented a small minority (perhaps between 10 and 20 percent) of the total population. In the mid-fifth century this minority made itself even more exclusive by a law introduced by Pericles that defined the conditions for citizenship yet more restrictively (Patterson 1981; Boegehold 1994; Hansen 1999: 52–54).

Before we convict the Athenians on this score, however, or even conclude categorically that their system was not a democracy at all, we should remember two points. One concerns the use of the term "democracy." We are simply not in a position to deny that the Athenians had a democracy, even if we believe that it does not fit *our* concept of democracy. After all, they invented the word, even if we are not entirely sure when and why they did it. Thucydides says explicitly, "Our constitution . . . by name is called a democracy" (2.37.1). He and the "Old Oligarch" (see note 6) use the word frequently; other late fifth-century authors clearly allude to it (Sealey 1974; Farrar 1988). Most of the arguments familiar from fourth-century theoretical discussions about democracy are mentioned by fifth-century authors, although none combines them into a systematic analysis (Raaflaub 1989b). Historically, the Athenians "own the copyright" for "democracy." All we can do is to state and explain the differences—and invent new terms for modern democracies (calling them, for example, "representative," "parliamentary," or "popular"). The other point is that women were politically enfranchised in the United States less than a century ago (and in other "old" democracies even much later), that descendants of slaves, though freed and legally enfranchised after the Civil War, achieved a respectable level of social and political equality only about fifty years ago, and that foreigners in the United States, even when enjoying resident status, can still not vote today (although, admittedly, naturalization is much easier in most modern democracies than it ever was in Athens). The Athenians thought and acted within the parameters that were generally accepted throughout antiquity and far beyond, until the very recent past (Strauss 1998: 147–54; Farrar, chapter 7 below, note 1). Within these parameters, though, they adopted an extraordinarily broad definition of "citizenship"—one that the vast majority of contemporaries found objectionable if not detestable and that posterity roundly condemned for over two millennia (Roberts 1994). In fact, for this and other reasons, the American Founders, among many others, explicitly rejected the Athenian model (Richard 1994; Roberts 1994: chap. 9). It is clear, therefore, that the Athenian democracy can be claimed only to a very limited extent as an ancestor of modern democracy. No direct line of development or descent leads from the former to the latter (Eder 1998: 107–9). Modern democracy has a varied—and, as Ellen Wood (1994) points out, ambiguous—ancestry; in Barry Strauss's view (1998: 141–47), it potentially has multiple genealogies that are all ideologically tainted. At any rate, upon sober reflection modern democracy's family tree, however it is reconstructed, does not originate in ancient Athens (Hansen 1994) or Sparta (Hornblower 1992: 1–2) or, for that matter, in the so-called primitive democracies of early Mesopotamian polities;[14] it is of much more recent origin. In terms of constitutional history, especially Athenian democracy, fiercely criticized already by contemporaries (Ober 1998a), feared and condemned by posterity (Roberts 1994), was an evolutionary dead end—even if Greek political theory and philosophy, decisively provoked by the experience of democracy (Farrar 1992), stimulated political thinkers, theorists, and philosophers through the centuries and does so even today.

Significance

Why, then, should we be interested in the origins of democracy in ancient Greece? What has it to do with us? Well, even if there is no direct evolutionary connection, democracy and the democratic idea still originated in Greece. They reached a high point in Athens in a time that gave rise to a most impressive flourishing of intellectual life and the arts (Boedeker and Raaflaub 1998), much of which survives. Despite painful gaps, overall Athenian democracy is exceptionally well documented. Moreover, a Greek *politeia* was not just a constitution or body of laws; it was the way a community chose to organize itself and to live its life, and thus it affected every aspect of communal life and politics. This was especially true for democracy: being an unprecedented and unsettling phenomenon, it compelled virtually every thinker and author at the time to confront it: works of history, oratory, philosophy and political theory, comedy and tragedy, and political pamphlets abound in reactions to democracy itself or its impact on politics and social life. We are thus in a position to study and analyze the "Athenian experiment" much more comprehensively than is usual in the realm of ancient history. Furthermore, many of the thoughts and ideas raised by fifth- and fourth-century authors, whether in connection with democracy or not, concern issues that aim at the core of human society and communal life: they are of timeless relevance. Directly or indirectly, Athenian democracy as an extraordinary experiment in social history thus stimulates our own thinking about crucial issues of our own democracy and society, incomparably more complex though they are. The point is precisely that the ancients help us focus on the essentials.

But Athenian democracy can do more for us than serve as a repository of ideas that stimulate our own thinking. As Paul Cartledge and especially Cynthia Farrar point out in chapters 6 and 7, dissatisfaction with the distance and disconnection caused by modern representative democracy, particularly in a country as large and diverse as the United States, has created a need to return to forms of more direct democracy, at least on the local, and perhaps even on a broader, level. Modern technological advances offer the means to meet this need. Farrar shows that early attempts to realize such opportunities bring us back to dimensions that are quite comparable to those in ancient Greece: towns and districts rather than states or nations. In this context, Athens, as by far the best-documented ancient democracy, can become for us the object of a case study or "historical laboratory." As Ober suggests, we can engage in a discussion "with its values, structures, and practice-based principles," and learn much from them (personal communication). We can ask how the Athenians did things, how they tried to resolve specific problems, what worked and what did not, and why so. From this perspective, their shortcomings and failures are as interesting and useful as their successes and achievements (Samons 2004). We can learn from them in ways that are comparable to how the American Founding Fathers learned from ancient writers about federal states and confederacies: not by imitating the ancient models (even though this, too, might occasionally be possible in the case of democracy) but by profiting from their experience in grappling with specific issues and problems and by understanding the differences between them and us. We might thus engage in a dialogue with Athenian democracy not as an ancestor but as a partner—a partner who, two-and-a-half millennia ago, was involved in a very similar quest for the best way of creating a good community that could foster a good life for its people.

Definitions

As Robin Osborne (forthcoming) observes, even "among the most careful of scholars the privileging of particular sources, as well as the privileging of particular criteria, predetermines the answer" to the question of when democracy came into being in ancient Greece (see also Eder 1998: 105–6). This answer will also depend largely on how we define democracy. Given the differences between ancient and modern democracies and the lack of continuity between them, modern definitions will be of limited use. Nor is there only *one* modern type of democracy: the range of systems that are called democracies today is even broader than it was in ancient Greece. What definition, then, should we adopt for our present purposes? Eberhard Ruschenbusch (1995) occupies one extreme of the spectrum: in his view, any system in which the people in assembly are involved in communal decision making is essentially a democracy. My own position is closer to the other extreme: in my view, democracy was realized when active citizenship and full political participation were extended to all adult male citizens, no matter their family background, wealth, education, or abilities, and when this (exceptionally broadly defined) citizen body through assembly, council, and law courts assumed full control over the entire political process, from the conception of policies to their realization and the oversight over those involved in executing them. Wallace's and Ober's positions are situated somewhere between these extremes. Accordingly, Ruschenbusch finds democracy already in the society described in the Homeric epics, while in my view the inception of democracy coincides with the period when the Athenians themselves, realizing either that they were about to step into uncharted territory and create an unprecedented system or that they had already done so, invented a new word for it: *dēmo-kratia*.

Yet we do not *know* exactly when this word was coined, nor should we exaggerate this aspect. This volume is about more than sparring with words and definitions. After all, if we believe that a system suitable to be termed a democracy came into being already as a result of Solon's reforms in the early sixth century, subsequent developments, as Aristotle suggests in *Ath. Pol.* 22.1, made this system even more democratic. If we reserve the term "democracy" for the fully developed system of the second half of the fifth century (or, with Eder 1998, even for that of the early fourth century), then previous systems as precursors of this democracy might aptly be termed "pre-" or "protodemocracies." Aristotle, we saw, registered for his time a great variety of types of democracy, ranging from near oligarchies to extreme popular governments. There is no absolute reason why his categories should not be applied diachronically as well, that is, to cover the entire range of constitutional development from the sixth to the fourth century (Robinson 1997). From this perspective, the system established by Solon and that fostered by Pericles 150 years later simply represent different forms of democracy. I personally think that this muddies the picture rather than clarifying it, but others have disagreed with me and will continue to do so.

This point seems to me important enough to be emphasized. Whatever term we use for the political system introduced by Solon in the early sixth century, clearly that established by Cleisthenes' reforms almost a century later transcended it by far and created fundamentally new realities and conditions for political thought and action that were inconceivable at Solon's time. Similarly, whether we decide to call systems of the "Cleisthenic type" egalitarian ("isonomic") or democratic, it seems again undeniable that the Athenians subsequently pushed institutional developments several decisive steps further and that the system they adopted in the mid-fifth century was, if perhaps not unique (although I believe it was at the time), certainly exceptional in its determined realization of the basic idea that all citizens should be politically equal.

Evolution, Process, and Ruptures

This volume, although mostly focusing on Athenian developments, in fact tries to answer two questions. One concerns the emergence of broadly egalitarian ("isonomic") political systems that, as Eric Robinson has shown (1997), although perhaps rarely as sophisticated as that of Cleisthenic Athens, became quite frequent by the end of the sixth century. They were probably not yet called democracies in contemporaneous parlance but in many ways fit into the range of democracies that was conceptualized by political theory in Aristotle's time. The other question focuses more closely on the case of Athens and tries to explain what made its more specific, mature, or fully realized form of democracy possible or even necessary.

None of the contributors to this volume thinks that democracy was instituted, so to speak, by the stroke of a pen at any one time by any one person.
We need not and do not want to imitate the Greeks in seeking the "first
inventor" (*prōtos heuretēs*) of democracy. Whether democracy was created by
a "revolution" is a different matter and one of our main points of debate.
Ober strongly believes that it was a popular uprising in domestic conflicts
between Cleisthenes and his rival Isagoras, who, moreover, received outside
support, that caused the breakthrough to democracy at the end of the sixth
century (chapter 4 below; see also Ober 1993, 1998b). Cartledge thinks
that "between 550 and 450 (at the outside)" something that should be
called "a political revolution took place at Athens" (personal communication). For various reasons, Wallace and I place this breakthrough even earlier or at the very end of this period. As Robin Osborne (forthcoming)
explains, this question has a long history and was answered variously by
many historians, from George Grote to our own day, often for reasons that
had as much to do with the political concerns and experiences of their own
time as with those of the ancient Greeks.

Yet this should not obscure another aspect on which we all agree. To put
it simply, historical processes advance by incremental change and by sudden
ruptures. This book is about the relative importance of three rupture
moments, but we all keep in mind the essential background of incremental
changes before, between, and after the rupture moments we each favor.

To explain, the democracy we know through a rich range of sources from
the late fifth and even better from the fourth century was the result of a long
evolutionary process that we can trace back to the early sixth century. As
chapter 2 shows, it had its roots even earlier, in mentalities, beliefs and values, ways of behaving, and institutions attested in the seventh and perhaps
late eighth centuries. This evolution, which I call here simply "the process,"
was stimulated powerfully, in a first moment of rupture, by social conflict
and the reforms enacted in the early sixth century by Solon, who, in trying
to resolve an acute social and economic crisis, established new parameters
of political thought and action (discussed in chapter 3). It was advanced by
measures introduced and policies pursued by the tyrants, Peisistratus and
his sons, who ruled Athens for much of the second half of the sixth century.
They did so at the expense of their fellow aristocrats and their centrifugal
tendencies. In deliberate contrast, the Peisistratids focused the citizens'
attention on the polis's center, Athens, by creating or enhancing shared
cults, festivals, buildings, and places, and thus helped integrate the polis.
Political evolution and polis integration were accelerated in a second
moment of rupture at the end of the sixth century, in reaction to renewed
aristocratic infighting and outside intervention and threats after the fall of
tyranny, by popular uprising and Cleisthenes' sophisticated reforms (analyzed in chapter 4). The polis, thus unified, stood its test immediately

against challenges by neighboring poleis and Sparta and, a few years later, against the lethal threat posed by Persian invasions. The process was further advanced by the changes caused by naval warfare, the creation of an Athenian empire, and the rise of Athens to become one of the leading powers in the eastern Mediterranean. A third moment of rupture was brought about by the reforms of the late 460s and 450s, championed by Ephialtes and Pericles, which were prompted precisely by these changes and by continuing aristocratic competition for the demos's leadership (chapter 5). For the purposes of this volume, we end our discussion with this third rupture point. The Athenians themselves identified the resulting system with democracy, and the authors of this volume agree that by then democracy, whenever it came into being, was in all essential respects fully developed.

Yet we are aware that the process continued even thereafter and reached its conclusion only much later, by reforms enacted early in the fourth century (Ostwald 1986: chaps. 9–10; Ober 1989: 95–100; Eder 1998) and again late in the century by Eubulus and Lycurgus (Ober 1989: 100–103). No one will underestimate the importance of the changes introduced after the Peloponnesian War (the collection and publication of the laws, the establishment of a board of lawmakers [*nomothetai*] to review existing laws and create new laws, the distinction between laws of general validity [*nomoi*] and decrees on immediate issues [*psēphismata*], and the introduction of pay for attendance of the assembly). Modern scholars have seen in these changes a "watershed" and Aristotle (*Pol.* 1274a7–11; cf. *Ath. Pol.* 41.2) characterized the fourth-century form of Athenian democracy as its *telos* (its furthest development). But, as Ober (1989: 97) observes, we should beware of overvaluing the constitutional aspects: "The constitution of the restored democracy retained all the major institutions that had guaranteed the ability of the common people to take an active role in governing the state." The Athenians reasserted the principles of political equality among all citizens and the exclusivity of the citizen body and, by introducing assembly pay, even realized them more comprehensively than before. It is only from the "point of view of political sociology" that Aristotle's assessment makes sense (96–98). Similarly, in subsequent decades "various constitutional adjustments" were made, but "no major changes in the sociology of Athenian politics" and no compromises "with the basic principles of the political equality and exclusivity of the citizen body, of the lottery, or of pay for state service." "Compared with the fifth century, the fourth century is remarkable less for its constitutional evolution than for its social and political stability. . . . This lack of fundamental change is why the author of the Aristotelian *Constitution of the Athenians*, written about 325 B.C., treats the period after 403 as a single constitutional epoch (*politeia*)" (102–3).

By contrast, Walter Eder emphasizes (1998: 105–6) that "in sharp contrast to the emergence of modern democracy, ancient democracy, pace

Josiah Ober, came into being without any obvious signposts of bloody civil war or radical revolution." Values such as liberty or equality were not discussed extensively and theoretically in advance, to be realized by a new constitution. Rather, democracy "arrived on tiptoes and in disguise," through a long series of reforms and changes initiated by aristocratic leaders

> who were both competitive and flexible and who were skilled enough to shape the polis and their position in it according to their interests, while assimilating to ongoing changes in politics and institutions. . . . All along they kept in touch with the growing demotic self-consciousness, which again was strengthened by ambitious aristocrats who took an ever increasing part of the demos into their *hetaireiai* (groups of followers). They did so to win political battles against their aristocratic rivals, until they finally had to realize that the demos had learned to manage its affairs independently of aristocratic guardianship. . . . In the end the demos was able to pick its leaders from among its own ranks; from being followers of the powerful, the common people evolved into a community of the powerful. (106, 136)

But to control power was not enough. "Rather, the sovereign people need to develop and to accept voluntarily some institutionalized procedures of self-control that are tied to existing norms and are apt to protect the community from arbitrary and hasty decisions" (111). Accordingly, Eder postulates, democracy was realized only when *both* the demos's independent action *and* effective self-control were secured, and this was achieved only by the reforms enacted after the Peloponnesian War (121).

Obviously, this view is based as well on privileging certain criteria (here intended to bring out those aspects that make ancient democracy most comparable to its modern counterpart [110–12]). Its major value lies in presenting a strong argument for placing the emphasis on process, evolution, and continuity at the expense of rupture and revolution: "There was no visible break in the constitutional development from aristocratic to democratic structures." This makes it difficult to assign a specific date to the birth of democracy, "but it provides the crucial answer to the more important question of why the first democracy in world history was realized without bloody fighting for liberty and participation" (137).

The question of how to assess the innovations introduced after the Peloponnesian War and the nature of fourth-century democracy will continue to stimulate debate (see also Rhodes 1980; Bleicken 1987; Eder 1995a, and the essays in Eder 1995b). Overall, the evolution toward democracy was not linear and even; rather it moved at different speeds, through leaps and interruptions, slowed down at times and accelerated at others, pushed forward by the consequences of changes in internal and external circumstances, and advanced dramatically by the activities of visionary individuals and the powerful, perhaps even revolutionary, expression of popular will. After each of these ruptures, Athens as a community differed massively from what it had been before: the Athenians related to each other, acted together, and confronted outside challenges in ways that would have been unimaginable even a few years earlier. Ultimately, due to an extraordinary constellation, from the mid-fifth century class relations and politics in Athens, as well as the polis's role in the concert of powers, were separated by a world of difference from what they had been 150 years or even a couple of generations before and what they could be in any other Greek polis.

The leaps and ruptures, the events, are thus as important as the process as a whole. Our purpose in this volume is to respect the latter but to focus on the former. We try to understand more precisely how the long-term development toward democracy (which, of course, was not recognized as such by contemporaries and was understood in its full significance only at its very end and then from hindsight) was advanced and focused by each of the three major "ruptures" and how such major advances were made possible by the interaction, observable in each case, between impersonal factors (such as ongoing social, economic, and political changes), popular will, and enlightened leaders. In good Greek tradition we try to achieve this goal competitively. Believing that the transformative events each of us is analyzing played a particularly important, perhaps the decisive, role in bringing about democracy, we plead our cases vigorously and in doing so expose weaknesses we perceive in the others' arguments. We do so, however, with the intention of fostering open and continuing discussion. We present the sources that are available for our analysis, and try to make explicit on what methodologies and approaches our cases are built. And with the same intention we expose our cases to the critical and sophisticated scrutiny of two of the most competent experts on ancient Athenian democracy, whose comments and further thoughts, we are sure, will stimulate the readers' own thoughts and further debate.[15]

NOTES

1. To give just a few examples, on the council of 500: Rhodes 1972; the Areopagus council: Wallace 1989; the law courts: Boegehold 1995; the assembly: Hansen 1987; see also Hansen 1983a, 1989a; on the history and working of democracy: Bleicken 1994 (1st ed. 1985); Hansen 1999 (1st ed. 1991); on developments in the fifth century: Ostwald 1986; Sealey 1987; on the historical context: vols. IV–VI of the 2d ed. of *CAH;* on the interaction between elite and masses: Ober 1989; on forms of political dissent: Ober 1998a; on terminology relevant to democracy: Ostwald 1969 on law, custom (*nomos*); Raaflaub 2004 (German ed. 1985) on freedom (*eleutheria*); Cartledge 1996a and Raaflaub 1996b on equality (*isotēs, homoiotēs*); Meier 1970: 7–69, 1990: 157–85 on the development of constitutional terminology (cf. brief discussions in Raaflaub 1995: 46–51, 1996b: 143–45). Sources: for inscriptions, see *IG* I³, ML, and Fornara 1983; commentaries: on Thucydides: Gomme et al. 1945–81;

Hornblower 1991, 1996; on Aristotle, *Ath. Pol.:* Rhodes 1981; Chambers 1990; on Plutarch, *Solon* and *Pericles:* Manfredini and Piccirilli 1977; Stadter 1989. On oligarchy: Ostwald 2000; on democracy and tyranny: McGlew 1993; Raaflaub 2003; democracy and religion: Versnel 1995; Jameson 1998; Boedeker 2007; democracy and law: Todd 1993; democracy and war: Hanson 1996, 2001; Strauss 1996; Raaflaub 2007; democracy and ideology: Meier 1990 (German ed. 1980); democracy and culture: Sakellariou 1996; Boedeker and Raaflaub 1998; the assessment of democracy through the ages: Roberts 1994; assessments from today's perspective: Samons 2004; Woodruff 2005; see also, generally, Rhodes 2003a.

2. All dates are B.C.E. unless indicated otherwise.

3. For earlier discussions of this issue, see Morris and Raaflaub 1998: chaps. 2–6. We have comprehensively rethought and reformulated the positions we defended in 1998. Walter Eder, who had argued that democracy really did not fully come into being before the constitutional reforms were enacted, in reaction to democratic crisis and two oligarchic coups, at the turn of the fifth to the fourth century (Eder 1998; see the last section of this chapter below), unfortunately decided not to join in this new venture.

4. Having initiated this project, I am most grateful to my colleagues for engaging in this ongoing discussion and for all the help they offered me along the way. I also thank them all for generous and valuable comments on an earlier draft of this chapter.

5. Some scholars conclude, therefore, that by the fourth century the Athenian political system had made the transition "from popular sovereignty to the sovereignty of the law" (thus the subtitle of Ostwald's 1986 book; cf. Sealey 1987 and comments in Eder 1998).

6. The anonymous late-fifth-century pamphlet surviving under the same title among Xenophon's writings offers not a history and analysis but a polemical critique of the workings of democracy; its author is therefore usually identified as Pseudo-Xenophon or the "Old Oligarch."

7. This section is written primarily for readers who are unfamiliar with the evidence. The informed reader may wish to skip to the next section.

8. For collections of Greek historical inscriptions, see Meiggs and Lewis 1988, covering the entire period from the late eighth to the end of the fifth century, and Rhodes and Osborne 2003, on the fourth century. Translations: Fornara 1983; Harding 1985.

9. Edited with French trans. in van Effenterre and Ruzé 1994–95; see Hölkeskamp 1999.

10. Van Effenterre (1985), trying to demonstrate with archaeological evidence that the Greek polis existed already in the Greek Bronze Age, offers a good example (see reviews by A. Snodgrass, *Classical Review* 36 [1986] 261–65; N. Ehrhardt, *Gnomon* 58 [1986] 711–15).

11. E.g., Raaflaub 2000; and see chapter 2 below.

12. For efforts to overcome narrow "Athenocentrism," see, for example, Kurke 1998; Morris 1998; Rhodes 2003b.

13. For discussion, see, for example, Hansen 1989e, 2005; Bleicken 1994: 323–34; Robinson 1997: 25–33; Ober 2004; Woodruff 2005; and Cartledge, chapter 6 below.

14. As proposed by Jacobsen 1970: 132–70; see Robinson 1997: 16–25; Strauss 1998: 145. For interesting discussions of "protodemocratic" features in Mesopotamia, see now Schemeil 1999; Fleming 2004.

15. I thank Mark Munn and two anonymous readers for valuable comments and suggestions, Jennifer E. Thomas for patient and thorough help in compiling and checking the bibliography, and David Yates for compiling the indices. All authors wish to express their gratitude for various generous subsidies (noted at the beginning of this volume) that helped reduce the price of this book.

Chapter 2

"People's Power" and Egalitarian Trends in Archaic Greece

Kurt A. Raaflaub and Robert W. Wallace

Democracy is constituted through institutions, practices, mentalities, and, eventually, ideologies. In Greece these different components of democracy reached their fullest development in the fifth and fourth centuries. If democracy means that all citizens, the entire demos, determine policies and exercise control through assembly, council, and courts, and that political leaders, attempting to shape public opinion, are subordinate to the demos, the first democracy that we can identify with certainty was that of Athens from the 460s, emerging as a result of historically specific and even contingent factors (see chapter 5 below). At the same time, the contributors to this volume agree, democratic institutions had a long prehistory, and their underlying mentalities and practices can be traced centuries earlier. Popular assemblies, a measure of free speech, a strong sense of community, and mentalities including egalitarianism, personal independence, self-worth, and a refusal to be cowed by the rich, powerful, or wellborn are reflected already in the earliest literary documents from archaic Greece. As we shall see in this chapter and in greater detail in chapter 3, in a number of poleis in the sixth and even late seventh centuries, the demos was prepared to rise up against their traditional rulers, to hand power over to a lawgiver or support a tyrant in seizing power, and according to some sources sometimes even to assume power themselves. Some ancient writers called these early constitutions democracies, although the meaning or accuracy of that designation must remain uncertain. Our inadequate sources for archaic poleis outside Athens and Sparta have obscured the nature of these polities, allowing us to conclude only that the impetus toward popular government was an early and Panhellenic phenomenon.

The purpose of the present chapter is to identify and analyze, through specific case studies, the early preconditions of classical Greek democracy as far as they can be recovered. We do not propose that fifth-century democracy evolved from such roots necessarily and inevitably. Rather, our case studies will help to illuminate how important institutions, practices, and mentalities emerged and evolved, before they were transformed through social and political crises and conscious political reform in the different stages of democratic development discussed in later chapters. Not least, these focused examinations of central topics in archaic Greece will help to balance the classical and Athenocentric perspectives that will necessarily prevail in later chapters.

We begin with one example that defines more sharply what we are looking for. Between 650 and 600 the citizens of a small polis (city- or rather citizen-state), Dreros on Crete, passed a law and had it inscribed on stone:

> This has been decided by the polis: When a man has been Kosmos, for ten years that same man shall not be Kosmos. If he should become Kosmos, whatever judgments he gives, he himself shall owe double, and he shall be useless as long as he lives, and what he does as Kosmos shall be as nothing. The swearers (to this shall be) the Kosmos, the Demioi and the Twenty of the polis. (ML 2; trans. Fornara 1983: no. 11)

This is one of the earliest extant polis laws in Greece. It represents the first instance (as far as we know, in world history) of a limitation being imposed upon the repetition of an office. The Kosmos apparently was the chief magistrate and judge of Dreros. The law prohibits him from repeating his office before an interval of ten years has expired and determines the punishment to be exacted for offenses against this restriction, involving material compensation and a serious reduction in the offender's status: he shall be "useless," that is, probably, deprived of various civic capacities, including the capacity to hold public office. Two groups of officials (the Demioi and the Twenty) are listed among those responsible for upholding the law.

In only a few lines, this law offers invaluable insight into the political and administrative structure of one early polis. More importantly in our present context, it reflects an effort by a community to gain control over its officeholders and leaders (Ehrenberg 1943: 14–18; Willetts 1955: 167–69; Hölkeskamp 1999: 87–95). The body that passed this law—most likely the assembly—is described simply as "the polis." The polis speaks, in its own voice: "This has been decided by [lit. was pleasing to] the polis" (*tad' ewade poli*). Comparable phrases are known, for example in a sixth-century honorary decree passed by Cyzicus in the Hellespont. Privileges bestowed upon the descendants of two citizens are introduced there by "The polis gave" (*polis edoke*), and the people, the demos, confirm this by an oath (*Syll.* no. 4; Ehrenberg 1937: 152; Hölkeskamp 1999: 172–73).

Whom does this simple formula comprise? All the citizens who meet specific qualifications, for example by being prosperous enough to equip themselves for the polis's infantry army? All the free adult male inhabitants of the polis? We simply do not know. Nor do we know how "the polis" decided upon these measures: upon the recommendation of a council or official, by acclamation or vote, with or without discussion, and if the former, who participated in the discussion. What the phrase does tell us, however, is important enough. This polis had achieved a marked sense of community and of communal organization, integration, and identification. A strong sense of community is one important precondition for the emergence of democracy.

How far will the extant documents or literary works of even earlier periods help us to find the roots of polis consciousness, egalitarianism, and other prerequisites of democracy, and trace their relations to "people's power"? Not so far as the Bronze Age, it would appear. Scanty sources from second millennium B.C.E. Greece (material remains revealed by excavations, including thousands of inscribed tablets) permit us to reconstruct in rough outline the administrative, social, and political structures of the society we call, after one of its most spectacular sites, Mycenaean (e.g., Chadwick 1976; Dickinson 1994). Even if they do not include the kinds of texts that illuminate the political and social practices and mentalities we are interested in, these materials make clear that the Mycenaean states were based on a centralized palace economy, hierarchically structured, and ruled by kings with strong political and religious prerogatives.[1] They reveal important analogies to Near Eastern polities of the second millennium and, overall, are mostly alien to the forms of communal organization that emerged in the early archaic period, after the destruction of the Bronze Age palaces (around 1200 B.C.E.) and a long period of turmoil and retrenchment often called the Dark Ages (encompassing, in various degrees, the time from c. 1200 to 750 B.C.E.; Snodgrass 1971; Morris 1997). Hence we turn first to our earliest texts from archaic Greece: the epics of Homer and Hesiod.

"HOMERIC SOCIETY"

Many scholars now agree that once we discount a handful of Mycenaean and Dark Age relics and the actions and events that are distorted by "heroic exaggeration," the "world" presented by the Homeric epics (*Iliad* and *Odyssey*) is consistent enough to reflect a historical society that can be dated and contextualized within the social evolution of early Greece. Homer's world reflects the world of the master poet(s) and singer(s), who composed these monumental epics in the late eighth or early seventh century, or that of a slightly earlier period that was still accessible by living memory and satisfied the poet's archaizing tendency. The universalizing (Panhellenic) nature of Homer's poetry does not permit us to place his society geographically. It is a society shorn of traces that are specific to particular regions and localities. Its characteristics and problems enabled audiences all over Greece to recognize them and identify with them.[2]

Homer focuses on heroic, elite leaders who compete for honor, status, and influence through combat and debate. "Speakers of words and doers of deeds" (*Il.* 9.443), their goal is "always to be the best and to excel among the others" (6.208).[3] In the elite's ideology and self-presentation, their heroics decide battles, their persuasive speech sways assemblies, and their class, separated by a wide gap from the commoners, dominates society in every respect. Yet as both epics demonstrate, this is only one side of a more complex reality in which the commoners and the community play a much larger and, in fact, crucial role (Raaflaub 1997b; 2001: 73–89).

This more complex reality is visible especially in descriptions of battle and related activities, and in the importance assigned to the communal processes of deliberation and decision making. We begin with Homeric fighting.[4] The *Iliad* spotlights duels between elite warriors and often seems to represent the masses of fighters as mere followers with little impact on the outcome of battle. The great heroes *alone* are able to decide the battle, defeat the enemy, or save the city and its people. Hector (the "holder, protector") bears this quality in his name, and the people call his son Skamandrios "Astyanax"—"lord of the city, since Hector alone saved the city" (6.402–3; cf. 22.506–7; Nagy 1979: 145–46). From this perspective, the leaders are profoundly different from the commoners (*laoi*, Haubold 2000), and this gap is emphasized frequently, especially in scenes where an individual rises to superb excellence (*aristeia*). Nothing else is to be expected in a heroic epic.

In fact, however, Homer also blurs this gap remarkably often. We hear frequently that all (*aollees*) the Trojans or Achaians attack or hold their ground (e.g., 13.136 = 15.306; 15.312), and that they fight in masses and crowds (*homiladon:* e.g., 15.277). In book 16, the 2,500 Myrmidons perform a collective *aristeia,* just as Patroclus excels in his individual one. While the latter readies himself for battle, Achilles goes around the huts of the Myrmidons and urges them to arm themselves (155–56). In their hunger for battle they are likened to wolves—a rare wild beast simile, typical of heroes, is here applied to masses of warriors (156–67). They are mustered: fifty ships with fifty companions (*hetairoi*) each have come to Troy, under five leaders (168–97). Achilles gives them a pep talk ("Myrmidons!" 198–209), making each man (*hekastos*) eager to fight (210–11), and including them all in his prayer (247–48). In their close formation they resemble a tight wall, in their aggressiveness a swarm of wasps (212–17, 257–67). Patroclus, too, addresses them: Myrmidons, *hetairoi* of Achilles, we must fight bravely to honor Achilles, who is by far the best among the Achaeans, "and so are we, his followers, who fight next to him" (*anchemachoi therapontes,* 268–75). So he fills each man (*hekastos*) with even more desire to fight: all together (*aollees*) they throw themselves upon the Trojans (275–76). All Myrmidons, including Patroclus, are presented as both "companions" and "followers" (*hetairoi* and *therapontes;* see van Wees 1997: 670; Donlan 1999: 345–57) of their leader Achilles. Odysseus himself well illustrates the fluidity and complexities of social status in his deceptive story to Athena, explaining that he refused to delight Orsilochos's father, Idomeneus, and be Orsilochos's *therapōn* in Troy, but instead "I commanded other *hetairoi*" (*Od.* 13.265–66).[5]

Of course, not every *hetairos* has equal status and is equally good and brave in battle. But no one is simply expendable: "We all know how to fight" (Il. 13.223); "there is work for all" (12.269–71); "there is a joint valor of men, even of very poor ones"—that is, combining their efforts, even the worst fighters can show valor (13.237). Overall, then, despite all the differences among the *hetairoi* who form the *laos* of the Myrmidons, each man counts and is taken seriously; each feels responsible for the success of the whole group and acts accordingly. The same concept recurs among Patroclus's victims, when Sarpedon, dying, calls upon the Lycian leaders and the entire *laos* to save his body (16.495–501; cf. 2.336–54).

Many additional indications suggest that Homer knows and assumes mass fighting by the people and considers it crucial for the success of battle. Various scenes and similes depict the army's march to battle, its formation and fighting. The poet's narrative technique alternates between "wide-angle" and close-up perspectives and never allows us to forget that the duels between heroic leaders he loves to describe in great detail are selected from a mass of similar duels that are being fought simultaneously along a widely extended battle line (van Wees 1994):

> And the men, like two lines of reapers who, facing each other,
> drive their course all down the field of wheat or of barley
> for a man blessed in substance, and the cut swathes drop showering,
> so Trojans and Achaians driving in against one another
> cut men down, nor did either side think of disastrous panic.
> The pressure held their heads on a line.
>   *Il.* 11.67–72

> The two sides closed together with a great war cry.
> Not such is the roaring against dry land of the sea's surf
> as it rolls in from the open under the hard blast of the north wind;
> not such is the bellowing of fire in its blazing
> in the deep places of the hills when it rises inflaming the forest,
> nor such again the crying voice of the wind in the deep-haired
> oaks, when it roars highest in its fury against them,
> not so loud as now the noise of Achaians and Trojans
> in voice of terror rose as they drove against one another.
>   14.393–401, trans. Lattimore

Other similes refer to forest or steppe fires, dark clouds and fog, storm winds and their effect on clouds and sea, swarms of birds or insects, herds of goats and sheep, woodcutters, leaves, flowers, and the sand on the shore. Before the battle, the dense formations of troops are compared with a solid wall built of stones set so close together that the force of storm winds cannot penetrate it (16.212–17). During battle, they are likened to a towering sea cliff that withstands the power of screaming winds and huge waves (15.614–22). In various combinations, these similes evoke the immense number of soldiers, the speed and violence of their advance or clash, and the horrendous noise caused by their movement and fighting. The exploits of the leaders—highlighted by a large set of different similes—would not create the visual and sound effects described by the mass similes.

The mass fighting described by Homer reflects only the beginning of a development that several generations later produced the hoplite phalanx (to which we will return). Yet already this poet is aware of an observation that lay behind the conception of the hoplite phalanx: avoidance of individual exploits and strict adherence to tight formations helped secure victory and greatly reduced losses: "Far fewer of the Argives went down, remembering always to fight in tight formation, friend defending friend from headlong slaughter" (17.364–65). This type of fighting reflects the transition, connected with the rise of the polis, from raids undertaken by elite warrior bands or larger groups of townsmen (e.g., *Od.* 9.39–61; 14.211–75; *Il.* 18.509–40; 11.670–761) to formal wars between neighboring poleis (e.g., *Il.* 11.670–761; 18.509–40), in which all able-bodied men fought who were capable of providing the requisite equipment. Such wars, usually fought for the control of contested land, are attested historically precisely from the late eighth century (Raaflaub 1997c: 51–53).

That such fighting presupposed basic equality among the fighters is confirmed not least by the modalities of the distribution of booty in the *Iliad*. The booty is brought into the middle (*es meson,* of the meeting place in the agora) and distributed by "the Achaeans," the *laoi* (*Il.* 1.123–29). Even if, for practical reasons, the leaders hand out the spoils (9.330–36; 11.685–88, 703–5), they do so on behalf and in the name of the community. Even lowly Thersites cries:

> Son of Atreus, what thing further do you want, or find fault with
> now? Your shelters are filled with bronze, there are plenty of the choicest
> women for you within your shelter, whom we Achaians
> give to you first of all whenever we capture some stronghold.
>   2.225–28

And Achilles complains:

> The share is the same for the man who holds back, the same if he fights
>   hard,
> We are all held in a single honor, the brave with the weaklings.
>   9.318–19

Apart from honorary gifts for the leaders, all soldiers thus receive equal shares.[6]

In view of all this, it is not surprising that the assembly plays a crucial role in both epics. Here, too, we need to look beneath the surface. At first sight, assemblies seem powerless and easily manipulated. They must be convened by an elite leader. Only the leaders (*basileis*, sg. *basileus*) speak. The assembled men are limited to expressing their opinion collectively, by shouting approval or displeasure, or else by "voting with their feet," as in the "temptation scene" of *Iliad* 2.142–54. Leaders as often as not seem to ignore such manifestations, dissolve the assembly, and do what they want anyway.

Again, however, closer inspection of a wide range of scenes and incidental remarks often reveals a different reality.[7] The assembly is a constant feature of Homeric society, embedded in its structures and customs, and formalized to a considerable degree. An assembly is called whenever debate of a public issue (*dēmion*, *Od.* 2.32, 44) is called for, in a polis or other social group (such as an army or warrior band). Leaders spend considerable time in the agora and in council. The speaker holds the leader's staff, thus assuming a position of high communal authority. Zeus (the king of the gods) himself and Themis ("Ordinance"), protectors of justice and divinely sanctioned customary law, watch over assemblies. Normally, the leader makes conscious efforts to convince the assembled men. Great importance is therefore attributed to his ability in persuasive speaking (*Il.* 9.440–43). The word that we translate as "obey" (*peithomai*) literally means "to be persuaded" and often has that sense, as in the formula "but come, as I speak, *peithōmetha*—let us all be persuaded." Agamemnon employs this formula when urging—not commanding—the troops to sail for home (*Il.* 2.139). As Mark Griffith observes (1998: 25–26), "the Greek moral and political vocabulary was always thin on words for 'obedience' or 'subordination.'" Submissiveness and blind obedience are not typical of the *laoi*.

True, there is no formal vote, hence no counting of votes, and no formal obligation to respect the people's opinion. Later, the introduction of such procedures and obligations will represent a big step toward institutionalized government in Greece. Even so, it is clearly in the leaders' interest to heed the assembly's voice. As the cases of Agamemnon (*Il.* bks. 1–2) and Hector (*Il.* 18.243–313; 22.99–110) illustrate, the consequences can be serious if leaders persist in ignoring the people or good advice and then fail to execute their plan successfully. Occasional comments suggest that the assembly has considerable power. When Odysseus weaves a tale of a life spent on Crete, he indicates that his community sent him to Troy, despite his reluctance, because of his demonstrated skills in fighting and ambush: "The harsh voice of the people compelled me" (*chalepē d'eche dēmou phēmis*, *Od.* 14.239).[8]

Overall, the assembly has an important function in witnessing, approving, and legitimizing communal actions and decisions regarding such matters as the distribution of booty, "foreign policy," and the resolution of conflicts (Raaflaub 1997a: 642–43). The middle (*meson*) is the communal sphere (*koinon*) shared by all citizens, elite and non-elite alike. It is here that the leaders debate and the masses raise their voice. The *meson* and *koinon* are symbols of communal integration. The demos's importance in this sphere confirms their importance in war.

One of these episodes of communal debate (in *Il.* bk. 2) contains a signal episode of free speech. Intending to test the resolve of his army, Agamemnon suggests in an assembly to abort the war against Troy and sail home. Contrary to his expectation, this prompts a mad rush to the ships, exposing a crisis in his leadership. Odysseus takes the initiative to restore order. He goes around, speaking to some *basileis* and distinguished men with soft words. But "when he saw some man of the people (*andra dēmou*) who was shouting, he would strike at him with his staff, and reprove him" (188–99):

> Now the rest had sat down, and were orderly in their places,
> but one man, Thersites of the endless speech, still scolded,
> who knew within his head many words, but disorderly (*akosma*);
> vain, and without decency (*ou kata kosmon*), to quarrrel with the princes
> with any word he thought might be amusing to the Argives. . . .
> Beyond all others Achilleus hated him, and Odysseus.
> These two he was forever abusing, but now at brilliant
> Agamemnon he clashed the shrill noise of his abuse. The Achaians
> were furiously angry with him, their minds resentful.
> But he, crying the words aloud, scolded Agamemnon. . . .
>   But brilliant Odysseus swiftly
> came beside him scowling and laid a harsh word upon him:
> "Fluent orator though you be, Thersites, your words are
> ill-considered. Stop, nor stand up alone against princes.
> Of all those who came beneath Ilion with Atreides
> I assert there is no worse man than you are. Therefore
> you shall not lift up your mouth to argue with princes. . . ."
> So he spoke, and dashed the sceptre against his back and
> shoulders, . . . and he sat down again, frightened,
> in pain, and looking helplessly about wiped off the tear-drops.
> Sorry though the men were they laughed over him happily.
>   *Il.* 2.211–70, trans. Lattimore

Homer makes every effort to discredit Thersites: he speaks out of order, he slanders the leaders to entertain the masses, he is the ugliest man (216–19) and the worst fighter in the army, he is hated by everybody, and his punishment delights the masses, who praise Odysseus extravagantly for silencing this "thrower of words, this braggart" (271–77). And yet Thersites speaks, has done so often, is skilled in speaking, and is not shouted down by the masses (Thalmann 1988). Moreover, he says exactly what Achilles had said the day before (1.121–29, 149–68, 225–32). Just as the Greek community at Troy in many ways resembles a single polis, so Thersites appears to represent public dissent against an aristocratic leader from amidst the assembled masses. Before Odysseus silenced the crowd, other "men of the people" apparently also spoke up, although the poet characterizes this as mere "shouting" (2.198).

Even though the commoners lack elite characteristics such as fine looks and virtues such as modesty (*aidōs*) and knowledge of what is "in order" (*kata kosmon*), they voice their opinions and sometimes speak up, in defiance of the aristocracy. When they fail to do so in Ithaca (in an important assembly scene in book 2 of the *Odyssey*), in full knowledge of the harm the suitors might cause not only to the estate of Odysseus but to the entire community, they are blamed for their passiveness (Raaflaub 2001: 83–86). Mentor says:

> I have no quarrel with the suitors. True,
> They are violent and malicious men,
> But at least they are risking their own lives. . . .
> It is the rest of the people I am angry with.
> You all sit here in silence and say nothing,
> Not a word of rebuke to make the suitors quit,
> Although you easily outnumber them.
>   *Od.* 2. 235–41, trans. Lombardo

In the administration of justice, too, the Homeric demos has a voice. A famous vignette on Achilles' marvelously decorated shield depicts an arbitration scene (*Il.* 18.497–508; Edwards 1991: 213–18 with bibliog.). A crowd has gathered in the agora. The issue is murder and a disagreement, perhaps about whether or not the family of the victim should accept the compensation promised by the killer.

> They were heading for an arbitrator
> And the people were shouting, taking sides,
> But heralds restrained them. The elders sat
> On polished stone seats in the sacred circle
> And held in their hands the staves of heralds.
>   501–5, trans. Lombardo

Although Homer's leaders are "men who safeguard the laws on behalf of Zeus" (*Il.* 1.238–39; cf. 2.205–6; 9.98–99), in this scene ordinary people speak and shout, in effect voting on the verdict each elder proposes. Moreover, despite Homer's bias, elite justice comes in for criticism—"there are cracks in the veneer," as Hans van Wees points out (1999a: 6). Van Wees observes:

Impartial justice turns out to be the *exception* rather than the rule when it is claimed that Odysseus "never did or said anything improper to anyone among the people, *as is the way [dikē] of godlike princes:* enemy to one man but friend to another" ([*Od.*] 4.689–92). . . . That personal interests may be upheld by means of violence or intimidation is evident from a simile which speaks of "men who, *by force,* judge crooked law cases in the agora, and drive out justice." (*Il.* 16.385–92)

Homer's *basileis* can be brutal (e.g., *Od.* 4.690–92). Achilles calls Agamemnon a *basileus* who "feeds on his people" (*dēmoboros: Il.* 1.231). In his grief about Hector's death, even Priam abuses his surviving sons as "shameful, boasters and dancers, the best men of the dancefloor, robbers of sheep and goats among their own people" (*Il.* 24.260–62, trans. van Wees).

The value system reflected in the epics further underscores the importance of the community. Although no one questions the *basileis*' status as leaders, they are constantly challenged by their peers. Their standing, honors, and privileges depend on their service to the community. If they fail, they suffer harsh criticism and disgrace (Raaflaub 1997a: 632 with references).[9] This "warrior ethic" (Redfield 1994: chap. 3) is exemplified by a conversation between two Lycian leaders, Sarpedon and Glaukos:

Glaukos, why is it you and I are honored before others
with pride of place, the choice meats and the filled wine cups? . . .
Therefore it is our duty in the forefront of the Lykians
to take our stand, and bear our part of the blazing of battle,
so that a man of the close-armoured Lykians may say of us:
"Indeed, these are no ignoble men who are lords of Lykia,
these kings of ours."
      Il. 12.310–19, trans. Lattimore

Hector eventually prefers to stand up to Achilles and risk death in honor rather than seeking shelter in the city and facing the Trojans' disapproval:

Ah me! If I go now inside the wall and the gateway,
Poulydamas will be first to put a reproach upon me,
since he tried to make me lead the Trojans inside the city
on that accursed night when brilliant Achilleus rose up,
and I would not obey him, but that would have been far better.
Now, since by my own recklessness I have ruined my people,
I feel shame before the Trojans and the Trojan women with trailing
robes, that someone who is less of a man than I will say of me:
"Hektor believed in his own strength and ruined his people."
      Il. 22.99–107

Similarly, Agamemnon and Achilles suffer because they failed to suppress selfish ambition and anger in favor of the common good (Raaflaub 2001:

80–83). Thersites rebukes Agamemnon in the assembly: "It is not right for you, their leader, to lead in sorrow the sons of the Achaians" (*Il.* 2.233–34).

Despite the elite's effort to emphasize distance and qualitative difference, Homer's language reflects no social contempt for the masses. Ordinary people are never called *kakoi* (low, bad, mean), as they are in later archaic poetry. Positive terms like *agathoi* (good, brave) or *hērōes* are used for them as well. Odysseus treats his men as comrades and friends (*philoi*) with care and respect: they are tied together by bonds of mutual dependence (see, for example, *Od.* 12.260–402). True enough, the ideal often clashes with reality. In the *Odyssey* the positive model of how members of Odysseus's household deal with poor people and outsiders is contrasted with the negative example of the suitors and unfaithful servants (Havelock 1978: chap. 9). Similarly, the kind offer of employment that the wicked suitor Eurymachus extends to the "beggar" Odysseus in *Odyssey* 18.357–61 has its counterpart in the broken promises of another elite employer in *Iliad* 21.441–52 (Finley 1977: 57–58). So, too, as we saw, the leaders can act despicably, but the ideal *basileus* is a "shepherd of his people" (*poimēn laōn*), not a brutal commander, distant ruler, or exploiter. For high status with concomitant honors and privileges he depends on the demos (Donlan 1999: 19–20).

This material suffices to demonstrate our point. In Homer, despite elite claims to the contrary, the demos's role is significant on the battlefield, in the assembly, and in society. Although equality is not yet formalized or confirmed by law or ideology, basic forms of egalitarianism are reflected in the weakness of aristocratic authority and social hierarchies, including class vocabulary. In fighting and in the assembly, each man can contribute, and none is happy to be subordinate or obey. Homeric society recognizes the value and humanity of each individual, even those of low social status. Although the elite may not like it, already men like Thersites are standing up in the assembly and addressing the gathered community. The sentiments of the people are a force to be reckoned with (*Od.* 16.371–82). Despite his elite focus and aristocratic bias, Homer already reveals some fundamental institutions, practices, and mentalities that would later form the core of Greek democracy.

HESIOD'S WORLD

Roughly contemporary with Homer and also addressing a Panhellenic audience, Hesiod presents himself almost as an "ideal type" of what must have been a significant Greek population of hardworking farmers, each with a wife and children, two oxen, a slave woman, and hired laborers, ideally prosperous, though in fact always close to the edge of subsistence (Millett 1984; Hanson 1995: chap. 3). Ian Morris (1996: 28–31; 2000) identifies this constellation of attributes as part of the "middling ideology" later shared by the *mesoi politai*, "middling citizens" of Athens' classical democracy. However authentic or generic autobiographic details in his epics may be (Nagy 1990: chap. 3), Hesiod purports to be a voice from the people. Unlike Homer's Thersites, his voice is not mediated through elite scorn. Especially *Works and Days* is in part a protest poem. Hesiod is sharply critical of aristocratic injustice and exploitation, and he implies that such criticisms were widespread (Morris 1996: 28–29):

> There is angry murmuring when right (*dikē*, or Dike, the goddess of justice) is dragged off wherever gift-swallowers choose to take her as they give judgment with crooked verdicts; and she follows weeping to those people's town and territories clad in darkness. . . . Often a whole community together suffers in consequence of a bad man who does wrong and contrives evil. . . . Zeus either punishes those men's broad army or city wall, or punishes their ships at sea. . . . Beware of this, lords, and keep your pronouncements straight, you gift-swallowers, and forget your crooked judgments altogether. (213–73, trans. adapted from West 1993)

Works and Days presents an image of independent, hardworking farmers standing up to a greedy and grasping elite: an important precondition for the emergence of people power. At the same time, Hesiod is suspicious of the polis's public sphere, advises his listeners to stay away from the quarrels of the agora, and urges them to focus on work, farm, and neighborhood (27–34, 342–52; cf. 493–501). Further complicating the picture, Hesiod's more greatly idealizing *Theogony* praises the *basileis*, whom the Muses give honey-sweet tongues so they can settle quarrels fairly, and who appear in the assembly like gods (79–93). By describing the just rule of Zeus, the *Theogony* offers Greek leaders a model to imitate (Raaflaub 2000: 35–36). These two Panhellenic songs are thus capable of reflecting alternative social visions. Just so, the *Odyssey* presents Odysseus as a model head of his *oikos* and fair leader of his community, while in the *Iliad* Odysseus appears as the tough leader and disciplinarian who beats and mocks the humble Thersites for not knowing how to speak *kata kosmon*.[10] Nonetheless, in neither of his poems does Hesiod make any claim to be equal to elite leaders or challenge their position in society. Empowered by the Muses, Zeus's daughters, he *does* claim to be an authority for what is right, just, and good (Nagy 1990: 67). A century later in Athens, Solon's poems still attest the people's outrage at injustice. By Solon's time, however, no one will call the aristocracy "honey-tongued" (Donlan 1999: chap. 2, esp. 68–75).

One striking aspect of Hesiod's message is his insistence on the farmer's independence and self-reliance. In particular, his world has no place for an institution that was frequent in other peasant societies. Patronage may be defined as an asymmetrical relationship involving the exchange of goods and services, which the more powerful participant (the patron) has the power to exploit. Although both useful and common in societies where many live near the margin of subsistence, in ancient Greece, with the exception of Sparta (Cartledge 1987: chap. 9), "instances [of patronage] are so peripheral and so few in number that they do not appear to exert any pronounced influence on the ordering of society" (Millett 1989: 16). Paul Millett associates the absence of patron/client relations with the citizens' independence characteristic of democratic Athens. As his essay reveals, the absence of such relations was typical of most of early Greece. Hesiod shows no awareness of patronage and emphasizes that dependency must be avoided (*W&D* 354, 366–67, 393–404, 408). Social equilibrium and the protections offered elsewhere by patronage were maintained through reciprocal relations of lending and borrowing between "friends" (*philoi*) and neighbors, that is, exchanges between people of similar status (Millett 1989: 43).

Hesiod thus contributes several further elements to our argument. While confirming Homer's evidence for the strength of the community and its individual members and feelings of resentment against abuses in the aristocratic administration of justice, Hesiod also documents the Greek farmers' deep-seated mentality of personal independence. Throughout their history, Greeks objected to being obliged to another and thus surrendering their freedom. People dependent on others were branded *kolakes* and *parasitoi*, "flatterers" and "parasites." Forced into slavery, Sparta's helots (according to tradition, the formerly free population of subjected territories; see below) revolted and kept their Spartiate masters on constant alert, finally winning freedom in the fourth century, when Sparta was defeated by Thebes and its power collapsed.[11] In Athens, the dependence of the serflike *hektēmoroi* was one of the main factors contributing to social conflicts and urging radical measures, including the abolition of debt bondage (Wallace, chapter 3 below). According to Aristotle (*Politics* 1269a36), "the *penestai* [serflike Greeks] in Thessaly often revolted against the Thessalians." Among the free, the Greeks' dislike of depending on another person for their living became even more pronounced in the fifth and fourth centuries, effectively barring the development of a free labor force (Humphreys 1978: 147).

HOPLITE IDEOLOGY

Although its roots are visible already in Homer, the hoplite phalanx developed in a long process and was fully formed only by the mid- to late seventh century.[12] It had a notable impact on the ideals and practices of communal cohesion. The poet Tyrtaeus (second half of the seventh century) sang to the gathered Spartiates:

Fear not the throng of men, turn not to flight,
but straight toward the front line bear your shields. . . .
Those who bravely remain beside each other

and press toward engagement at the front
die in less numbers and save the ranks
behind; of those who run all virtue is perished.

    11.3–4, 11–14 West 1992; trans. adapted from West 1993

It benefits the whole polis and demos,
when with a firm stance in the foremost rank
a man bides steadfast, with no thought of shameful flight,
laying his life and stout heart on the line,
and standing by the next man speaks encouragement.

    12.15–19 West; trans. adapted from West, our emphasis

Massed in close ranks together, hoplites fought in strict discipline, shoulder to shoulder, shield to shield. Even if hoplite warfare evolved gradually and itself did not constitute a social and political revolution, it reflected social relations in several important ways. First, phalanx fighting was inherently communitarian, cooperative, and egalitarian. Elites and *mesoi* fought side by side as equals, in defense of the polis. They learned to trust each other and work together. This furthered a sense of community not conditioned by birth, wealth, or other social distinctions. Second, and related to this point, hoplite warfare offered no room for aristocratic *aristeiai,* as the Greeks imagined were typical of "heroic" fighting. The best fighters were placed in the first rank, irrespective of status and class. Hence every hoplite had a chance to be recognized as the best (*aristos*). The soldier's *aretē* (excellence), as Tyrtaeus illustrates so impressively, could no longer be claimed exclusively by the elite. *Aretē* was communalized. Even if still at the end of the archaic period, after the great Persian War battle at Plataea, the bravest fighters were singled out and honored (Herodotus 9.71), all the Greek hoplites who had fallen in this battle were celebrated as heroes and collectively compared with the epic heroes of the Trojan War (Simonides 11 West; cf. Boedeker 2001). Third, the polis supervised training and decided when and where to fight. Although raids by elite warrior groups and private military actions against neighboring communities still occurred, henceforth the hoplites formed the principal military force of all Greek poleis, and hoplite warfare was communal, conducted by the polis as the collectivity of its citizens.

The need for mass warfare was surely in part conditioned by the growing populations of eighth- and seventh-century Greece, and the resulting scarcity of land and development of the concepts of territoriality and fixed boundaries. The hoplite phalanx evolved in an interactive process with the polis and land ownership (Raaflaub 1997c, 1999). At the same time, many scholars have observed that rigid lines of heavily armed troops were not ideally suited to a country with many more hills and mountains than level plains. Quintessential qualities of the hoplite phalanx were the massed equality of all warriors, the equal bravery demanded of everyone together, and the will of each hoplite to acquire armor and fight for his community.

To substitute for the glory of single combat, the aristocracy turned to competitive athletics. At the Olympic games boxing and the pankration were introduced in the first half and middle of the seventh century. The latter was a violent, sometimes deadly mix of boxing and wrestling that barred only biting and gouging out the eyes. We can only speculate about the collective psychology that lay behind the aristocracy's adoption of such a "sport" (Poliakoff 1987). The synchronicity with the development of egalitarian hoplite warfare is surely no coincidence.

SPARTA'S WORLD OF *HOMOIOI*

With all this in mind, we now take a closer look at Sparta's bold, in some ways even startling revolution. In a process poorly documented by our late and distant sources, Sparta in the late eighth century had conquered not only the area on its own (east) side of the Taygetos mountain range (Laconia) but also Messenia in the west. Sometime in the second half of the seventh century, the Messenians rose in revolt and brought Sparta to the brink of defeat. Even earlier, Sparta seems to have suffered another major defeat, by its neighbor and hated rival Argos (traditionally dated to 669). Fragments of the poetry of Tyrtaeus (collected in West 1992: 169–84; trans. in West 1993: 23–27) offer tantalizing insights into this crisis and reflect the desperate efforts of Sparta's army to defeat the rebels. In response to these major military threats to its survival, the Spartan community began to transform itself into a hoplite state. The details of this process have been much discussed recently, in a comprehensive effort at reevaluation. Many of the traits characteristic of the militaristic society for which Sparta was famous evolved over time and were probably not in place before the mid-sixth century or even later. Yet some elements, including a few that are crucial for our present purposes, resulted from a conscious communal effort of polis reform that can be dated to the seventh century.[13]

Sparta's survival depended on the ability of its citizens (the Spartiates) to defend their polis and control the areas and populations subjected in recent wars. A strong and ready army was thus indispensable. It is no accident, therefore, that fighting in the hoplite phalanx continued to be perfected during the second half of the seventh century, and that Argos and Sparta (perhaps in response to Argos) were believed to have been the leaders in this development.

Yet Sparta's bold response to the dangers confronting it was not only military, but economic, ideological, and political. The strength of a hoplite army lay not only in its discipline but also in numbers. Whether or not the Spartiates had to provide their own equipment (Cartledge 2001a: 165), it was in the polis's interest to make sure that a sufficient number of citizens owned enough property to meet the requirements of the hoplite class. The seventh-century crisis revealed alarming deficiencies in this respect. As Aristotle reports, "a poem of Tyrtaeus called *Eunomia* ("Good Order") [shows that] some people impoverished by war were demanding that the land should be distributed" (*Politics* 1306b37–1307a2; cf. Tyrt. 2 West). As a result, the Spartiates made sure that each citizen had sufficient land to free him for military service and to provide his contributions to communal meals. Subjected helots worked this land, thus providing the Spartiates with the means to keep them in subjection.

The hoplite army's egalitarian ideology came to be expressed in the Spartiates' classification of themselves as *homoioi,* "alikes" or "similars" (Cartledge 1996a). To be sure, for much of the archaic period Sparta was less "abnormal" than has long been thought, in this and other respects. Social and economic differences were not abolished (Sparta was no utopia), and continuing differentiation much later became the main cause of a massive decline in citizen numbers and military power (Hodkinson 1983, 1993, 2000). Yet on a basic level, and especially concerning military preparedness, social differences were suppressed and obscured early on: the Spartiates presented themselves as equals. Thucydides observes: "It was the Spartans who first began to dress simply and in accordance with our modern taste, with the rich leading a life that was as much as possible like that of the ordinary people" (1.7).

Sparta's transformation was reflected (and effected in part) by a new constitution, the so-called Great Rhetra—the world's first written constitution, attesting to the Greeks' electrifying discovery that a community could change its traditional form of government by writing down new rules. The *rhētra*'s provisions are reflected in a poem by Tyrtaeus (4 West, quoted by Diodorus Siculus) and in Plutarch's *Life of Lycurgus* (chap. 6, perhaps based on Aristotle's lost work on the Spartan constitution). Although problems of text and content have been endlessly debated, few scholars doubt the *rhetra*'s essential authenticity.[14] It was normal procedure to sanction political change by religious authority, usually of Apollo's oracle in Delphi. Tradition has turned this causal relationship around and made the *rhētra* itself an oracle:

> After dedicating a temple to Zeus Sullanios and Athena Sullania, forming *phulai* and creating *obai,* and instituting a Gerousia of thirty, including the leaders (*archagetai*), then from season to season they shall *apellazein* between Babyka and Knakion so as to propose and stand aside (*eispherein, aphisthasthai*). But to the people (*damos?*) shall belong the authority to respond (?) and power (*kratos*). (Plut. *Lyc.* 6.2, trans. adapted from Talbert 1988)

The gods' epithets remain unexplained—or else have been emended, for example, to *Hellanios/a. Phulai* and *obai* are subdivisions of the citizen body, perhaps tribes and districts or villages. *Archagetēs* is an archaic title of the Spartan kings, who are usually called *basileis.* Since the assembly was held on

Apollo's feast day, *apellazein* (celebrate the feast of Apollo) came to mean "hold the assembly" (Welwei 1997; Cartledge 2001b: 30–31). Babyka and Knakion must be topographical indicators, defining the place where the assembly was to meet. *Eispherein* (making proposals) seems unproblematic, while the obscure *aphisthasthai* (to stand aside) has been the subject of much speculation, none of it provable. The first part of the last sentence is mangled in the manuscript tradition. If proposed emendations are correct,[15] the *damos* was entitled to respond to proposals made by others. *Kratos* is undisputed: power was in the hands of the *damos*.

Tyrtaeus says the following about the *rhētra:*

> The god-honored kings shall be leaders of the council (or perhaps rather:
>   first in debate [*archein boulēs*]),
>   they who care for the lovely city of Sparta,
> and the elders of revered age (*presbugeneas gerontas*), and then the men of
>   the people (*dēmotas andras*),
>   responding in turn to straight proposals (*eutheiais rhētrais
>   antapameibomenous*).
> They shall speak what is good and do everything justly
>   and counsel nothing for the city (that is crooked).
> Victory (*nikē*) and power (*kratos*) shall accompany the mass of the people
>   (*dēmou plēthei*).
> For Phoibos has so revealed this to the city.
>   4.3–10 West, trans. adapted from Fornara 1983

Apollo's oracle prophesied in hexameters; Tyrtaeus wrote elegiac couplets. His pentameters add nothing essential to the hexametric lines and thus are perhaps "fillers," enabling the poet to integrate the oracle into his elegy (West 1974: 184–86). At any rate, some essential points seem clear enough. Here and elsewhere possibly a kings' man (Murray 1993: 169), Tyrtaeus says there will be a hierarchy of speaking: first the kings, second the other members of the *gerousia* (the council of elders), last the common citizens. Nonetheless, he continues to stress that the full assembly shall have the final decision (*nikē*) and in this sense, power (*kratos*). If our understanding of the pentameter in line 4 ("responding to straight proposals") is correct, the poet's interpretation would seem to confirm the emendations (mentioned above) of the corrupted phrase in Plutarch's text—if, that is, we are right in taking Plutarch and Tyrtaeus as complementing each other.

Many "ifs," but they should not obscure the significance of this document. By the terms of the Rhetra, the *damos* of Spartan citizens was to be divided into tribes and villages. The introduction of such civic subdivisions is known from other communities (notably Athens and Rome) and seems to reflect communal adjustments necessitated by the formalization (even after a long evolution) of hoplite fighting (Raaflaub 1999: 135). The citizens

were organized into military units according to their residence and registered with their property. The polis thus had a clear sense of the manpower
available, and the army could be mustered quickly and efficiently by local-
ity. This reorganization was sanctioned by the introduction of new cults of
Zeus and Athena, traditionally the protectors of communities.

On the political side, the institutions and processes of decision making
were formalized as well. The council of elders was to consist specifically of
thirty men, including the two kings and twenty-eight *gerontes* who were distinguished by age and experience, being at least sixty years old (Plut. *Lyc.*
26.1). The place and the dates of mass assembly meetings were fixed. The
assembly was the place where proposals were introduced and decisions were
made. That the *damos* was to have the supreme power to decide is uncon-
tested. The kings and elders were to speak first in deliberation. They were
to introduce proposals. Was there open discussion in the assembly? That is,
did the "men of the *damos*" participate in the debate or merely answer the
proposals collectively, by voting? The evidence of Plutarch and Tyrtaeus is
not entirely clear, but the latter's words make better sense if there was open
debate. Furthermore, according to Plutarch the final provision of the *rhētra*
was later amended by a rider: "But later when the people by subtractions
and additions perverted and distorted the motions, the kings Polydoros and
Theopompos added the following *rhetra:* But if the people speaks crooked,
the elders and the *archagetai* are to be rejecters" (*Lyc.* 6.7–8; trans. Murray
1993). The rider implies that individual Spartans had been speaking up
from the floor, amending proposals and affecting the assembly's agenda.

Was Sparta, then, as some scholars have argued, the first democracy?[16]
"To the mass of the *damos* belong *nikē* and *kratos*." In the fifth century, the
juxtaposition of *dēmos* and *kratos* in a suitable context of one of Aeschylus's
tragedies is often taken to circumscribe the word *dēmokratia,* which does not
fit the poetic meter (Raaflaub, chapter 5 below). Crucial aspects of the *rhētra*
are that it fixed the dates, place, and powers of the Spartan assembly, which,
even in the classical period, exercised the power by acclamation to decide
issues that were brought before it. In a meeting reported by Thucydides
(1.87) in 431 B.C.E., following a mass deliberation (1.79), the assembly
voted in favor of the ephor Sthenelaidas's proposal for war, and against King
Archidamus. In addition, we know from other sources that the assembly
chose members of the powerful *gerousia* through collective shouting, a form
of popular vote in which those who gauged the levels of noise for each candidate were not supposed to know the latter's identity (Plut. *Lyc.* 26; Flaig
1993; Lendon 2001). Those who define democracy mainly by the assembly's power to make final decisions will count Sparta as a democracy. Oswyn
Murray writes: "The original *rhetra* itself records the assertion by the assembly of Equals of their dominance in the state" (1993: 168–69). As he also
notes, "the Spartans were always remarkably free in criticism of their kings

for alleged irregularities of birth or conduct, and were able to depose or exile them" (162). Even those who consider these criteria insufficient to define a democracy will admit that the "protodemocratic" features of Sparta's system are striking.[17]

Yet despite such "democratic" elements in Sparta's constitution the rider shows that free speech from the assembly floor proved problematic. As a consequence, the *damos*'s power was in some way reduced. The *damos*'s decisions could not perhaps be overruled, but *gerontes* and kings apparently received some sort of veto power. Whether they could suspend a decision by the assembly with which they disagreed or refuse to accept modifications proposed from amid the *damos*, and what was done next about such contested issues, we simply do not know.[18]

What role the five ephors played in this system is unknown. This office is often dated to the sixth century, but it may have existed from the early seventh and been enhanced in the sixth.[19] Elected for one-year terms by the assembled Spartiates and with no formal restrictions on eligibility, the ephors in some measure represented the *damos* and formed a counterweight to the aristocracy represented in the *gerousia* (Cartledge 2001d: 60) and to the power of the kings. They alone did not rise from their chairs of office in the kings' presence. Every month, they swore an oath on behalf of the people, to retain the kings as long as they abided by the laws. Every ninth year they watched the night sky for shooting stars. If they saw one, the king was suspended until the oracle in Delphi could be consulted (Plut. *Agis* 11). How much of this originated in the seventh century and what exactly prompted the increased role of the ephors, traceable from the late sixth century, is anyone's guess. This does not, of course, preclude the conclusion that some of the characteristics of this office suggest for a much earlier period an enhanced valuation of the *damos*'s role in the community.

Unquestionably, however, by the late sixth century Sparta had progressed a long way on the path toward a militarized society. No doubt, the ideology of the *homoioi* and the equality bestowed on the citizens by Sparta's early institutions are remarkable: the assembly's authority was formally recognized, members of the *gerousia* were elected, and the ephors came to act as a powerful check on the kings. Yet Sparta did not develop into "rule by the people." We mentioned the restrictions imposed on the assembly by the rider to the *rhētra*. Although every Spartiate could participate in the assembly, it remains unclear to what extent individual Spartans took advantage of this opportunity. M. I. Finley (1982: 33) may have identified the difficulty: "Can we imagine that the obedient, disciplined Spartan soldier dropped his normal habits on the occasions when he was assembled not as a soldier but as a citizen, while he listened to debates among those from whom he otherwise was taught to take orders without questioning or hesitation?"

The early historians (Hdt. 1.65.2–66.1; Thuc. 1.18.1) noted that Lycurgus (the legendary lawgiver) changed Sparta from a bad order (*kakonomia*) to a good one (*eunomia*). Collectively, at the expense of the helots' slavery (Plut. *Lyc.* 28.11), the Spartiates enjoyed the freedom, privileges, and values typically associated with aristocracy in Greece (31.1). But no one mentions the individual freedom (*eleutheria*) that characterized classical democracies, or freedom of speech. The discipline required in the army soon pervaded all dimensions of communal and even private life.[20] Plutarch writes that in Sparta "no man was allowed to live as he wished," but "as in a military camp," all were constantly engaged in public service to their polis (*Lyc.* 24.1; cf. Aristotle *Nichomachean Ethics* 1180a24–28). Xenophon states that Lycurgus

> laid down an inflexible requirement to practice all political virtue. Those who carried out their legal duties were given an equal share in the polis. He did not take into account physical weakness or poverty. If anyone shrank from carrying out his legal duties, Lycurgus indicated that he should no longer be considered one of the *homoioi*. (*Constitution of the Lacedaemonians* 10.7–8; trans. adapted from Moore 1975: 86)

The most important virtue in Sparta was obedience. As Xenophon observes, in contrast to other states where this is considered to be *aneleutheron* (unfree, that is, not befitting one's social status), "at Sparta the most powerful men (*kratistoi*) show utmost deference to the officials; they pride themselves on their humility, believing that, if they lead, the rest will follow along the path of eager obedience" (*Lak. Pol.* 8.1–2). In a well-known episode, Herodotus (7.104.4–5) points to the rule of "master" law (*despotēs nomos*) that supersedes freedom and explains Spartan bravery—an assessment that is ambivalent in several ways (Millender 2002). Restrictions imposed on the Spartiates' personal life promoted strength and discipline in the interest of the community's survival. Such restrictions could be coercive; they are described in detail in Plutarch's *Life of Lycurgus* and in Xenophon's *Constitution of the Lacedaemonians* and need not be summarized here. In addition, as Finley (1982: chap. 2) and others have observed, fatal contradictions were built into the Spartan system, in particular, inequalities of wealth, birth, and honor.

For all these reasons, the "democratizing" elements in Sparta's early development did not survive past infancy. Yet, under admittedly extraordinary circumstances, Sparta demonstrated the potential inherent in the polis's egalitarian structures.

OTHER PHENOMENA PROMOTING EGALITARIANISM AND "PEOPLE'S POWER"

More briefly, we mention several other developments that are important in the present context.

First, paradoxically, tyranny to some extent furthered the growth of "people's power" in archaic Greece. Whatever the origin and early use of the term *turannos* (Salmon 1997; Parker 1998), autocratic rule by an individual spread rapidly through a number of poleis during the century after 650. Tyrants monopolized power and honor, elevating themselves above all others, especially rival aristocrats. Thus, in part, tyranny reflected continuing hierarchic mentalities and ambitions widespread among the elite (Connor 1977). At the same time, many tyrants at least began as the people's men, supported or even put forward by the demos to defend them against aristocratic abuses and the impact of destructive rivalries, and securing communal peace and prosperity (Murray 1993: 144). The sixth-century poets Solon and Theognis and many fifth- and fourth-century historians reiterated the close links between demos and tyrants.[21] In these poleis, the people were not yet ready to seize power but they were ready to have a voice in deciding about those who would govern them. As far as the sources indicate, most early tyrannies began as popular dictatorships relying on the support of the demos.

A related form of autocratic office helps illuminate the demos's role in resolving social crises (see Faraguna 2005; Wallace 2007). In *Politics* 1285a29–b2 Aristotle mentions

> a third type of monarchy, which used to exist among Greeks of old. This third type is called *aisumnētēs* and was in rough terms an elective tyranny. . . . The rulers held office sometimes for life, sometimes for a stated period or until certain things should be accomplished: for example, the people of Mytilene elected Pittacus [c. 650–577] for the purpose of repelling the exiles who tried to come back led by Antimenides and the poet Alcaeus. That Pittacus was chosen is clear from one of Alcaeus's banqueting songs in which he grumbles that "with mass-adulation they appointed low-born Pittacus to be tyrant of their easy-going and unlucky state." (trans. Sinclair and Saunders 1981)

Although Pittacus was the first and most famous *aisumnētēs*, others are attested in sixth-century Miletus and Olympia, and "lawgivers" were active in many other archaic poleis (Hölkeskamp 1999; and see below). An early-fifth-century inscription from Teos forbids the appointment of an *aisumnētēs* even if the majority (*polloi*) wish it (van Effenterre and Ruzé 1994–95: 1.105, lines 22–24).

On archaic tyrannies, two further points are worth emphasizing. One is that tyrannies typically lasted no more than two generations. Sons often failed to demonstrate their fathers' abilities, met resistance, became abusive, and were overthrown—often by the demos. The other is that tyrannies had the effect of enhancing communal cohesion and strength and furthering the rise of the *mesoi*. As the example of Athens illustrates especially well, an extended period of tyranny weakened the elite's social and economic power and the local and regional structures that had supported their political dominance. As a result, communities prospered, and the citizens learned in a new way to focus on the community and its center. If tyrannies suggest that the demos was not yet ready to govern, the "age of the tyrants" was important in unifying the polis and creating the potential for independent communal action (Anderson 2003; Raaflaub, chapter 5 below). Tyranny was thus an important stage in the process toward democracy (Stahl 1987; Eder 1988, 1992).

Second, political upheavals by the demos in archaic Greece sometimes had more direct consequences. Eric Robinson (1997; see also O'Neil 1995) has examined comprehensively all the evidence that survives from the archaic period for the existence of institutions and laws that attest to egalitarian political structures and popular involvement in polis government. Based on the broad range of democratic constitutions discussed in Aristotle's *Politics* and other criteria, he identifies these early polis systems as democracies. He concludes:

> A pan-Hellenic movement towards egalitarianism, detectable early in the archaic period, preceded democracy's appearance; our investigation . . . revealed fully eighteen states for which convincing evidence exists for popular government before 480 B.C. Certainty was not possible, for political history in the archaic period must be constructed from the thinnest scraps of testimony. . . . Of these eighteen, we found the most compelling cases for actual functioning democracies in Achaea, Croton, Acragas, Ambracia, Argos, Chios, Cyrene, Heraclea Pontica, Megara, Naxos, and Syracuse. . . . Most of them can demonstrate institutions characteristic of Greek democracy. These include mechanisms for the control of magistrates, low or nonexistent property qualifications, a representative council, and active popular participation in juries and legislative bodies. At the least, evidence shows the *demos* to have been *kyrios*, the single most crucial test. (1997: 126)

Investigating the causes of the emergence of such early "democracies," Robinson states: "Most early popular governments . . . share one feature regarding their genesis: they arose as a result of an extraordinary political crisis. . . . The conclusion seems inevitable that early forms of democracy only took root as a result of severe political upheavals" (129). "Such results," Robinson concludes, "accord well with the idea of an emerging pan-Hellenic egalitarianism in the archaic period, for such ideals would seem to be a prerequisite for the autonomous formation of democratic governments" (129).

As Robinson himself recognizes, the evidence for these archaic democracies is often tenuous. Others, noting the absence of reliable contemporary information and applying more specific definitions to "democracy," might prefer to categorize them as "pre- or protodemocracies." Aristotle himself notes that the governments that "we call *politeiai*"—mixtures of oligarchy and democracy (Robinson 1997: 42)—"earlier men called democracies" (*Pol.* 1297b22–28). Nevertheless, Robinson's findings are important.[22] As we shall see in greater detail in chapter 3, in some archaic poleis the demos itself was ready to seize power, even if the precise nature of these revolutions can no longer be identified. Approaching this issue from a different angle and mostly using different evidence, Ian Morris has also argued for a widespread movement toward egalitarianism especially in the second half of the sixth century.[23]

Third, colonization provided a powerful incentive to establish egalitarian political and social structures. Colonies were newly founded communities, often combining people of different origins, both geographically and socially. These people left their homes for various reasons, including social dissatisfaction and economic misery. Except for the colony's founder (*oikistēs*), who received certain privileges and, after his death, might be worshipped as a hero, all colonists started from scratch, on the same level, and with the same opportunities. As we saw above (note 5), the settlers of Cyrene were to sail "on equal and fair terms." In quite a few colonies the equal distribution of plots for houses and fields is reflected in the plan of the main settlement and the network of roads and paths. This experience in turn had a powerful impact on egalitarian thinking and demands for redistribution of land "back home" in the Greek mainland.[24]

Fourth, we return to our starting point (the law of Dreros on Crete). Archaic laws (collected by van Effenterre and Ruzé 1994–95 and interpreted by Hölkeskamp 1999) provide important evidence for the development of institutions, for early efforts to limit aristocratic freedom of action, and for an evolving sense of community and joint communal action. True, the elites themselves certainly played an important role in initiating and realizing such efforts, not least because they were able to provide leadership and expertise and were interested in preventing destructive rivalries and the rise of tyranny (Eder 1998, 2005). But clearly such regulations, which often resulted in incisive innovations, must have been prompted by strong pressure from within the polis to limit abuses by the elite and secure equal treatment for all (Gehrke 2000). As we shall see in chapter 3, the Athenian lawgiver Solon states this clearly. Equal for all, laws helped address the problem of "gift-devouring *basileis*" about whom Hesiod complained earlier (*W&D* 39). The formalization of institutions, the enactment of written law, and the appointment of mediators and legislators with extraordinary power were supported by the entire polis, as the means to overcome social crises and promote civic justice (Raaflaub 1999: 140 with bibliog. in n. 58).

All this had a leveling effect, curbed arrogant abuses of aristocratic power, and promoted equality and security of justice. Such equality affected both the aristocracy and broader citizen classes. In fact, there is much to suggest that an explicit political terminology that stressed not similarity or relative equality (*homoiotēs*, as cultivated by the Spartan *homoioi*) but full or absolute equality (*isotēs*, as in *isonomia*, equality of political shares, or *isēgoria*, equality of speech in communal affairs) emerged in elite circles, who saw themselves deprived of equality by a tyrant's monopolization of power. Once this terminology existed, it could be applied to political systems that were designed to empower broader citizen groups in the interest of stabilizing the polis. The reforms the Athenians enacted under the leadership of Solon at the beginning, and of Cleisthenes at the end, of the sixth century are prime examples, but legislation and political regulation with similar purposes were widespread in archaic Greece.[25]

Fifth, as Hesiod's *Works and Days* illustrates impressively, day by day, for most Greeks local life, household affairs, working in the fields, and recreation including communal festivals and village dancing were far more significant than the politics of the agora. The Greeks in part transferred to politics what W. Robert Connor (1996a, 1996b) calls "a preexisting democratic culture," that is, mentalities developed in kinship and neighborhood groups, cult worship, managing their villages (Thuc. 2.15; Schmitz 1999, 2004), and business associations, where working relationships connected individuals as equals, whether brothers or partners. Connor calls attention to the organizations (some of them little understood) that are mentioned in a law attributed to Solon: "If a deme or members of a phratry or *orgeōnes* of heroes or members of a *genos* or *sussitoi* (messmates) or funerary associates, or *thiasōtai*, or pirates, or traders make arrangements among themselves, these shall be binding unless forbidden by public texts" (1996a: 219; the law is cited in *Digest* 47.22.4).

Connor suggests that not all of these associations were organized on hereditary or hierarchical principles. He also points to a provision in the homicide law enacted by the Athenian lawgiver Draco in 621, that pardon may be granted by father, by brother, and by son, or "the one who opposes it shall prevail" (*IG* I³ 104, lines 13–16). This provision appears to reflect the lawgiver's awareness that patriarchal authority was lacking, or even that equality prevailed, among the males of a family: even one recalcitrant son could veto what the father had proposed. The uncertain authority of the heads of household (*kurioi*) in dealing with other household members is well known from classical Athens, especially in regard to protecting family property (Hunter 1994: 9–42). Even women could come forward to guard the interests of family members. Connor also points to democratic attitudes in the worship of Dionysos, including the carnival atmosphere of free speech and the worship of Dionysos as "the god who in equal measure to rich and humble gives griefless joy of wine" (Euripides *Bacchai* 421–23; cf. Connor 1989). Egalitarian rather than hierarchic mentalities were thus influential in spheres outside politics.

Finally, Jean-Pierre Vernant has long drawn our attention more generally to egalitarian elements in Greek polis society (e.g., 1982: esp. chap. 4). As he observes,

Greek society was egalitarian, not hierarchical. The city defines those who
compose it by placing them in a group on a single horizontal plain. . . . Each
individual, if he is a citizen, is, at least in principle, able to fulfill all the social
functions. . . . There is no priestly or warrior caste. . . . The citizen of the classical *polis* belongs not to *Homo hierarchicus* but rather to *Homo aequalis*. (1991:
319–20)

Again, Sparta is a partial exception, but Vernant is surely right in pointing out
that social equality and independence are reflected in a wide range of phenomena throughout Greek life, from the power of *ho boulomenos* (every person who wanted, including slaves) to decide himself whether to be initiated
into the Mysteries at Eleusis (Hdt. 8.65.4) to the subjectivity of poets and
thinkers. Sappho writes: "Some say a host of cavalry, others of infantry, and
others of ships, is the most beautiful thing on the black earth, but I say it is
whatever a person loves" (fr. 16 Campbell 1982). Here, Vernant observes,

the subjectivity of the poet questions established norms and socially recognized values. It also serves as a touchstone for individual evaluations: the beautiful and the ugly, the good and the bad. . . . There exists then a relativity of
communally held values. In the last resort, the criterion of values falls to the
subject, the individual—what he or she has personally experienced—and this
is what forms the substance of the poem. (1991: 319–20, 324, 327)

In these and other ways, in early Greece political and military equality,
the personal independence and autonomy especially of "middling" citizens,
the Greeks' refusal to subordinate themselves to patrons, overlords, or abusive aristocrats, the characteristic openness and tolerance of individuals'
opinions and choices, and personal freedom as balanced by a strong egalitarian commitment to the community: all of these qualities lay at the root of
Greek democracy. They were necessary although not sufficient conditions
for developments that eventually resulted in democracy. It is the purpose of
subsequent chapters to discuss the factors that helped realize this potential
at various stages in the history of Athens.[26]

NOTES

1. Central palace economy: Finley 1982: chaps. 12–13; Kilian 1988; Laffineur
and Niemeier 1995; Thomas and Conant 1999: xxv–xxvii, 1–16; Galaty and Parkinson 1999; Voutsaki and Killen 2001. That villages or towns in the territory of the various late Bronze Age palace states or in "marginal" areas not reached by them
retained structures of self-administration (with leaders and possibly council and
assembly) is likely even if only scant references to officials survive; see, for example,
Deger-Jalkotzy 1995; Thomas 1995; Parker forthcoming; and various contributions
in Galaty and Parkinson 1999 and Voutsaki and Killen 2001 (we thank Sigrid Deger-
Jalkotzy for some of these references). Such features are visible on the margins of

some Mesopotamian states (e.g., Mari: Fleming 2004; see, more generally, Schemeil 1999). On Jacobsen's theory of "primitive democracy" (1970: 132–70), see Robinson 1997: 16–22; Fleming 2004: 15–16, 235–41.

2. See Finley 1977; Murray 1993: chaps. 3–4; Morris 1996; Raaflaub 1997a: 625–33; 1998a. The translations in this section come from Lattimore 1951 and Lombardo 1997.

3. Adkins 1960; 1972: 10–35; Stein-Hölkeskamp 1989: chap. 2; van Wees 1992; Redfield 1994; Donlan 1999: 1–34.

4. See recently Snodgrass 1993; van Wees 1994, 1997, 2000; Raaflaub 1997c, 2005a; see also Cartledge 2001a.

5. In the late-seventh-century foundation decree for Thera's colony at Cyrene (preserved in a fourth-century copy, ML 5, lines 25–27; trans. Fornara 1983: 23), "it has been decided by the Therans to send Battos off to Libya, as Archagetes and as King, with the Therans to sail as his companions (*hetairoi*). On equal and fair terms shall they sail . . ."

6. Cf. *Od.* 9.39–42; Detienne 1965; Nowag 1983. This does not preclude, of course, that some commoners, like Thersites in the previous passage, envy the leaders for their special shares. Similarly, in *Od.* 10.38–42 Odysseus's men complain that they are coming home empty-handed, while Odysseus has amassed many treasures.

7. For details and references, see Raaflaub 1997b; Ruzé 1997: pt. 1.

8. For other examples, see Raaflaub 1997b: 19, 22–23.

9. Even criticism of the leaders' material privileges is not infrequent (e.g., *Il.* 2.225–38; *Od.* 10.41–48).

10. Obviously, though, as *Od.* bk. 24 shows, Odysseus's revenge against the suitors is excessive and brings the community to the brink of civil war. The resulting conflict between Odysseus's family and the other elite families of Ithaca and surrounding areas can only be resolved by divine intervention and will require atonement on the part of Odysseus himself: see S. West in Heubeck et al. 1988: 51–62, and bibliog. in Russo et al. 1992: 354.

11. Parasites: e.g., Xen. *Mem.* 2.8; Arist. *Rhet.* 1367a32; Isai. 5.39; Isocr. 14.48; Dem. 57.45. Helots: Talbert 1989; Ducat 1990; Cartledge 1991; Luraghi 2001a, 2002; Luraghi and Alcock 2003.

12. Cartledge 2001a; Raaflaub 1999: 132–41; van Wees 2000. Krentz (2002; see also van Wees 2001) believes that pure hoplite fighting emerged even much later (see Raaflaub, chapter 5 below). On hoplite fighting, see Hanson 1991, 1995, 2000; Mitchell 1996; van Wees 2004: chap. 13.

13. For a survey of widely accepted views before recent reevaluations, see Oliva 1971. Hodkinson has led the recent effort: see esp. 1997, 2000; furthermore, e.g., Nafissi 1991; Kennell 1995; Thommen 1996; and, for the helot problem, Luraghi 2002. For discussion of Sparta's early expansion and wars, see Cartledge 2001c: chap. 8; Murray 1993: chap. 10; Meier 1998. See also, generally, Finley 1982: chap. 2; Cartledge 2001b.

14. For discussion with bibliog. see Raaflaub 1993b: 64–68; Meier 1998; Cartledge 2001b: 29–34. Van Wees (1999) argues that Tyrtaeus's poem has nothing to do with the Rhetra. *Contra:* Meier 2002 (with van Wees's response [2002]); Link 2003; Raaflaub 2006.

15. For the unintelligible *gamōdangorianēmēn* of the MSS, e.g., *damōi d'antagorian ēmen* or *damōdōn antagorian ēmen.*

16. "The history of European democracy begins, arguably, . . . in Sparta" (Hornblower 1992: 1; cf. Isocr. 7.60–61, 12.153–55). Hansen remarks (1994: 33) that if the emended Rhetra "is a genuine document of the seventh century, we need not have any difficulty in trusting Aristotle and all the other fourth-century sources who hold Solon responsible for the introduction of democracy in Athens in the beginning of the sixth century. And if that is true, democracy must have originated in Sparta in the seventh century, not in Athens more than a century later."

17. Among other criteria to be considered here we mention (a) the severe limitation of full citizenship to a few thousand privileged Spartiates, while not only (and obviously) helots and *perioikoi,* but also other Spartiates were excluded who failed to meet the requirements of the *homoioi;* (b) the unusual authority of kings and *gerontes,* who were elected for life, although their power was to some extent balanced by the ephors (see below); and (c) continuing uncertainties about procedures in the assembly.

18. We should point out that some scholars do not accept Plutarch's explanation of the "rider" as a separate and later regulation but consider it an integral component of the original *rhētra;* for discussion and bibliog., see van Wees 1999: 20–22; Welwei 2000: 45–46, 59. We should also point out that recent scholarship (e.g., van Wees 1999, 2002; Meier 1998, 2002) seems to place much stronger emphasis than we do on the aristocratic nature of the Rhetra.

19. Plutarch (*Lyc.* 7) dates the ephors' introduction 130 years after Lycurgus, although the dating is controversial. For a detailed discussion of the ephorate, see Richer 1998.

20. "There is one political ideal that Sparta cannot be made to reflect—the radical belief in individual liberty, issuing in liberal democracy" (Rawson 1969: 11).

21. Theognis lines 39–52; Solon frr. 9, 11, 34 (= *Ath. Pol.* 12.3) West. See later, for example, Hdt. 3.82.4; 5.92 (with Forrest 1966: 111); Arist. *Ath. Pol.* 12.3; *Pol.* 1305a, 1315b. On tyranny, see recently Murray 1993: chap. 9; Stein-Hölkeskamp 1996.

22. See Hansen's comment (*Bryn Mawr Classical Review* 1999.09.17): "Robinson's impressive collection of evidence adds up to a strong 'wigwam' argument, i.e., one built of a number of not very strong parts that gathered together add up to a strong argument."

23. Morris 1996; 2000: chaps. 4–5. See also Hanson 1995: chap. 5, and discussions in Schuller, Hoepfner, and Schwandner 1989 about Greek equality, based on egalitarian polis architecture (see Hoepfner and Schwandner 1994).

24. Colonies: Asheri 1966: 7–16; 1975; Vallet 1968: esp. 74–78, 94–107; Leppore 1973; Murray 1993: 113–15. Founder's cult: Malkin 1987: pt. 2. Impact on Greece: Link 1991; Malkin 1994.

25. See, for legislation, Gehrke 1993, 2000; Hölkeskamp 1999 (and earlier articles listed in his bibliog.). On the origin of *isonomia* and *isēgoria,* see Raaflaub 1996b: 143–45.

26. We thank Paul Cartledge, Mark Munn, Eric Robinson, and two anonymous readers for generous comments and suggestions.

Chapter 3

Revolutions and a New Order in Solonian Athens and Archaic Greece

Robert W. Wallace

This chapter discusses the history of political and legal reform, mass revolution, and the reports of various people's governments in Greece during the archaic period. Its greater focus on Athens is dictated by the state of our evidence, meager in any case but more extensive for that city, and by Athens' importance in the history of democracy. At the same time, many scattered references in Aristotle's *Politics* make clear that if we possessed the 157 other *Constitutions* reconstructed in his school in addition to the *Constitution of the Athenians*, Athens' revolutions and early experiments with people's power would join a large variety of such experiments across a number of major poleis. Some of these developments are indicated below. Democracy was invented by the Greeks, not by several Athenian politicians.

CONDITIONS IN PRE-SOLONIAN ATHENS

In the seventh century an aristocracy calling itself *eupatridai,* "the sons of good fathers," dominated the territory of Attica. These aristocrats were part of a Panhellenic elite, linked across poleis by marriage, guest-friendship, costly competitions in the Olympic games, and the orientalizing luxury of the symposion.[1] The Eupatrids' lavish burials, now mostly out of fashion elsewhere in Greece, have been interpreted as a retrograde attempt to recreate the Dark Age order (Morris 1996: 25). Within Attica, Eupatrid domination and exploitation caused significant economic, political, and social problems, which came to a head early in the sixth century. Echoing traditional categories of criticism, the poet and later lawgiver Solon calls the Eupatrids "you who have pushed through to glut yourselves with many good things" (fr. 4c.2 West 1992 [henceforth W]).[2] Athens' rulers "do not know how to restrain their greed or how to order their present festivities in the

49

peacefulness of the banquet" (fr. 4.9–10 W).³ In the century before Solon's 594/3 reforms, Attica's uncertain archaeological record shows a decreasing number of burials but an increase in remote sanctuary activity (Osborne 1989). While difficult to interpret, these data could suggest that the inhabitants had returned to an older, elite style of selective burial (ibid. 319). The unpopulated state of the one area that has been systematically explored, the deme Atene along the southwest coast (Lohmann 1992, 1993), cannot be typical (Osborne 1997). Developments elsewhere in Attica are unknown (cf. Foxhall 1997), although Solon's reference to the Eupatrids' seizing "public possessions" (fr. 4.12 W) may suggest that they occupied land that was previously open to others. In any case, Eupatrid extravagance and other bad behavior certainly brought great economic pressure especially on men called *hektēmoroi* ("sixth-parters," perhaps indentured serfs) and *pelatai* (perhaps "dependents"), whose lives were bound to the upper classes by economic dependency.⁴ Showing detailed knowledge of Solon's laws and poems—according to Hesychios, Aristotle wrote five volumes "On Solon's *Axones*" (that is, on the law code named after the rotating whitened boards on which the laws were written)—and reflecting a sympathetic bias toward the downtrodden, the Aristotelian *Constitution of the Athenians* (*Athēnaiōn Politeia* or *Ath. Pol.*) offers this summary:

> The Athenian polity was oligarchic in all other respects, and in particular the poor were enslaved to the rich—themselves and their children and their wives. The poor were called dependants and sixth-parters, since it was for the rent of a sixth that they worked the fields of the rich. All the land was in the hands of a few, and if the poor failed to pay their rents both they and their children were liable to seizure.⁵

Economic burdens drove some dependent farmers to the breaking point. Some were sold abroad into slavery. "Of the poor, many make their way to foreign lands, having been sold off in bondage, fettered by shameful chains" (Solon fr. 4.23–25 W). Even for independent farmers, inheritance practices put pressure on land-holding, by distributing property equally among heirs, thus subdividing farms into ever smaller portions. Solon's reforms also make clear that many non-Eupatrids were prospering, both at the highest economic levels and among "middling" residents of Attica. Greeks typically linked greater political status (*timē*) with greater wealth. It was difficult for prosperous non-Eupatrids to achieve such status under the oligarchy.

The Eupatrids' oppressive domination extended well beyond economic injustice. In the same breath Solon mentions their "love of money" and their "arrogance" (fr. 6.3 W). Subsequent events will justify the observation that "for the many, the harshest and bitterest aspect of the *politeia* [the communal state of affairs] was their enslavement. . . . It could be said that there was nothing in which they had a share" (*Ath. Pol.* 2.2). "Sharing in the polis" defined citizenship, membership in the community (e.g., *Ath. Pol.* 42.1). Late-seventh-century Attic society was far more polarized and hierarchic than the world of Odysseus a century earlier, as we saw in chapter 2. In Homer, the masses had an important role in assemblies and sometimes also in dispute settlement. Elite families were not so removed from the communities in which they were embedded.[6] Under the Eupatrids, the Attic demos came to lose their traditional portion of *timē*. Even Solon, stout defender of the lower classes, calls them *kakoi*—since Homer the word meant "base," "ugly," "worthless" (LSJ)—while minimizing distinctions between social classes (Anhalt 1993: 95–101). Later, his defensive, even self-contradictory claim, "to the people I gave as much privilege (*geras*) / power (*kratos*) as sufficed them, neither taking away *timē* nor holding out still more" (fr. 5 W = *Ath. Pol.* 12.1 / Plutarch *Life of Solon* 18.5), reveals that in 594 the popular revolutionaries were demanding greater political standing. It also shows that Solon's reforms did not satisfy their political aspirations.

ARISTOCRACIES IN CRISIS

When in the early sixth century the Athenians looked out beyond their borders, they saw many traditional aristocracies disrupted. One or two generations before Solon, Sparta's constitutional reforms, introducing a hoplite state, showed how inherited governments might be changed and how such changes might lead to military victory. As we saw in chapter 2, these reforms undercut upper-class justifications for social superiority and wealth (Glaucus and Sarpedon in *Iliad* bk. 12). They proclaimed the "alikeness" of the Spartiates, fixed the place and times of Sparta's assembly, and declared the people's voice authoritative: "the victory and power of the demos." Sparta makes clear that the cause of such reforms was not only hostility to the old order, but the positive effects of civic egalitarianism and the confidence and strength of the Spartiate demos.

In subsequent decades, popular revolutions upturning aristocracies and kings roiled many communities. Everyone heard the news when neighbors drove out rapacious and oppressive aristocracies, inspiring other communities to act. In redressing their social problems, three paths were open to archaic poleis: a single ruler, legal and constitutional reform, or popular revolt and what the sources call mass government, however we understand that concept.

First, as we saw in chapter 2, in many poleis the demos welcomed an aristocratic "single ruler," either as "tyrant"—the word still lacked pejorative connotations—or as an elected *aisumnētēs*, willing to address the mass's grievances and needs. In Argos perhaps in the first quarter of the seventh century, Pheidon gained power as tyrant or king. In Corinth perhaps around 655, Cypselus seized control from the Bacchiad clan and "brought justice" to the city (Herodotus 5.92b, quoting the Delphic oracle). A little later, Orthagoras gained power in Sicyon; one of his successors at the end of the seventh century bore the remarkable name Isodamos, "Equal-People."[7] Perhaps in the 640s and after tremendous popular turmoil, the Megarian demos drove out their aristocratic government and handed power to the tyrant Theagenes. Megara had grown wealthy through sheep-raising. According to Aristotle (*Pol.* 1305), Theagenes gained the trust of the demos and became their leader "by slaughtering the livestock of the rich." Sometime before Solon, Tynnondas became tyrant in a city in Euboea that Plutarch (*Sol.* 14.7) does not name. Many larger city-states experienced tyranny in the seventh or sixth century (Murray 1993: 138; Osborne 1996: 193).

Right in the midst of these revolutions, c. 632, Attica also had a brush with tyranny, although the demos was not yet ready to go down that road. Cylon was an Athenian aristocrat, an Olympic victor in 640, and husband of an elite foreigner, the daughter of Theagenes, tyrant of nearby Megara. In the first known episode in Attic history, Cylon seized the Acropolis and attempted to become Athens' tyrant. Among varying accounts of these events, Thucydides writes:

> When the Athenians got to hear of [Cylon's action], they came in from the countryside en masse (*pandēmei*) to thwart the conspirators, whom they surrounded and besieged. As time passed, the Athenians grew tired of the blockade, and most of them went away, entrusting the nine archons . . . to supervise the siege, with full powers to make whatever settlement they thought best. (1.126)

The striking element in Thucydides' account is that, unlike in other poleis, the demos was responsible for a potential tyrant's failure. They came en masse to blockade the Acropolis. Then, returning to their farms, they arranged for Cylon's defeat through the archons to whom they gave full authority. Most of the Cylonians were killed, an act for which the Alcmaeonid family was later exiled.

How far can we rely on Thucydides' story? As Thucydides himself (1.20, 6.54) and Rosalind Thomas (1989: 272–81 for Cylon) have argued, oral traditions are liable to distortion, and historical narratives can quickly become anachronistic. In addition, Thucydides' description of the relations between demos and archons seems inconsistent with the Eupatrid oligarchy mentioned in *Ath. Pol.* Herodotus (5.71), writing a generation earlier, tells a different story, that Cylon and his companions failed to seize the Acropolis and were dealt with by some officials, "*prutaneis* of the *naukraroi*," who (he says) were then in charge of Athens and had promised the Cylonians they would not be killed. Herodotus is silent about the demos and the circumstances of the Cylonians' failed attempt. He notes that the Alcmaeonids were blamed for their deaths.

Many will draw only limited conclusions from this early and shadowy

nothing

episode. On the other hand, written sources, including Solon's poetry (which fifth-century school children memorized and recited in public: Plato *Timaeus* 21b), and songs performed at symposia such as those of Theagenes' fellow Megarian Theognis, could have supplied near-contemporary perspectives on Cylon's activities. In addition, some prominent Athenians—the Alcmaeonids' enemies—had excellent reasons for remembering the Cylonians, as the curse on the Alcmaeonids for killing them still carried political weight in the later fifth century. How do the accounts of Herodotus and Thucydides compare? Thucydides, a serious historian aware of source problems and unsympathetic to the demos, seems deliberately to contradict Herodotus, a non-Athenian. Herodotus simply does not explain the Cylonians' failure. The *naukraroi* may have been local financial officials (*Ath. Pol.* 8.3, 21.5; Pollux 8.108; Bekker, *Anecd. Gr.* 1.283) rather than political leaders; and how could their *prutaneis* promise anyone immunity from execution? Although consensus on these issues has proved elusive, Thucydides' account supplies a context and background for mass political action in 594, when (we shall see) a powerful, vocal majority of the Attic population rejected traditional aristocratic leadership, forcing the Eupatrids to surrender their monopoly of power, and there was only halfhearted support for a tyrant.

On any account, in 632 the demos rejected Cylon. For whatever reason, Cylon failed to ignite popular indignation against the aristocracy, as other Greek tyrants had done. According to Thucydides, he managed to ignite indignation only against himself. When the Alcmaeonids had the unpopular Cylonians killed, they may have aimed to strengthen their political standing with the demos, as the Alcmaeonid Cleisthenes did several generations later. Those killings led to tremendous political strife within the ruling elite, lasting for years, down to Solon (Plut. *Sol.* 12.3–9; *Ath. Pol.* 1). A judicial settlement before Solon's archonship resulted in the Alcmaeonids' exile under a curse. "The bodies of the original offenders were cast out of their graves" (*Ath. Pol.* 1).

In addition to tyranny, a second path open to archaic poleis in redressing their grievances was legal and constitutional reform. Outside Sparta, such reforms are attested first through the many fragments of archaic laws and constitutional measures surviving on stone or other durable materials (van Effenterre and Ruzé 1994–95; cf. Hölkeskamp 1999). Chapter 2 opened with a seventh-century law from Cretan Dreros, in which the polis sought to regulate its principal judicial official (the Kosmos) by ensuring that he did not hold office longer than one year (van Effenterre and Ruzé 1994–95: no. 81). In another seventh-century decree (or law) from Dreros, after consulting (?) with the tribes the polis stipulates that an official called the *agretas* not punish a certain category of offender (no. 64). Other early Cretan laws mention the *damos,* the *polis,* or the people of a city in the genitive case (e.g., *Gortuniōn*) in the sanctioning formulas of written laws.[8] An obscure late-seventh- or early-sixth-century regulation from Tiryns mentions various officials, the popular assembly (*aliia*), and also "the crowd" (*ochlos*) (no. 78). The famous Chios inscription (Robinson 1997: 90–101), itself dated between 600 and 550, indicates that some time previously the Chians had instituted a people's council, probably of two hundred citizens; this text mentions and grants further powers to the popular assembly, here designated "the demos called together" (*dēmos keklēmenos*); *dēmos* and its cognates (*dēmarchos, dēmosiē*) recur often in this text; as we shall see, one official is charged with "safeguarding the laws of the demos." Eric Robinson concludes that "true power" resided with the assembly and a representative popular council (99, 101). Solon's contemporary at Mytilene, the *aisumnētēs* Pittakos, combined the functions of single ruler, lawgiver, and *sophos*, sage, passing laws that limited the expense of aristocratic funerals and doubling the fines for offenses committed while drunk, perhaps by aristocratic symposiasts (Plut. *Moralia* 155f). Presumably as *aisumnētēs*, he did not himself devise a new constitution (Arist. *Pol.* 1274b18–21).

Before the fifth-century development of the ideologies of political type (such as democracy or oligarchy), the Greeks had no names to designate different approaches to constitutional reform, or to help conceptualize coherent or consistent political solutions. As Karl Hölkeskamp (1992, 1999) has shown, archaic laws and political reforms display no overall coherence: their solutions to legal and other difficulties were ad hoc. Instead of legal or constitutional content, this path was identified by the figure of the reformer, through the overlapping categories of lawgiver (*nomothetēs, thesmothetēs*), mediator or arbitrator (*diallaktēs, aisumnētēs, katartistēr*), wise man or sage (*sophos, sophistēs*) skilled in politics. To quote Hölkeskamp, "in this sense alone the famous 'arbitrators' were true 'lawgivers'. Their task was to propose and implement concrete and durable solutions for those totally different, but always new and alarming problems that had made the appointment of a *katartistēr* necessary in the first place" (1992: 93). Extraordinarily, a number of poleis entrusted their rebuilding to a single individual judged to be wise and politically astute. A number of these men became famous throughout Greece.

Traditionally, the first of these early Greek lawgivers was Zaleukos, publishing his laws in western Locri in 662 B.C.E. (but not to press the date). Aristotle wrote:

> When the Locrians asked the oracle how they might find relief from the considerable turmoil they were experiencing, the oracle responded that they should have laws enacted for themselves, whereupon a certain shepherd named Zaleukos ventured to propose to the citizens many excellent laws. When they learned of these and asked him where he had found them, he replied that Athena had come to him in a dream. As a result of this he was freed and was appointed lawgiver. (fr. 548 Rose, trans. Gagarin)

The fanciful material in this account reflects traditional elements: for example, the lawgiver as outsider, in this case living in the wilderness like other folk heroes (from Achilles to the Lone Ranger); also, the divine authority of his laws. Most of the traditions about these earliest lawgivers are invented (Szegedy-Maszak 1978). Nonetheless, well-documented cases, including Solon and Pittakos, prove that such figures existed.

Having rejected a tyrant in 632, the Athenians themselves then chose a lawgiver, Draco, traditionally in 621/0 (Stroud 1968).[9] Of Draco's laws, only the law for unpremeditated homicide, republished in 409/8, remains more than a vague allusion. Probably a confluence of differing forces was responsible for Draco's appointment. Many scholars (e.g., Humphreys 1991: 20–22) link Draco's homicide laws with the ongoing strife after Cylon, as the Alcmaeonids' enemies avenged their sacrilege in killing the Cylonians, who had put themselves under Athena's protection (Plut. *Sol.* 12, probably from the lost beginning of *Ath. Pol.*). Laws prohibiting homicide would have benefited the Alcmaeonids, who therefore had reason to support Draco. To be sure, the principal concern of the single extant law on unpremeditated homicide is that of pardoning killers; and pardon is forbidden unless every member of a family concurs (*IG* I[3] 104, lines 13–19; Fornara 1983: no. 15). This provision might or might not have reduced civic strife or helped any Alcmaeonids or others who had fled Athens. This interpretation of Draco's homicide laws will also not explain his non-homicide legislation.

Another perspective has suggested that the traditional severity of Draco's measures represented an aristocratic reaction against mounting social chaos and any challenge to the traditional order. Solon's repudiation of almost all of Draco's laws (*Ath. Pol.* 7.1) confirms that they were felt to be too harsh. Solon granted amnesty to almost everyone previously exiled (Plut. *Sol.* 19.4). Alternatively or in addition, many early laws can be seen as regulating power relations within the elite (Eder 1986; Osborne 1996: 186–90). Draco's laws may have shared a similar purpose.

In addition to these possibilities, the fixed penalties and procedures implied by written law necessarily limited the arbitrariness of judges' sentences. As we saw in chapter 2, already Homer and Hesiod—Panhellenic texts—complained of some aristocrats' "crooked justice." A generation after Draco (we shall see), Solon proclaimed that he wrote down laws "alike," *homoiōs*, for upper and lower classes. He also legislated that verdicts by the *archontes*, Athens' public authorities,[10] could be appealed to the people (*Ath. Pol.* 9.1). By 594, therefore, the demos was concerned about unfair justice and unacceptable sentencing by aristocratic judges. Draco's laws were a step toward equal justice. Nonetheless, after Draco the problems of harsh and unequal justice remained. As Solon's poems and legislation show, Draco's laws indicate—and provoked—popular discontent with the administration of justice, and the power of the discontented to effect change.

The third path open to archaic poleis to redress their grievances was out-right popular revolt and some form of mass government, apparently first attested in Athens' neighbor Megara. Perhaps in the 620s the Megarian aris-tocracy succeeded in driving out the tyrant Theagenes but after "a short time," according to Plutarch, was itself driven out by the demos. Echoing sources contemptuous of democracy (including the poems attributed to Theognis and Aristotle's *Constitution of the Megarians* [Robinson 1997: 115 n. 184]), Plutarch writes:

> When the Megarians had expelled Theagenes their tyrant, for a short time they were sober and sensible in their government (*politeia*). But later when the popular leaders (*dēmagōgoi*) poured out untempered freedom for them, as Plato says, they were completely corrupted, and, among their shocking acts of misconduct toward the wealthy, the poor would enter their homes and insist upon being entertained and banqueted sumptuously. But if they did not receive what they demanded, they would treat all the household with violence and insult (*hubris*). Finally, they enacted a decree whereby they received back again the interest that they happened to have paid their creditors, calling the measure "return interest." (*Mor.* 295c–d)[11]

This passage attests the hatred of the Megarian demos for the aristocracy's greed and lavish symposiastic lifestyle, paid for on the backs of the people, as we also saw in Athens. "Return interest," *palintokia,* suggests that economic exploitation by the aristocracy was a major issue, as it had been when Theagenes earlier gained the tyranny. Plutarch's mention of a decree could suggest that in this version the demos had taken over the *politeia;* just so, in *Moralia* 304e–f Plutarch directly calls Megara's government at the time of the "return interest" an "untempered democracy"—whatever the exact meaning of that term. As I have said, Plutarch may well have derived his information about archaic Megara from Aristotle; in *Poetics* 1448a Aristotle writes that comedy was invented in Megara "at the time of their democracy." The *Marmor Parium* (*FGrHist* 239 A39), at any rate, dates comedy's invention sometime between Damasias's second archonship in 581 and Peisistratus's first tyranny twenty years later. In undated passages in the *Politics* Aristotle twice refers to the destruction of this *dēmokratia* led by demagogues because of its *ataxia* (dis-order) and *anarchia* (1302b30, 1304b34–40; see also 1300a16–19): the wealthy nobles who overthrew it then installed an oligarchy.

Although the poems attributed to the Megarian Theognis form a com-posite text posing many problems, one of the arguably original "Cyrnus" poems also complains that Megara had degenerated. Blue blood has now yielded to the unwashed masses, who seem to have taken over the adminis-tration of justice:

> Cyrnus, this polis is still a polis, but its people are different. Formerly they knew nothing of legal decisions or laws but wore goatskins around their

REVOLUTIONS AND A NEW ORDER   57

flanks—wore them to shreds—and grazed like deer outside this polis. And now they are *agathoi* [upper class] . . . , and those who were formerly *esthloi* [noble] are now *deiloi* [base cowards]. Who could bear to look upon this? . . . They cheat one another as they laugh at one another, since they do not know the distinctive marks of *kakoi* [base] or of *agathoi*. (53–60 W)

What was the date of Megara's radical government? Plutarch says that after Theagenes' overthrow, the aristocracy ruled for "a short time." As Theagenes' daughter married Cylon sometime before 632, she cannot have been born much after 650, and thus her father cannot have been born much after 680. His tyranny is commonly dated from the 640s to the 620s (Legon 1981: 93–103; Aristotle's list of long-serving tyrants does not include him [*Pol.* 1315b]). When did the demos expel the subsequent, "short-lived" aristocracy? In an episode that Ronald Legon (1981: 122) and Thomas Figueira (1985: 287–88) reasonably date c. 600, the Megarians attacked the piratical Perinthians, who were colonists of Samos. According to Plutarch (*Moralia* 303e–304c = *Quaestiones Graecae* 57), Samos was then governed by the arch-aristocratic "Landowners" (*geōmoroi;* see also Thuc. 8.21), who sent help to Perinthos and defeated the Megarians. The victorious Samian generals, however, "conceived the project of overthrowing the oligarchy of the Landowners at home" and persuaded their six hundred Megarian prisoners to help them "free the city." "When the city was freed, those of the Megarians who wished they made citizens." It is hard to decide whether the Samians were inspired to ask the Megarians to help expel their oligarchy because the Megarians had already expelled their own, or whether the Megarians were reluctant to return home because their city was still oligarchic. In the latter case, the Samians' success against the Geomoroi could well have inspired the mass's revolt in Megara. Even so, it remains possible that the Megarian revolt followed the Athenians' in 594/3 and was inspired by it.

Whatever its precise date or structure, Megara's radical government lasted at least down to the end of the *Marmor Parium*'s period, 581–561. In 560 Megara founded a colony at Heraclea Pontica on the Black Sea. According to Aristotle, Heraclea's government was also a democracy controlled by anti-elite demagogues, but so radical it was quickly overthrown: "At Heraclea, too, the democracy was brought low just after the foundation of the colony—and all because of their own leaders, whose unjust treatment of the notables caused them to leave; finally the exiles gathered forces, returned, and put down the democracy" (*Pol.* 1304b31–34).

SOLON'S DECISION

With reforms, upheavals, and mass revolutions blazing across Greece, now it was Athens' turn. "When the *politeia* was organized in this way and the many were enslaved to the few, the people rose against the notables. The strife was fierce, and they held out against one another for a long time" (*Ath. Pol.* 5.1–2). Solon himself remarked the people's forceful involvement in the uprising. "They came with a mind to plunder" (fr. 34.1 W). "Another man would not have held the demos in check" (fr. 36.20–22 W = *Ath. Pol.* 12.4). Although he later says he tried to restrain the demos, Solon makes clear that even if he was a Eupatrid (*Ath. Pol.* 5.3; Plut. *Sol.* 1.2–3), before his reforms he viewed the crisis amidst the demos in revolt. Before his archonship he lambasts the Eupatrids and predicts justified violence:

> The minds of the leaders of the demos are unjust; soon they will suffer the many pangs of great arrogance (*hubris*). They cannot control their greed and enjoy the cheerful feast at hand in peace. . . . Their wealth depends on crime. . . . They seize and steal at random, not in any way sparing holy possessions or public possessions, nor do they protect the sacred foundations of justice. (fr. 4.7–14 W)

He calls upon the Eupatrids, "exhorting the wealthy not to be avaricious" (*Ath. Pol.* 5.3). "Restrain your mighty hearts in your breasts, you who have pursued every good thing to excess, and let your pride be in moderation; for *we* shall not obey, nor will these things be perfect for you" (fr. 4c.5–8 W = *Ath. Pol.* 5.3). Aristotle notes: "Solon always assigns the fundamental responsibility for the civil war to the rich. That is why even at the beginning of the elegy he says that what has alarmed him is their 'love of money and excessive pride,' the implication being that these had been the cause of the bad feeling."[12]

Observing developments elsewhere, many among the demos wanted Solon to become tyrant (*Ath. Pol.* 6.4: "He frequently mentions it in his poetry"; Plut. *Sol.* 14–15.1). Solon, however, declined, rejecting the use of violence. "Nor was it my pleasure to act through the violence of tyranny" (fr. 34.7–8 W = *Ath. Pol.* 12.3); "I spared my native country, and did not lay my hand on tyranny and implacable violence" (fr. 32.1–3 = Plut. *Sol.* 14.8; these passages may be the first to link violence with tyranny). Instead Solon chose the path of the *sophos*, *nomothetēs*, and *diallaktēs*, the path of constitutional reform based partly on Sparta in the preceding century. As a young man Solon had seen the demos welcome a lawgiver. He knew they had rejected tyranny. As in the great text that Stobaios calls "On Justice" (fr. 13 W), his poems again and again return to themes of justice (Manville 1990: 150–54; Sakellariou 1993). "Justice, even if slow, is sure" (fr. 13.8 W). "*Eunomiē*, lawfulness, puts all things into good order and makes them sound, and often places shackles about those who are unjust" (fr. 4.32–33 W). His amnesty law (Plut. *Sol.* 19.4) expressly denied amnesty to anyone previously convicted of attempted tyranny. Chosen lawgiver, mediator, and archon by all sides together (*Ath. Pol.* 5.2; cf. 7.1), Solon worked to resolve Athens' economic problems, wrote new laws and enacted remedies for judicial abuse, and established a new government that was equitable for all Athenians. The

Eupatrids accepted Solon's mediation as he swore not to become a tyrant—
anathema to the aristocracy—and his appointment defused a violent civil
war. Over the next thirty years, as we shall see, they may have outfoxed him,
but only to be trumped by the demos.

SOLON'S REFORMS

Debt Relief

As we saw, Attica's crisis was in the first place economic. Solon's poetry
describes a clash between the demos and the wealthy, land-hoarding upper
class. In 594 the poor demanded and received their farms free and clear,
and public lands ("public possessions," fr. 4.12 W) were reopened. The
dependent statuses of *pelatēs* and *hektēmoros* were eliminated. At a stroke
Solon's so-called *seisachtheia*, "shaking off of burdens," abolished all debts.
"Black earth, from whom I removed the boundary-markers fixed in her in
many places, before enslaved, now free" (fr. 36.5–7 W = *Ath. Pol.* 12.4).
Henceforth no Athenian could legally be compelled to work at the bidding
of another. Attica became a land of independent farmers, each working for
himself. Possibly offering compensation to their owners from the public silver (*Ath. Pol.* 8.3), Solon even summoned back Athenians who had been
sold abroad into slavery—"this one justly, the other one unjustly . . . speaking no longer their Attic tongue. . . . And others, suffering base slavery even
here, trembling before the humors of their *despotai*, I set free (*eleutherous*)"
(fr. 36.8–15 W). Henceforth no Athenian could be sold into slavery.
Permanent subordination or exploitation by "masters" was forbidden, and
the institution of debt bondage was eliminated. To judge from Solon's
poems and reforms, all Athenians, including the poorest, were involved in
this struggle. Even *hektēmoroi* and *pelatai* exerted political pressure and had
a voice in shaping the new community.[13]

New Laws

Solon wrote new laws for Athens, with penalties reportedly much less severe
than Draco's. For example, Solon stipulated that the penalty for theft was
not death but double the value of the item stolen if it was recovered, ten
times its value if it was not; five days in the stocks might also be imposed at
the court's discretion (frr. 23a–d in Ruschenbusch 1966b [henceforth R]).
Other, sometimes quite detailed measures promoted social order and
reflected systematic thought. For example, one law specified the minimum
distance from a neighbor's property of a house, wall, ditch, well, beehive, or
certain kinds of trees (frr. 60–62 R). Another law forbade speaking ill of the
dead (fr. 32a R). Solon enacted significant protections for all Athenians by
permitting "anyone who wanted" (*ho boulomenos*) to prosecute crimes affect-

ing the community (Fisher 1990; Todd 1993: 110–12), in case the immediate victim was weak or helpless (*Ath. Pol.* 9.1). Solon's concern for even the humblest Athenians is once again apparent; even if his source or inspiration is unknown, Plutarch rightly remarks: "The lawgiver correctly accustomed citizens to understand and sympathize with one another as parts of one body" (*Sol.* 18.6). Although the legal sources for other poleis are deficient, there is no reason not to suppose that many of Solon's laws were innovations. At the same time, detailed regulations on a wide variety of small problems were characteristic of archaic legislation (Hölkeskamp 1992: 90). Whatever motivated Draco's law code a generation earlier, Solon says he wrote his laws "for base and noble alike, and set straight justice over each" (fr. 36.18–19 = *Ath. Pol.* 12.4). Solon's laws were equal for everyone: justice admitted no social hierarchies.

Solon also provided that verdicts by the *archontes* could be appealed to the *ēliaia* or public court. *Ath. Pol.* 12.1 lists judicial appeal to the demos as one of Solon's three most democratic measures. In part on the basis of two laws in Demosthenes, Mogens Hansen (e.g., 1991: 259–60) suggests that Solon's *ēliaia* (which he distinguishes from the assembly) also heard cases of first instance. This reform gave final judicial authority to the assembled demos, not to elite judges. Provisions for appeal to the "popular council" and the assembly are also attested in Chios some time between 600 and 550 (Robinson 1997: 95–97).

Constitutional Reform

In addition to his economic and legal reforms, Solon transformed the structure of political authority from an informal oligarchy determined by heredity and traditional social class to a legally fixed government based on law, economic status, and a formal political role for all Athenians. His *politeia* combined Greek timocratic hierarchies of public authority (*archē*), now based on wealth not birth, with the public recognition and expansion of the demos's traditional voice in the assembly and now also in court. A number of his provisions giving formal power to the demos are paralleled in other poleis, but Solon's mix was also unique. As was typical of these early Greek lawgivers, an extraordinary self-confidence drove his vision of his city's future. Seven reforms established Athens' first constitutional government.

1. The Timocratic Classes.   Before Solon, the Attic population consisted of an untidy melange including richer and poorer Eupatrids, *hektēmoroi*, free farmers, craftsmen and traders, prosperous non-Eupatrids, slaves, *pelatai*, and foreigners. How far any mobilization of hoplites—not attested for Athens before the later seventh century—was independent of Eupatrid local organizing is unknown. Solon created four new social classes (*Ath. Pol.*

7.3). So far from *isomoiria* (equal shares [of land]), Solon's classes were distinguished not by birth but exclusively by agricultural production and (in three of the four classes) by the military service corresponding to it: "five hundred bushel men," "horsemen" with more than 300 bushels, and "yoke men," probably hoplite soldiers, with more than 200 bushels. These figures should be taken as ideals of civic prosperity—even including wine, Attica was not so productive—and of a particular type. As Oswyn Murray observes (1993: 194), Solon's highest class "was a deliberate provocation of the old aristocracy: the nobility of the 'men of good birth' was to give way to a nobility of five hundred bushel men." Solon abolished the old aristocracy in favor of a graded timocracy based on wealth and military status. Regarding the function of these classes, Martin Ostwald writes:

> When Solon divided the citizen-body into the so-called four "property-classes," he did not set up a system of graduated entitlements: his purpose was to determine the degree of service the state could expect of each group of citizens, since there was no public pay for public service: only the highest class . . . could be expected to serve as treasurers . . . ; the lowest class could be called on only for attendance and voting at assembly and at jury meetings. Membership in each of these classes was not a precondition for graduated rights: the Athenians' name for "property-class" was *telos,* derived from the verb *teleō,* which denotes the fulfillment of a public obligation, such as the payment of a tax. Thus, belonging to a given class did not describe a "right" . . . but the expectation the community had of a member. (1996: 56–57)

Even the thetes, the lowest class, had civic responsibilities in the assembly and court. As in Lycurgan Sparta, the demos's role was now formally recognized and made explicit, just as written laws made explicit the rules of justice. Solon emphasized the civic importance of every Athenian, rich or poor. "Public ill comes home to every single man, and no longer do his courtyard gates avail to hold it back; high though the wall be, it leaps over and finds him out unfailingly, even though in his flight he may hide in the farthest corner of his chamber" (fr. 4.26–29 W). Every citizen, rich or poor, was expected to involve himself in public affairs (Raaflaub 1996c: 1060), not least in times of civic strife (*Ath. Pol.* 8.5), or be expelled from the civic body. In Solon's conception, through his reforms "all people will win" (*nikēsein pantas anthrōpous,* fr. 32.4–5 W).

2. *The Offices.*   Athens' public authorities, its *archai,* among whom *Ath. Pol.* 7.3 lists archons, treasurers, *pōlētai* (sellers), the Eleven (prison officials), and *kōlakretai* (collectors of hams), were now elected or pre-elected (see 3 below) by the demos from the upper two or three of Athens' four new classes. *Archai* were no longer co-opted by and from the Eupatrids. As happened earlier in Sparta and other poleis, the structure of polis leadership was transformed.

According to *Ath. Pol.* 8.1, the demos voted by tribe. Attic tribes were based on mythical claims of blood relation, not geographical proximity. It is impossible to determine what influences might have shaped tribal voting—in particular, whether the tribes were bastions of upper-class power, as perhaps they were by the end of the century. In any case, most non-Eupatrid "five hundred bushel men" will have had no hereditary followers on whose support they could rely. These men necessarily appealed directly to the people.

From 594, men of hoplite standing were entitled to hold any office except the archonship (opened to them in 457: *Ath. Pol.* 26.2). In the settlement after Damasias's usurpation of power in the late 580s, Eupatrids shared the archonships equally with men whom *Ath. Pol.* 13.2 calls "peasants" (*agroikoi*), and "craftsmen" (*dēmiourgoi*). The pejorative names suggest a hostile aristocratic source. The settlement suggests how far Solon's reform broke the aristocracy's monopoly on power. As we have seen, the important timocratic element in Solon's *politeia* was typically Greek. *Archai* conferred power and honor, *timē*. Aristotle remarks: "We call the *archai timai*," and adds: "If the same persons hold the *archai* all the time, the rest must be without *timē*" (*Pol.* 1281a31–33). The community always had higher expectations of wealthier members, recompensed by greater honor. We never entirely leave the world of Glaucus and Sarpedon.

3. Election by Lot.   According to the writer of *Ath. Pol.*, who had studied this aspect of Solon's reforms, the demos elected forty candidates for the archonships, ten per tribe, and from these forty, nine archons were chosen by lot. *Ath. Pol.*'s report remains controversial, not least because Aristotle's *Politics* had earlier contradicted it.[14] If allotment was Solonian, it certainly was not the symbol of democracy it later became in classical Athens. In 594 the lot will have had three causes or consequences. It helped to insure diversity among archons, a valuable principle also for aristocrats. It mitigated any threat of social violence resulting from offended *timē* when powerful men lost elections. Finally, it diluted the force of political ambition and aristocratic tradition. This dilution inevitably increased the power of other political elements, whether or not this was Solon's intention.

4. Scrutiny of Officials.   Aristotle decisively (*Pol.* 1274a15–17, 1281b32–34) and Isokrates (7.26, 12.147) both say twice that after 594 the demos scrutinized (*euthunein*) the *archai* after their terms of office.[15] In passages seeking to minimize Solon's democratic reforms, Aristotle remarks that the demos was to *euthunein tas archas*, to hear *tas euthunas tōn archontōn*. This provision is perfectly Solonian, giving the demos some measure of control over the public authorities who had previously outraged them. Since the demos had elected the *archai*, who better might examine their conduct following their term in power (*archē*)? The demos also had the power to overturn judicial verdicts by archons. A series of fragmentary laws from Tiryns apparently from the late seventh century (*SEG* 30.380; see Osborne 1996: 186–87) provide an elaborate series of controls on different *archai,* including supervision by the people. In Aeschylus's *Persians,* a decade before Ephialtes' reforms, Atossa calls the Persian king Xerxes *oukh hupeuthunos polei,* "not answerable to the city" (line 213). As H. D. Broadhead comments (1960: 85), Atossa is "made to speak like an Athenian," thus distinguishing Xerxes from "Athenian magistrates." Late in the sixth century, according to information apparently from Timaeus, at Croton the Pythagoreans were overthrown and land was redistributed, debts cancelled, offices and the assembly were opened to all citizens, and representatives chosen by lot from "all" the demos examined (*euthunein*) the officials (Iamblichus *De Vita Pythagorica* 257; Robinson 1997: 76). In the fifth century accountability to the demos was a key aspect of democratic ideology (Hdt. 3.80.6).

5. Participation in the Assembly.   As the Rhetra did in Lycurgan Sparta, Solon formalized the composition and functions of the people's assembly. Henceforth, all citizens had the power to participate in the assembly and vote (*Ath. Pol.* 7.3). This equality of voting power, reinforced in every assembly as speakers appealed for the demos's support, must have had significant psychological consequences both for the demos and for their leaders. We cannot know how often the assembly met, or how many people attended, in the thirty-three-year interval between Solon's reforms and Peisistratus's tyranny. However, there is no reason not to suppose that the assembly's vote was final in all matters that were put before it. Before Peisistratus seized power in 561/0, he asked the assembly for a bodyguard of fifty club-bearers, on a proposal by a certain Aristion (Hdt. 1.59.4; *Ath. Pol.* 14.1). It is striking that a wealthy and powerful aristocrat asked the assembly for these men, instead of simply supplying them from his own dependents.

According to *Ath. Pol.* 7.3, Solon formally designated political participation and a vote also for the thetes, lesser landowners and hired laborers (not, as they are called elsewhere in this volume, "subhoplites," which is a pejorative non-Greek term). How far this measure merely institutionalized the traditional, inclusive nature of the assembly is unknown. In any case, the sources preserve no trace of opposition by any Athenians to the formal opening of Athens' assembly even to former *pelatai* and *hektēmoroi.* Far more important than a man's wealth or social position was his Athenian blood (Solon frr. 2, 4.21–22, 4a W). Even slaves, if Athenian, were restored to freedom and their just place in the community. As Solon said, through his reforms "all people will win" (*nikēsein pantas anthrōpous,* fr. 32.4–5 W).

6. Powers of the Assembly and Solon's People's Council of 400.   How far did Solon intend the people to have power, rather than simply to approve or disapprove what different leaders recommended? Traditional aristocracies were governed by small and informal elite councils. In Lycurgan Sparta, by contrast, "to the *damos* shall be victory and *kratos*," and some years later the assembled *damos* was judged to be speaking "crookedly"—perhaps, that is, with too much free speech. To be sure, we do not know how far the Solonian *archai* could act on their own initiative without consulting the demos. Indeed, the potentially extensive executive powers of the *archontes* must constitute the principal distinction between Solonian government and full democracy, even though the demos had the power to examine the public authorities after their terms of office. In any case, the importance of Athens' newly constituted assembly is indicated by Solon's institution of a probouleutic council of 400 to set the assembly's agenda (*Ath. Pol.* 8.4, cf. 21.3; Plut. *Sol.* 19.1; Rhodes 1972: 208–9). As an *archē* (*Ath. Pol.* 8; see also Arist. *Pol.* 1317b30–31), it is perfectly conceivable that membership in Solon's council was not extended below the zeugite class. Nonetheless, this probouleutic people's council was dramatically more inclusive than Sparta's probouleutic Gerousia. The institution of this council was a further measure preventing traditional leaders from dominating assemblies. Even the skeptical Charles Hignett went so far as to assert that the evidence for Solon's people's council "would be a decisive proof that he intended the ekklesia to develop into the effective sovereign of the state" (1952: 92).

Following Hignett, some have doubted the existence of this council, mainly because its first indisputable attestation is linked with Athens' oligarchic revolution of 411. At that time the Cleisthenic council of 500 was replaced by a council of 400, as part of a program to restore "the forefathers' government" (*Ath. Pol.* 31.1). It is unfortunate for sixth-century history that the oligarchs of 411 chose to imitate this particular aspect of Athens' early *politeia*. Yet their misuse of Solon's council need not imply that they invented it. Both *Ath. Pol.* 8.4 and Plut. *Sol.* 19.1–2 attest that council's existence. Writing well before 411, Herodotus (5.72.1) also referred to the council in his narrative of 508/7, when the Spartan Cleomenes tried to replace it with a council of 300. Solon himself may well have referred to it, in a metaphor for the Areopagus and people's council as the two anchors of the ship of state.[16] Finally, other early people's councils are attested, in particular the "people's council," *bolē dēmosiē*, in Chios sometime between 600 and 550. That council was at the center of Chios's government (Robinson 1997: 99). The Chios constitutional inscription indicates that it was "chosen fifty from each tribe." If the Chians were divided into the standard four Ionic tribes, their council consisted of two hundred citizens—and Chios was far smaller than Attica.

As we shall see, the importance of Solon's council for the demos was made clear in 508/7, when Cleomenes' attempt to dissolve it sparked a popular backlash. I note the tradition, admittedly only in Diogenes Laertius

(1.49–54), that when Solon opposed Peisistratus's tyranny before 561, the council, "being supporters of Peisistratus," said he was mad.

In classical Athens, the power of all citizens to address the assembly was an important democratic principle. Did non-elites speak in early-sixth-century assemblies? Free speech is often thought to have emerged among the aristocracy, as nobles vied to be "best in battle and in council" (e.g., *Il.* 1.258; Raaflaub 1990/91: 13). The main Athenian evidence for this notion is the name of Cleisthenes' aristocratic opponent Isagoras, "Equal-Speaker," at the end of the century. Isagoras was born at a time when most scholars at least used to believe that the people did not yet have an important role in government. On the other hand, when Isagoras and Cleisthenes began to struggle, Cleisthenes was no democrat, and we know nothing of the politics of Isagoras's father. On general grounds scholars also argue that before Athens' fifth-century democracy, no one except the elite would have mustered the courage to speak in the assembly. Josiah Ober (1989: 79) suggests that free speech was extended only later in the fifth century, as the institutional bases of power broke down and political activity was no longer dependent on political office. "The pre-Cleisthenic noble was likely to hold an official position (e.g. as an Areopagite) that gave him the legal or traditional (it does not really matter which) privilege of addressing the citizenry in formal Assembly." That model better fits Republican Rome than the looser class structures and psychological egalitarianism of archaic Athens.

Athens' democratic ideology of free speech may well have emerged in the later sixth or early fifth century (Momigliano 1973: 258–59). Freedom to speak out, however, was not dependent on ideology. At a minimum, J. D. Lewis (1971: 133) must be right in observing that "there may never have been a clear prohibition of the ordinary citizen addressing the assembly." Moreover, in the revolutionary crisis before his reforms, Solon indicates that the revolutionaries were calling out for the equal distribution of land (fr. 34 W = *Ath. Pol.* 12.3). He mentions "assemblies of the demos" where he laid out his program (fr. 36 W = *Ath. Pol.* 12.4). Presumably, many people, including emboldened *hektēmoroi*, spoke out at these meetings (cf. *Ath. Pol.* 12.3: "Their talk was vain"), some men calling for Solon to become tyrant. Eupatrids certainly did not monopolize these meetings—if they even attended. Are we to suppose that in other assemblies these outraged farmers suddenly became too shy to speak, or that after 594 they spoke no longer? It may be that Sparta's Lycurgan reforms were followed by what later seemed excessive free speech by the assembled Spartiates. Arnaldo Momigliano rightly suggested that the necessarily more open debate in Athens' council of 400 will have accustomed many citizens to speak before their peers, grappling with issues confronting the city (1973: 258).

A law attributed to Solon stipulates that men over fifty might address the assembly first (Aeschines 1.23, 3.2–4; cf. Plut. *Mor.* 784c–d). As Momigliano observed (1973: 257–58), its age provision indicates this law's antiquity; so does its archaic verb *agoreuein* (Kapparis 1998). By inviting men over fifty to speak first, the herald's proclamation suggests that anyone over fifty could speak, that assembly speakers were not chosen according to birth, wealth, or public office (as they were in the Roman Senate). This measure also implies that before its passage, many men under fifty were speaking. Solon's legal innovation that *ho boulomenos*, "anyone who wanted," could prosecute in cases important to the community, would appear to mean that "anyone who wanted" could prosecute. This law, too, said nothing of wealth or birth. Fifth-century articulations of freedom reflect not new phenomena but the conceptualization and political development of practices already visible in Homer. Democracy's "free, frank, and equal speech," *parrhēsia* and *isēgoria*, were epiphenomena based on long-standing Greek mentalities. If Eupatrids attempted to control the assembly, Hesiod and Thersites had long since shown how ineffective those attempts might be.

7. The Areopagus Council.   According to our sources' nearly unanimous testimony, Solon transformed a venerable homicide court on the Areios Pagos (at that time "massive hill," not "hill of Ares") into the Areopagus Council, composed of all ex-archons.[17] Solon's provision on the age of assembly speakers indicates his respect for elders. As we have seen (in note 16), he conceived of this council as the "second anchor" for his ship of state. Whether newly established or reconstituted, Solon's Areopagus was assigned a number of powers, beginning with *nomophulakein*, "guarding the *nomoi*" (*Ath. Pol.* 8.4). The reference of *nomoi* is uncertain. If it refers to (or includes) statute laws—and Solon's major accomplishment was the institution of statute laws—we may ask, "guard" against whom? As we have seen, the demos are said to have examined (*euthunein*) the *archai* after their terms of office. Did Solon specify that a body of ex-archons should watch over *archai* during their year in power, to make sure they followed the law? The "Constitution of Draco" in *Ath. Pol.* 4.4 states that the Areopagus "was guardian of the laws, and watched over the *archai* to see that they exercised their *archai* according to the laws. A man who was wronged could make a denunciation to the Council of the Areopagites, indicating the law under which he was wronged." This "Constitution" was probably fabricated in the late fifth century, and indicates how the early competence of the Areopagus was understood at that time. Similarly, a decree proposed by Teisamenos in 403 authorized the Areopagus to "take care of (*epimeleisthai*) the laws, so that the *archai* may employ the laws that have been passed" (Andocides 1.83–84). Philochoros reports that, probably after 462/1, the Athenians instituted a board of *nomophulakes* to "force the *archai* to abide by the laws."[18] As in the seventh-century law from Dreros, a common purpose of archaic legislation was regulating *archai* (e.g., Hölkeskamp 1992: 94; Osborne 1996: 186–88). Thus an early-sixth-century *rhetra* of the Eleans specifies: "If he who holds the highest office and the princes (*basileis*) do not impose the fines," they themselves are fined, and "let the Hellanodikas enforce this and let the body of demiurgi enforce the other fines" (Buck 1955: no. 61, his trans. mod.). In the Chios inscription, Robinson (1997: 95) interprets as populist the official who *dēmou rhētras phulassei*, "guards the laws of the people." Granting any individual official power over his peers usually aroused Greek anxieties. In Athens' classical democracy, monthly scrutiny of officials by the demos replaced this aspect of *nomophulakein* by the Areopagus and the board of *nomophulakes*. Alternatively or in addition, *nomophulakein* may have authorized Solon's Areopagus to check improper actions by the newly powerful assembly. This power would resemble the power of Sparta's Gerousia to "set aside" if the assembly spoke "crookedly." In the passage cited, Philochoros added that the fifth-century board of *nomophulakes* also "sat in the assembly and council . . . , preventing the enactment of things disadvantageous to the city."

Finally, if in this context *nomos* had a wider sense than statute law, as, for example, "the condition of an orderly, civilized society" (cf. Ostwald 1969: 22, 33–37), the Areopagus may have had some authority regarding broader social concerns, for example, by enforcing Athens' early "law against idleness," to ensure that heads of households continued to cultivate their lands on behalf of other family members and heirs.[19]

According to *Ath. Pol.* 8.4 the Areopagus was also charged with "protecting the popular government" (*dēmos*) through a *nomos eisangeltikos*, "a law on giving information." Although the word *dēmos* may be anachronistic, Aristotle had studied Solon's *nomoi*, and there is no reason to dispute that Solon provided for the protection of Athens' government (Wallace 1989: 64–66). Cylon, Peisistratus, and the many revolutions across Greece showed that fears for the government were well founded.

SOLON'S POLITEIA: AN ASSESSMENT

What Kind of a Politeia?

How are we to classify Solon's *politeia,* and how did he? A basic dilemma, for him and us, lay in the absence of developed political concepts and vocabulary. Although Solon knew the abstract noun "tyranny" (fr. 32.2, 34.7), sixth-century Greeks had not yet defined the different types of constitutions or specified their components or linked them with ideologies, except perhaps very broadly with *eunomia,* "good order." Once these developments had started (essentially in the fifth century), some fourth-century observers judged that "Solon was an excellent lawgiver who broke the over-exclusive nature of the oligarchy, ended the slavery of the common people, and established the ancient democracy with a well-balanced constitution. For they regard the Council of the Areopagus as oligarchic, the elected offices as aristocratic, and the law courts as democratic" (Arist. *Pol.* 1273b). The analysis is perceptive, although it omits one essential component of Athens' government—the people's assembly. Structurally, Solon's reforms created a mixed timocratic/democratic system of institutions, transferring power from an abusive aristocracy into the hands of an upper tier of men, as determined by wealth and military service, and to all Athenians, in the assembly and the *ēliaia,* possibly under the guard of a council of ex-*archai.*

What was Solon's conception of his reforms? He had no words like "mixed," "aristocracy," or "democracy." It is unclear how far *eunomia* carried any constitutional content, although the influence of Sparta is apparent. Then the most powerful and prestigious polis, some decades earlier Sparta had produced the first revolution involving specific constitutional reforms, installing "*kratos* by the *damos*" among *homoioi* (alikes, peers). Solon also used the term *homoios,* and Doric *ēliaia.* His Areopagus shows important parallels with Sparta's Gerousia. Both councils had a homicide competence (see Arist. *Pol.* 1275b), both were elected by the people and served for life, and both may have been authorized to set aside decisions of the demos. Spartan territory was divided among the Spartiates; in *Pol.* 1307a Aristotle states that in Sparta "the poem of Tyrtaeus called *Eunomia* [shows that] some people impoverished by the war were demanding that the land should be distributed." According to Solon, in 594 some of Athens' revolutionaries were also demanding *isomoiria,* the equal distribution of land (fr. 34 W = *Ath. Pol.* 12.3). Solon resisted this demand but sang of *eunomia.*[20]

Beyond the constitutional content of Solon's various reforms, political roles were important. Solon refused to become a tyrant, accepting instead the position of archon, lawgiver, and mediator. In those personae and that of *sophos* (sage: see Wallace 2007) he addressed Athens' problems. Before his archonship, Solon spoke out from among the revolutionaries. His actions in 594/3 reflect a more complex stance. Chosen to mediate by the oligarchs and the revolutionary demos "together" (*Ath. Pol.* 5.2), he embraced this role, at once helping and restraining the demos, the new rich, and also the old order.

The Demos Empowered

In the economic sphere, Solon resisted the revolutionaries' extreme demands for violence, plundering, and the redistribution of land (*Ath. Pol.* 12.3). At the same time, he "set the land of Attica free" and abolished hektemorage and debt bondage. Thus in a balanced way he worked to resolve Athens' economic difficulties.

The *archai* continued to exercise great powers (*Ath. Pol.* 13). At the same time, reinforcing the new authority of executive public government as opposed to aristocratic privilege, Solon is reported to have commanded "obey the *archai*, right or wrong" (fr. 30 W). Furthermore, the new rich shared in the *archai*, as did the hoplite class; the demos elected the *archai;* and the Areopagus Council and the demos, through scrutinies and judicial appeal, watched over the *archai* to prevent the abuse of their authority.

Understanding the extent of the demos's power is perhaps the hardest aspect of Solon's reforms. In addition to relief from oppression, Solon gave significant powers to the council of 400, to the assembly (now formally constituted from all citizens), and to the people's court. On the face of it, it seems remarkable and indeed revolutionary that henceforth the demos elected Athens' powerful *archai*, that a large group of citizens prepared the assembly's agenda, and that in the assembly and the court the people's voice was decisive (*kurios*). These measures seem much more extensive than merely restoring the demos's traditional voice, which in the seventh century the Eupatrids had stifled. Of course, as scholars rightly stress, we must resist evaluating Solon's *politeia* in the reflected light of Athens' later democracy. Solon had no idea how dominant the fifth-century assembly or council would become as a result of contingent historical factors. Still, on the face of it, Solon's demos was given great power. Solon created the basic institutions of Athens' democracy.

The Demos Restrained

Solon's words, however, suggest a more restrained interpretation of his reforms. First, this was not Athens' fifth-century democracy:

> This is how the demos can best follow its leaders
> if it is neither unleashed nor restrained too much.
> For excess breeds *hubris*, when great prosperity comes
> to men of unsound mind.
>   fr. 6 W = *Ath. Pol.* 12.2

Solon's demos should follow their leaders. He does not conceive of a government without leaders, run only by the people:

> I gave to the demos as much esteem (*geras*) / power (*kratos* [Plut. *Sol.* 18.5])
>   as is sufficient,
> not detracting from their honor (*timē*) or giving out more.
> To those who had power (*dunamis*) and were admired for their wealth,
> I also declared that they should have nothing unseemly (*aeikes*).
>   fr. 5 W = *Ath. Pol.* 12.1

When Solon lists what he promised the people in revolt (fr. 36 W), he does not mention political power:

> But as for me, which of the things for which I called
> the people together did I not attain before I stopped?
> . . . I took up the boundary stones. . . .
> I brought back many men who had been sold off. . . .
> Those here at home . . . I made free.
> Laws, too, . . .
> I set down in writing.

After his reforms, Solon's poems repeatedly proclaim his mediating intentions. If anyone else had gained his post,

> he'd not have held the people back, nor stopped
> until he'd stirred the milk and lost the cream.
> But I took up my post in No-Man's Land
> just like a boundary stone.
> fr. 37.6–10 = *Ath. Pol.* 12.5

> Both sides I strove to surround with a strong shield.
> I did not permit an unjust victory to either's demands.
> fr. 5 W = *Ath. Pol.* 12.1

> Yet had another held the goad as I,
> a man of bad intent and filled with greed,
> would he, like me, have held the people back?
> Had I supported what then pleased their foes
> or even what their own extremists planned,
> Athens had been bereaved of many men.
> Therefore I warded off from every side,
> a wolf at bay among the packs of hounds.
> fr. 36.20–26 = *Ath. Pol.* 12.4

"Some say that Solon received the following oracle at Delphi: 'Take your seat now in mid-ship; yours is the work of direction; for many in Athens support you'" (Plut. *Sol.* 14.6). Another poem "argues the case of each side in turn against the other and goes on to exhort them to join in putting an end to the quarrel that had arisen" (*Ath. Pol.* 5.2).

Resolving the Contradiction

How do we explain the apparent contradiction between the increased powers that Solon gave the demos, and the more moderate tone of his verse? Three points may be remembered. First, Solon was more moderate than the extremists wanted. He gave the demos a good deal, including what the demos had gotten in other poleis, but not, for example, the equal distribution of land. Second, when Solon claims that he neither gave nor took away *geras / kratos* and *timē* from the demos, this need not mean that he did nothing for them. He gave the demos what he thought was right for them, neither more nor less; and he took away from the Eupatrids what he judged to be "unseemly." Third and perhaps most important, like much archaic poetry except epic and Hesiod, Solon's poems (including his love poetry) were part of the world of aristocratic literary performance and were written for the symposion, a focus of aristocratic cultural life.[21] Solon himself was an aristocrat and will have shared many complex aristocratic mentalities in addition to his anger at the Eupatrids and his concern for civic justice. It is striking that in the *geras / kratos* poem, composed in the aftermath of his reforms, he mentions "those who had power and were admired for their wealth." To an audience of aristocrats Solon could certainly emphasize how moderately he had responded to the demos's demands. Before his reforms, we remember, Solon was adamant in his opposition to the greedy, overbearing Eupatrids. Antony Andrewes rightly warns against "overinterpreting" Solon's poetry to signify impartiality to the demos, in the light of how much he gave them (1982a: 390).

Standard explanations for Solon's institutions look forward rather than back. Those scholars who accept the evidence for Solon's constitution believe that its democratic elements were largely Solon's own idea, and that he was ahead of his time. Psychologically the people were not yet prepared to use the power that he willed upon them. Oswyn Murray states that Solon's reforms were "too advanced for his society": they merely set Athens "on a . . . course towards social justice" (1993: 200). George Forrest remarks: "Solon could not have conceived of a self-confident mass of ordinary men" (1966: 172). "It seems clear that [Solon's constitutional] measures *were intended* to increase participation by the demos, and they were combined with *a strong effort* to raise the citizens' political awareness, sense of responsibility, and involvement" (Raaflaub 1998b: 38, my emphasis; cf. earlier Meier 1990: 46–47). From this perspective, Solon's constitutional reforms were different from his economic reforms, in that they were not intended to resolve a violent revolutionary situation by striking compromises between competing demands. Solon was a visionary educator of the citizens whom he was attempting to politicize, although he failed in this endeavor. When the demos again became fed up with the aristocrats in 561, they did not establish a democracy but a tyranny.

These teleological assessments seem to presuppose that before 508 nonelite Athenians were more or less downtrodden masses, lacking confidence and a sense of self-worth. They were not yet free from a traditional dependence on a hereditary aristocracy, although Solon wanted to encourage this. These views resemble the paternalistic conception of society idealized by fifth- and fourth-century Athenian conservatives, of the demos as children, guided by all-knowing *patres* (see, for example, *Ath. Pol.* 28.5). This elitist, paternalist model has influenced modern thinking about the origins of democracy, in part because of familiar conceptions about the West's transition from medieval social and political hierarchies to the modern participatory state, and in part because of apparent parallels with certain contemporary societies where for centuries (we are told) downtrodden masses have been subservient to an arrogant, all-powerful upper class and democracy has proved difficult to cultivate.

Does this model fit any polis in archaic Greece? As we saw in chapter 2, already in our earliest sources non-elites display self-confidence, egalitarianism, and individualism; they spoke out, acted as they thought right, and balanced community needs against their own intense feelings of freedom, self-worth, and independence. In Athens, even *hektēmoroi* and *pelatai* helped to effect political and economic changes, gaining formal power in assembly and court despite their poverty. Fundamental mentalities of egalitarianism, self-worth, and independence explain why democracy was an invention of the Greek people. They had listened to Hesiod and others on the rapacity of the aristocracy. They had seen fellow countrymen expel their traditional rulers. The Spartans redistributed land and established the people in power by a new constitution. The rapid diffusion of written laws suggests that Hesiod's indignation against unfair justice by the *basilēes* reflected widespread and enduring sentiment. Against standard reconstructions based largely on aristocratic sources and self-serving aristocratic perspectives, Solon's constitution balanced ordinary people's demands not to have others control their lives, with measures of empowerment, restraint, and sharing.

Solon was not attempting to politicize the people. His poems show that they were politicized already. His task was to mediate between the demos and the Eupatrids by legislation that would pacify the revolutionaries and restore the people's voice. In a dangerous situation threatening violence, mediators as a rule do not make dramatic, even spectacular concessions of direct and immediate political power to people who are not demanding power. Earlier demonstrations of people power in the wider Greek world suggested what measures were available against the hated old order.

In 594 the demos, including the humblest, forced change, freeing their lands and bodies from abuse by the aristocracy, and taking for themselves a strong measure of political power in assembly and court. Solon's constitutional measures were a consequence of citizens' political awareness, their sense of responsibility and civic involvement, and the need for a new dispensation of power. This fundamental mentality explains why democracy first appeared in Greece and came to be adopted widely as a form of government.

THE AFTERMATH OF SOLON'S REFORMS

If a vocal mass of people demanded and received a good share of power in 594, why did they not make greater use of it in later decades? In fact, for some years the struggle continued. According to *Ath. Pol.* 13, politics after 593 was marked by conflict among various political groups, especially over the archonship, which for two years went unfilled. The settlement after Damasias's two-year usurpation in 582–580 awarded half its power to "peasants" and "craftsmen"—whatever those terms may mean. The Eupatrids were clearly reluctant to surrender control. Damasias's usurpation also helps to contextualize the seventh-century Dreros law that prohibited the Kosmos from occupying his office for more than one year. In other ways as well, Solon's attempt at mediation and balance was not completely successful. We hear of no activity by the Areopagus Council until after 480. The exclusion of thetes and hoplites from the highest offices could have caused difficulties, although we must bear in mind that neither Cleisthenes nor Ephialtes addressed this structural problem. The archonship was only extended to hoplites in 457 and was never formally opened to thetes. *Ath. Pol.* 13.3 describes various difficulties in the post-Solonian period: some men were impoverished by the cancellation of debts; others disliked the new *politeia;* personal rivalries were serious. The settlement after Damasias is the last we see of the demos for some twenty years, except in factions led by elites.[22]

People's Revolutions in Sixth-Century Greece

Elsewhere, mass revolutions continued to break out, some of them quite possibly influenced by Solonian Athens. These developments must be especially interesting for those who question Greek "people power" before the fifth century.

We have already noted the revolutions of late-seventh- and early-sixth-century Megara, lasting down into the 550s. Another archaic poem of Theognis laments that the "good vineyard of the Lelantine plain [in Euboea] is being destroyed, the *agathoi* are fleeing and the *kakoi* manage (*diepein*) the city" (lines 891–94 W). This passage seems to describe a popular revolution that roiled Euboea, Athens' near neighbor to the north. Off the west coast the Corinthian colony Ambracia, founded c. 625, was ruled by Gorgus the son of Corinthian Cypselus, and then by his son Periander. Afterwards, "the demos joined with the tyrant Periander's enemies to throw him out and then took over the *politeia* itself" (Arist. *Pol.* 1304a31–33). This action is dated c. 580 or a little earlier (Robinson 1997: 80). Aristotle notes that "in Ambracia the property qualification for office was small, and was gradually reduced and became so low that it might as well have been abolished altogether" (*Pol.* 1303a22–24). In Argos according to Diodorus (7.13.2; see also Pausanias 2.19.2), after a serious military reverse at the hands of Sparta, "the demos rose up against" the last of Pheidon's successors because he had not divided the land among them by lot. He was driven out, and, not later than 550, an inscription indicates that nine *damiourgoi* (who are named) ruled (*anassein*) the city, the bold verb signalling that they had inherited their power from kings.[23] In *Politics* 1304a29–31 Aristotle writes that "in Chalcis the demos together with the notables destroyed the tyrant Phoxon and straightway took hold of the *politeia*" (Robinson 1997: 88–90).

Finally, again in the mid-sixth century, Delphi sent the Mantinean Demonax to Cyrene after a disastrous military defeat. Demonax first enacted tribal reforms, which probably increased the size of the citizen population. "Then, assigning to the *basileus* Battos certain special lands and priestly offices, all the other things which the *basileis* previously had he put in the middle for the demos" (*es meson tōi dēmōi:* Hdt. 4.161.3). Elsewhere Herodotus appears to use this phrase for popular government (3.80.2, 3.142; Robinson 1997: 103), although the constitutional details must escape us.

Solon's Failure?

In the midst of all this revolutionary fervor across the Greek world, why did the Athenian demos not retain its ardor, exploit the assembly's constitutional powers, and develop Solon's institutions into a full-fledged democracy? Many reasons may be suggested. The aristocracy remained rich and powerful, and continued to provide the city's leaders. Solon had not broken the old order, as history shows successful revolutions must. In addition, Solon's institutions were new and needed time to function. Perhaps above all, most Athenians were peasant farmers. Before 594, they were furious at their abuse by arrogant and greedy aristocrats, without recourse in the assembly or court. In 594 they forced reforms to solve these problems, freeing their lands and bodies from the grasp of the aristocracy and obtaining a good measure of political and judicial power. Once their immediate grievances had been resolved, however, they went back to farming, as they had in the Cylonian crisis. Why should men routinely waste valuable time away from their fields, especially when in the sixth century, month by month, few issues of great consequence will have come before the assembly? Earlier, the "middling" Hesiod had given the same advice to his brother Perses (*Works and Days* 28–29). As Aristotle remarks, farmers are too occupied to attend political meetings (*Pol.* 1319a). When political issues did not affect their livelihoods, most Athenians worked at their living.

It is also clear that in the years after Solon's reforms the squabbling between aristocrats had intensified. According to the sources (Hdt. 1.59.3; *Ath. Pol.* 13.4–5; Plut. *Sol.* 13.1–2; see Rhodes 1981: 179; cf. Lavelle 2000; Anderson 2003: 18, 31–32, 67), the demos and aristocracy broke into three regional sections, each contending against the others. The aristocrats continued to indulge in lavish lifestyles (Morris 1996: 34). Hippocleides, archon in 566, spent a year in Sicyon courting, ending up by dancing drunk on tables (Hdt. 6.129). Finally, as Peter Rhodes (1981: 127) and others note, "Solon may even have made life harder for some of the poor in that they would probably find it more difficult to borrow after his reform."

The Path to Tyranny

By 561, as in 594, the demos had had enough. Now, however, they chose a different solution. Going down the well-worn path that Solon had declined, abandoning their government even though just at this time popular governments were emerging around the Greek world, they ended the squabbling by supporting Peisistratus as tyrant. "Since cities at that time were not large and the demos lived in the countryside fully engaged in making their living, when the leaders of the demos became warlike, the demos grasped for tyranny" (Arist. *Pol.* 1305a). Solon himself attests that the demos wanted Peisistratus and were responsible for his tyranny. He warned them:

> From great men a city is destroyed, and into the slavery
> of a single ruler (*monarchos*) by ignorance the demos falls.
>> fr. 9.3–4 W = Diod. 9.20

Once Peisistratus gained power, Solon blamed the demos:

> If you have suffered terrible things through your own baseness (*kakotēs*),
> do not put the blame for this on the gods.
> For you yourselves increased these men, giving pledges,
> and through these things you have evil slavery.
> Each one of you walks in the tracks of the fox,
> but for you altogether your mind is empty.
> You look to the tongue and to the words of a flattering man,
> but do not look to the deed that arises.
>> fr. 11 W = Diog. Laert. 1.52; Diod. 9. 20

The demos voted Peisistratus a bodyguard, and when he seized the Acropolis, they pointedly did not besiege him there, as they had besieged Cylon. All this supports Aristotle's express statements that the demos trusted Peisistratus from their hatred of the rich (*Pol.* 1305a), and that he was *dēmotikōtatos* (*Ath. Pol.* 14.1), perhaps "most inclined to the demos." Rhodes observes (1981: 186): "It is likely that Pisistratus, drawing support from the part of Attica that was poorest and farthest from Athens, claimed to represent the interests of various kinds of unprivileged Athenians and is not unfairly described as *demotikotatos*."

Of course Peisistratus did not champion the poor simply out of disinterested benevolence. They were his constituency, they wanted what he gave them, and for this reason other aristocrats ultimately failed to drive him out. Aristocrats continued to be powerful down until the Peloponnesian War (431–404 B.C.E.). Their failure to eliminate Peisistratus, however, suggests no strong public support for their type of governing. Two points are striking. First, although Peisistratus was a tyrant, the sources are emphatic that he "administered everything according to the laws" (*Ath. Pol.* 16.8; see also Hdt. 1.59.6; Thuc. 6.54.6). Such was the strength of Athens' inheritance from its lawgiver Solon. (For this same reason, in later Athens most laws were called Solonian.) Second, Peisistratus is reported to have been especially concerned for the economic well-being of ordinary Athenians, for example, by making loans to assist them with farming (*Ath. Pol.* 16.2–3), something that may have been difficult after Solon's *seisachtheia*, as we have noted. Aristotle remarks rather cynically that the tyrant helped the people succeed in farming the countryside, so that they would not worry about public affairs. Put less pejoratively, being comfortably off suited Attica's peasant farmers very well. They needed to farm and were happy to prosper. Powerful himself, Peisistratus also represented them and worked for their prosperity. In classical Athens his tyranny came to be praised as a golden "age of Kronos" (*Ath. Pol.* 16.7 and see references in Rhodes 1981 ad loc.; cf. [Plato] *Hipparchus* 229b3–7).

Cleisthenes and After

In two generations the demos had risen up twice to change their government, in 594/3 and 561/0. They did so a third time in 508/7. After the Alcmaeonids and Spartans drove out Peisistratus's unpopular son Hippias in 510, Athens again was beset by aristocratic infighting, this time between Cleisthenes and Isagoras. When Isagoras won the archonship of 508/7, Cleisthenes "added the demos to his group of supporters" (Hdt. 5.66.2). That is to say, the assembly voted Isagoras into office but then immediately shifted its allegiance.

How did Cleisthenes win over the demos? First, he reversed the aristocrats' recent expulsion of many people whose civic status had become uncertain, perhaps because they did not belong to phratries (*Ath. Pol.* 13.5; cf. now Anderson 2003: 41). It is noteworthy that the demos apparently welcomed the integration of these persons. Second, he proposed to reconstitute and reorganize the army, which the tyrants had weakened or even disbanded (van Effenterre 1976; Frost 1984). The extraordinary popularity of this measure is indicated by the army's brilliant success in 506, defeating the Boeotians and the Chalcidians on a single day (Hdt. 5.77–78). Cleisthenes reorganized the army by creating ten new tribes. He simultaneously weakened regional loyalties by ensuring that each of these tribes was constituted from different regions of Attica (*Ath. Pol.* 21). He used his tribes to rebuild the people's council, expanding it from 400 to 500, 50 men per tribe. Replacing the old *naukrariai* (*Ath. Pol.* 21.5), Cleisthenes reorganized deme or village government, establishing a hundred or more local goverments around Attica (Osborne 1997: 245–47). Each of these local governments had a demarch ("deme authority"), a treasurer, a meeting place, control of the citizenship lists, and so forth. This reform indicates the deep desire by large numbers of ordinary, rural Athenians to govern themselves. Finally and not least, in 508/7 Cleisthenes must have promised the demos not to institute an oligarchy but to strengthen the people's government.

Just as Solon's Athens was not isolated from events in the wider Greek world, so Cleisthenes' reforms parallel developments elsewhere. The archaeological record, in particular the cessation of lavish aristocratic burials, has suggested that egalitarianism was now emerging in many poleis (Morris 1996: 39–40), as it had earlier in Sparta. So, too, was democracy.

When Cleisthenes won over the demos, Isagoras and the Spartans countered by demanding the expulsion of those "accursed" after the Cylonian conspiracy, especially the Alcmaeonids. Remarkably, the Alcmaeonid Cleisthenes now withdrew into exile. When the Spartans arrived with a small force, they procured the exile supposedly of seven hundred families (a conventional number). The Spartan king Cleomenes now "tried to dissolve the people's council and entrust the government to three hundred of the supporters of Isagoras. The council, however, stood firm in resisting him. Cleomenes, with Isagoras and his faction, occupied the Acropolis. The rest of the Athenians, thinking the same things, besieged them for two days" (Hdt. 5.72.1–2). The crisis was resolved, and Cleisthenes and the others returned. In the following chapter Ober well describes the marvellous response of the demos, uniting to save their polis. In 5.3 Herodotus uses the same phrase, "thinking the same things," to express a broad sense of political unity. This was not the first time the Athenian demos had so acted. The pattern is familiar. At critical threats to Athens, the demos en masse went into action—in 632, in 594, in 561, and now again in 508: barring the intermezzo of Peisistratus's popular tyranny, once every generation.

Nonetheless, we probably should not make too much of these episodes, dramatic as they were. As Kurt Raaflaub says in his chapter below (see also Anderson 2003: 78–80), Cleisthenes had won the demos over earlier, by offering them a *politeia* that gave them what they wanted: citizenship for many, an army, a democracy, and local government. Institutionally, the Cleisthenic *politeia* was not very different from Solon's, except in its geographical diversification, expansion of deme government, and organization of the army. The mentalities that drove these democratic reforms we have seen before. In Athens, however, tyranny had now been discredited, the aristocracy had long been out of power, and the wider Greek world was moving toward egalitarianism. It was time for Athens' democratic constitution to come into its own.

Did Athens' so-called subhoplites, the thetes, share in Cleisthenes' reforms? In one sense this issue is not critical. The number of thetes is uncertain, but the many thousands of hoplites were enough to make Cleisthenes' government a democracy. Nevertheless, there is no good reason to deny that thetes participated in Cleisthenes' reforms. Except in Solon's timocratic scale (which persisted long into the fifth century and was never formally abolished), there is no evidence that Athens' hoplites ever distinguished themselves from the lower classes. Ober (1998b: 73) has ably argued this point for the Cleisthenic period, Raaflaub himself (1996b) has done so for the 460s and later; Geoffrey de Ste. Croix (1981: 290–92) and Victor Hanson (1996: 295–96) have done so for the last decade of the fifth and the following century. In 462, the Spartans sent Cimon's hoplites back to Athens, fearing lest they side with the helots (Thuc. 1.102). Murray writes (1993: 144): "The absence of any established distinction of status between hoplites and the rest of the people meant that, in acting for themselves, the hoplites acted for the *dēmos* as a whole." Even with land producing less than 200 bushels per year, many thetes had adequate farms. As a group they were not a landless proletariat. Many poorer Athenians surely regarded themselves as fully Athenian, many of them as *mesoi,* "middling citizens." They were welcomed as equals by citizen hoplites. As Jean-Pierre Vernant observed (e.g., 1982: chap. 4), Greek society was largely nonhierarchical.

In addition to Ober's (1998b: 78–81) and Greg Anderson's (2003: 52–57, 112–14) surveys documenting the demos's confidence before the Persian Wars, our sources preserve a web of traditions that illustrate the people's newly strengthened voice after Marathon in 490. *Ath. Pol.* 22.3 mentions the confidence that their victory gave to the demos. According to Plutarch, when Miltiades asked the assembly for a crown of olives because he had won the battle, Sophanes of Dekelea, "rising up from the middle of the ekklesia," objected: "Let Miltiades ask for such an honor for himself when he has conquered the barbarian single-handed" (*Life of Cimon* 8.1). The people sided with Sophanes. Although Plutarch is no infallible source for this period (for a defense of his report see Lewis 1971: 136–37), his story is consistent with a later tradition in Aeschines (3.183–85). After the Athenians had won the battle at the river Strymon, probably in 476/5, the generals asked to be honored by the assembly. The assembly agreed, voting them three stone Herms "but on condition that they should not inscribe their own names upon them, in order that the inscription might not seem to be in honor of the generals, but of the people." Aeschines quotes the epigrams on these Herms, praising Athens' soldiers. If Aeschines' anecdote is suspect, the epigrams did not praise the generals, but Athens' soldiers. Anderson (2003: 151–58) discusses a number of contemporary public epitaphs in honor of the city's armies.

Miltiades' troubles with the demos were not yet done. In 489 he convinced them to grant him a fleet of seventy ships, promising only to enrich them. In traditional aristocratic fashion, he used this fleet for private purposes, to punish Paros because one Parian "had slandered him to Hydarnes the Persian." He failed to accomplish anything at Paros and on his return was prosecuted "before the demos for deceiving the Athenians"—a noteworthy legal charge for the history of democracy. The demos condemned him to the extraordinary fine of fifty talents—charging to him the riches that he had promised them and that his son Cimon later paid (Hdt. 6.132–36). The following year, according to *Ath. Pol.* 22.3, "now that the demos was confident, they used for the first time the law about ostracism." Six times in seven years the demos now tasted the pleasure of banishing powerful aristocrats from Athens' great families, including the Peisistratid Hipparchos, the Alcmaeonid Megacles, Xanthippos the father of Pericles, and Aristeides, later the architect of the Delian League. In 487/6 the demos also instituted a constitutional change: "for the first time since the tyranny the nine archons were appointed by lot on a tribal basis, from a short list of five [more likely one] hundred elected by the members of the demes" (*Ath. Pol.* 22.3). Although various aspects of this reform have been much debated, it certainly weakened the political importance of Athens' leading political offices, henceforth denied to ambitious politicians as a basis for political power. In our earliest abstract description of democratic government, Herodotus mentions first that offices are filled by lot (3.80.6).

As for free speech, Herodotus (7.142–44) reports a freewheeling assembly debate in 480 on the meaning of the Delphic oracle's reference to "wooden walls" in the context of the Persian invasion of Athens:

> When the messengers had left Delphi and laid the oracle before the people, there was much inquiry concerning its meaning, and among the many opinions which were uttered . . . Some of the elder men said that the god's answer signified that the Acropolis should be saved, for in ancient times the Acropolis of the Athenians had been fenced by a thorn hedge. . . . But others supposed that the god was referring to their ships. . . . Expert readers of oracles (*chrēsmologoi*) took the verses to mean . . . But Themistocles . . . and the Athenians judged his advice to be better. . . . And they accordingly resolved . . .

The demos probably indicated its judgment by more than simply voting. Victor Bers concludes that "fairly early in the fifth century *thorubos* [mass hubbub] was common at large official meetings" (1985: 3). In *Farmers* (fr. 101 Kassel-Austin 1984), perhaps of 424 or 422, Aristophanes included the following joke: A. "They really used to sing their pleas?" B. "By Zeus, they did. I'll give you proof: whenever someone defends himself badly, the older men, seated in court, say 'you're singing.'" This passage suggests that outbursts by the dikasts had once been common but perhaps were old-fashioned in the 420s.

By 508/7, the demos had made four decisive interventions in government. In a subsistence agricultural economy, most farmers will have thought governing not so important as putting food on their tables. In consequence, day by day most people did not preoccupy themselves with community government. As Aristotle and Raaflaub (in his chapter below) have noted, this changed after Athens' naval victory in 480, and the reasons are not far to seek. First, the point raised by the "Old Oligarch" (1.2) and Aristotle (*Pol.* 1279b, 1321a5–14, 1329a1–12, 1304a33ff.; cf. 1288a), that those who defend a state gain political power, may well have applied to Athens. Although history offers plenty of people's armies in nondemocratic states (Ceccarelli 1993; Wolin 1996; Ober 1998b), Raaflaub rightly observes that Athens' navy quickly became a standing (or "floating") fleet, with thousands of citizens drawing pay from the polis in return for fighting. It seems reasonable that such men took an active role in deciding polis policy, as our sources note. Even more importantly, a larger number of ordinary Athenians now became involved in city politics because politics had become interesting, with major issues to decide, and especially because the empire brought in large amounts of allied silver. This Attica's peasant farmers found well worth paying attention to. "Now that a large amount of money had been collected, Aristeides advised the Athenians . . . to leave the fields and live in the city: there would be maintenance for all, some on campaign, some on guard duty, others attending to public affairs. . . . The Athenians were persuaded. . . . They provided ample maintenance for the common people, so that more than twenty thousand men were supported from the tribute, the taxes and the allies " (*Ath. Pol.* 24.1–2; cf. Plut. *Aristeides* 22, 25). Some time before Ephialtes' reforms, Damon coined the slogan "to give the people their own," when recommending the introduction of dikastic pay (*Ath. Pol.* 27.4). In contrast to the modern world, it is a remarkable measure of the power and standing of ordinary Athenians that the imperial riches that poured into the city after 477 were openly distributed even to the poorest citizens, instead of being seized by the rich.

Finally, the decade from 462/1 saw a series of institutional reforms, beginning with Ephialtes' transfer of the Areopagus's political powers into the control of the demos. The aristocratic Kimon opposed these reforms, as he did his rival Ephialtes. These changes do not reflect the increased standing specifically of Athens' thetes. Indeed, Solon's timocratic principle was retained, as in spite of their greater participation in the public realm, thetes continued to be denied access to Athens' highest offices. In 457 such access was extended to the zeugite or hoplite class, which had been especially powerful since Cleisthenes. Just as there was no seventh-century "hoplite revolution," so there was no thetes' revolution before or after 462/1. Rather, the demos as a whole, and also its leaders, benefited from these measures. Ephialtes' reforms, the 457 reform of the archonship, and the appearance of democratic ideology in the 460s all reflect the development and expansion of the demos's standing generally, at the expense of the traditional aristocracy. As the last of this series of measures, Pericles' citizenship law of 451/o outlawed marriage with foreigners, an aristocratic custom.

Since Cleisthenes and in fact since Solon, Athens' constitution had empowered the demos to dominate government. Usually, the demos made little use of this power, in part because governing held little interest or profit. For these reasons, fully active, day-to-day democracy at Athens followed the establishment of the Delian League. On the other hand, at no time is it appropriate to speak of ordinary Athenians or other Greeks as lacking self-confidence, feeling inferior to wealthier men, or failing to understand and exploit their own political strength. In these mentalities lay the roots of Greek democracy.[24]

NOTES

1. On the transition from warrior to orientalizing symposion, see Fehr 1971: 26ff. and passim.

2. Translations of Solon are taken or adapted from Rhodes 1984 and Miller 1996, those of *Ath. Pol.* from Rhodes.

3. On the intensification of the Greek aristocracy's search for wealth and luxury, see Starr 1977: 46–54.

4. For a good discussion, see Murray 1993: 189–94.

5. *Ath. Pol.* 2.1. I am prepared to dispute Rhodes's view (1981: 118–19) that *Ath. Pol.* took its account of Solon largely from a single source. Among other points, its exposition partly reflects Peripatetic political theories and research interests (Wallace 1999: esp. 243–48). Raaflaub (1996c: 1054) rightly points out that *Ath. Pol.*'s description of seventh-century Attica disregards the substantial number of landowning farmers who later became Solon's hoplite class. If this disregard reflects contemporary sources, it may indicate the absence of class sentiment between Attica's poorer and its middling citizens (see below).

6. Sounding almost like Hesiod, Odysseus tells an arrogant suitor: "Eurymachos, I wish there could be a working contest between us . . . out in the meadow, with myself holding a well-curved sickle, and you one like it, so as to test our endurance for labor, without food, from dawn till dark, with plenty of grass for our mowing. Or if it were oxen to be driven, . . . and there were four acres to plow . . . there you would see if I could carve a continuous furrow" (*Od.* 18.366–75, trans. Lattimore).

7. Nik. Dam. *FGrHist* 90 fr. 61.4; cf. Paus. 6.19.1–4 with Griffin 1982: 40–42.

8. See, for example, *IC* IV, 43 Ba (Gortyn), 78 (Gortyn); *Bulletin de correspondance hellénique* 109 (1985) 163, cf. 177–78 (Lyttos: van Effenterre); 61 (1937) 334 (Dreros); *Kadmos* 9 (1970) 124 with 127–28 comm.: law-making requires the authorization of the polis which published the decree.

9. As we saw in chapter 2, unfair justice by the *basileis* was a long-standing issue in early Greece. In Athens sometime after 682, six annual officers called *thesmothetai*, literally "lawgivers," were appointed to administer justice (*Ath. Pol.* 3.4). Unfortunately, we cannot determine the circumstances behind their institution.

10. The translation "magistrate" is inappropriately modern and Roman. "Official," while less problematic, omits the power and authority implied by *archē*. See Wallace 2005.

11. Pl. *Rep.* 562d refers not specifically to Megara but only to democracy.

12. Despite Aristotle this was not class warfare. Solon states: "As for wealth, I long to have it, but to possess it unjustly is not my wish: assuredly Justice comes at a later time" (fr. 13.8–9 W; see also lines 10–14). The shameful thing is when the rich behave badly.

13. "In Greece and Rome the debtor-class rebelled. . . . Abolition came . . . as a direct consequence of of struggle from below, at times reaching genuinely revolutionary proportions" (Finley 1982: 162).

14. *Ath. Pol.* 8.1, 47.1, cf. 22.5, defended, for example, by Rhodes 1981: 146–48. Contrast *Pol.* 1273b34–1274a3, 1274a16–17, 1281b25–34. *Ath. Pol.*'s chapters on Solon are in many ways its masterpiece. By contrast, *Politics* can be hasty (e.g., 1266b14–16: Solon equalized the possession of property in Athens). Hansen's principal argument (1991: 49–52) against the lot, that the Athenians would never have thus chosen their military commander, is damaged by Hdt. 6.109.2 (a passage he knows), which states that in 490 Kallimachos was chosen polemarch by lot. Under the tyranny, the Athenians reverted to electing archons (Thuc. 6.54.6; *Ath. Pol.* 22.5).

15. See Wallace 1989: 53–54, followed by Rihll 1991: 113 n. 85; also Wallace 1998.

16. Plut. *Sol.* 19.2: see Rhodes 1981: 153 and Hansen 1990: 98 with nn. 120–21. For possible archaeological traces of the Solonian council, see Camp 1992: 38–39.

17. Wallace 1989: chaps. 1–2, and appendix on the name "Areios Pagos." Now formally composed of all ex-archons serving for life and with legally specified functions, this council was necessarily Solon's institution. Had the Eupatrids' informal oligarchic council also met on the Areopagus? We can scarcely imagine why Athens' aristocrats would have trooped up from the city to meet on a barren rock beside a shrine to the Semnai, underworld deities of the female curse. The failure of Solon's Areopagus Council was in part the product of its novelty.

18. *FGrHist* 328 fr. 64; see Wallace 1989: 56. Everyone agrees that if this board is historical, it was short-lived. We never hear of it elsewhere or again.

19. Wallace 1989: 61–64. For this wider use of *nomos* (including customs, traditions, and oral principles) in early Sparta, see Gagarin 1986: 57–58.

20. It is therefore interesting that Sparta supported Solon and the Athenians against the Megarians, in their dispute over Salamis (Plut. *Sol.* 10).

21. See, for example, Schmitt-Pantel 1990: 20–25, with references in nn. 41, 47, and 48.

22. "There are in other places constitutions that according to law incline toward democracy but by reason of their customs and training operate more like oligarchies. This is especially apt to happen after a change of constitution. The citizens do not immediately discard their old ways, but are at first content to gain only moderate advantages from their victory over the opposing side" (Arist. *Pol.* 1292b).

23. *SEG* 11.336 = van Effenterre and Ruzé 1994–95: no. 87, see also no. 88; Robinson 1997: 82–84; for *damiourgoi* at Mycenae c. 525, see no. 101.

24. For comments my thanks to Andrzej Chankowski, Robin Osborne, Eric Robinson, audiences at Florence and Nijmegen, the excellent referees for this volume at both Princeton and California, and not least my fellow authors. Peter Rhodes sent speedy and helpful responses to queries.

Chapter 4

"I Besieged That Man"

Democracy's Revolutionary Start

Josiah Ober

In searching for the "origins of Athenian democracy" I have avoided the individualist, institutionalist, and foundationalist premises undergirding much historical work on Athenian political history.[1] My approach to the history of Athenian democracy cares relatively little for the motivations of Cleisthenes or (e.g.) Solon, Ephialtes, Pericles, or Demosthenes, since I do not think that democracy was "discovered" or "invented" by an individual. Rather I suppose that these (and other) highly talented individuals responded creatively to what they correctly perceived as substantial changes in the Athenian political environment, and that these changes were the direct result of collective action. The responses of creative individuals had much to do with the shape of Athenian political culture but should not be simply equated with it. Next, while I acknowledge that institutions are very important in that they allow for the stabilization of a new order of doing things and thus provide a basis for subsequent evolution (see below), I suppose that democratic institutional practices arose in response to a historical rupture, to an "epistemic" sociological/ideological shift—that is, a substantial and relatively sudden change in the ways that Athenians thought, spoke, and behaved toward one another.[2] And finally I suggest that we should replace the notion that Athenian-style democracy was the product of a constitutional "foundation" with a view of *dēmokratia* as pragmatic, experimental, and revisable: originally a product of action on the part of a socially diverse body of citizens and subsequently sustained and revised by the decisions and practices of the citizenry.

What I am seeking, then, is an epistemic shift, and an event that crystallized that shift and thereby motivated individuals to design institutions capable of framing and giving substance to a dramatically new understanding of society. I will argue here that the key shift occurred in the last decade of the sixth century, and that the decisive event was an uprising by the Athenian demos. That uprising took place in response to an attempt by a foreign invader and his quisling Athenian supporters to dissolve the existing Athenian government in 508/7 B.C.E. Democracy comes into existence with the capacity of a demos to act as a collective historical agent. In Athens, that came about when "I, the people" did something that really mattered, by besieging a Spartan king for three days on the Athenian acropolis.

TWO ANCIENT ACCOUNTS
OF THE ATHENIAN REVOLUTION

The most complete and earliest account of these events is by Herodotus, who did the research for his *Histories* in the mid-fifth century B.C.E., just within living memory of the uprising itself.

> [After the last of the tyrants had been deposed by the Spartans] two men were especially powerful (*edunasteuon*): Cleisthenes, an Alcmaeonid, who was reputed to have bribed the Pythian priestess, and Isagoras, son of Tisander, a man of a notable family. . . . These men were engaged in a civil conflict over power (*estasiasan peri dunamios*). Cleisthenes was getting the worst of it in this dispute and brought the demos into his group of comrades (*ton dēmon pros-etairizetai*). After that he divided the Athenians into ten tribes instead of four as formerly. . . . When he had associated (*prosethēkato*) the Athenian demos, formerly utterly despised (*apōsmenon*), with his side (*moiran*), he gave the tribes new names and increased their number, making ten phylarchs in place of four, and assigning ten demes to each tribe. . . . Having brought over (*pros-themenos*) the people, he was stronger by far than his rivals in the civil conflict (*tōn antistasisiōteōn*).
>
> Isagoras, who was on the losing side, devised a counterplot, and invited the aid of Cleomenes, who had been his guest-friend since the besieging of the Peisistratids. It was even said of Cleomenes that he regularly went to see Isagoras's wife. Then Cleomenes first sent a herald to Athens demanding the banishment of Cleisthenes and many other Athenians with him, the Accursed, as he called them. This he said in his message by Isagoras' instruction, for the Alcmaeonids and their faction were held to be guilty of that bloody deed while Isagoras and his friends had no part in it. When Cleomenes had sent for and demanded the banishment of Cleisthenes and the Accursed, Cleisthenes himself secretly departed.
>
> Afterwards, however, Cleomenes appeared in Athens with a smallish force. Upon his arrival, he, in order to take away the curse, banished seven hundred Athenian families named for him by Isagoras. Having done so, he next attempted to abolish the council (*tēn boulēn kataluein epeirato*),[3] and to transfer political authority to a body of three hundred supporters of Isagoras. But when the council resisted and refused to obey (*antistatheisēs de tēs boulēs kai ou boulomenēs peithesthai*), Cleomenes, together with Isagoras and his supporters,

occupied the Acropolis (*katalambanousi tēn akropolin*). However, the rest of the Athenians (*Athēnaiōn de hoi loipoi*), who were of one mind (*ta auta phronē-santes*) [regarding these affairs], besieged them [on the Acropolis] for two days. But on the third day a truce was struck, and the Lacedaemonians among them were allowed to leave the territory [of Attica].

[Cleomenes] was thus again cast out together with his Lacedaemonians. As for the rest [of Cleomenes' men: Timesitheus of Delphi is the only one named], the Athenians imprisoned them under sentence of death. . . . These men, then, were bound and put to death. After that, the Athenians sent to bring back Cleisthenes and the seven hundred households banished by Cleomenes. (Hdt. 5.66–73.1)

The Aristotelian *Constitution of Athens* (*Athēnaiōn Politeia* or *Ath. Pol.*), written a century after Herodotus, in the late fourth century B.C.E., offers a gener-ally compatible and indeed largely (although not entirely) derivative account of the events of 508/7:

When the tyranny had been put down, there was a period of faction-strife between Isagoras, son of Teisander, who was a friend of the tyrants, and Cleisthenes, who belonged to the family of the Alcmaeonids. Cleisthenes, hav-ing got the worst of it in the comrade-groups (*hetaireiai*), enlisted the demos on his side, offering to hand over the government to the multitude (*plēthos*).

Isagoras began to lose power, so he again called in the aid of Cleomenes, who was a great friend of his, and jointly persuaded him to drive out the curse, because the Alcmaeonids were reputed to be a family that was under a curse. Cleisthenes secretly withdrew, and Cleomenes with a few troops proceeded to expel as accursed seven hundred Athenian households.

Having accomplished this, he tried to put down the council and set up Isagoras and three hundred of his friends with him in sovereign power over the state. But the *boulē* resisted (*tēs de boulēs antistasēs*), and the multitude gath-ered itself together (*kai sunathroisthentos tou plēthous*),[4] so the supporters of Cleomenes and Isagoras fled for refuge (*katephugon*) to the Acropolis, and the demos invested it and laid siege to it for two days. On the third day they let Cleomenes and his comrades go away under a truce, and sent for Cleisthenes and the other exiles to come back.

The demos having taken control of affairs (*kataschontos de tou dēmou ta prag-mata*), Cleisthenes was their leader (*hēgemōn*) and stood first with the people (*tou dēmou prostatēs*). . . . These were the causes, therefore, that led the demos to trust in Cleisthenes. And when this time he had become chief of the multi-tude (*tou plēthous proestēkōs*), in the fourth year after the deposition of the tyrants, in the archonship of Isagoras [he enacted various institutional reforms]. These reforms made the constitution much more democratic than that of Solon; for it had come about that the tyranny had obliterated the laws of Solon by disuse, and Cleisthenes, aiming at the multitude (*stochazomenon tou plēthous*), had instituted other new ones, including the enactment of the law about ostracism. (*Ath. Pol.* 20–22.1)

RETELLING THE STORY

There are many ways a contemporary historian of ancient Greece might retell the story of Athens in the eventful year of the archonship of Isagoras. Modern accounts tend to emphasize elite personalities and interelite conflict, and to see the democratic institutional "foundation" as the invention (whether for altruistic or self-interested purposes) of elite individuals—most notably, of Cleisthenes himself.[5] By contrast, my story about 508/7 centers on a revolutionary uprising that takes place without leadership in the traditional sense. In my story Cleisthenes' leadership and the successful implementation of the reforms associated with his name are *responses to* the revolutionary situation, and so it is not Cleisthenes but the Athenian demos (qua citizen body) that is the protagonist.[6] Cleisthenes plays an important role in my story, but he is not the lead actor. The events of the year 508/7 constitute a genuine rupture in Athenian political history, because they mark the moment at which the demos stepped onto the historical stage as a collective agent, a historical actor in its own right and under its own name.[7]

In the aftermath of the expulsion of the tyrants in 510 B.C.E. the political battlefield of Athens was initially disputed between rival aristocrats, supported by coteries of limited size and heavily weighted to the upper end of the socioeconomic spectrum. Isagoras and his supporters sought to narrow the existing (Solonian/Peisistratean) "constitution," first by restricting the body of those entitled to citizenship,[8] and then by turning over political power to a small and homogeneously pro-Spartan elite. Isagoras's main opponent was Cleisthenes, a leading member of the politically prominent Alcmaeonid family. There is no reason to suppose that Cleisthenes was a "protodemocrat" in the era before 508/7. His prior political record suggests no deep ideological commitments: Cleisthenes had been willing to accept the high office of archon under the tyranny, although some elements of the Alcmaeonid family had probably been active in resistance to the tyrants in subsequent years.[9] Cleisthenes may have felt that his family's antityrannical activity had earned him a position in the subsequent political order. But in the event, it was Isagoras, with his Spartan connections, who was elected archon for 508/7 B.C.E.[10]

In what was probably an improvised and rather desperate response to Isagoras's election, Cleisthenes brought the "formerly despised" demos (the mass of Athenian citizens—including free subhoplites) into his group of comrades—his *hetaireia*. His surprise move suggests that he was aware of a desire for political recognition on the part of the demos. The aetiology of that desire is complex, but we may assume that (inter alia) the constitutional reforms of Solon and the civic festivals sponsored by the tyrants had undercut traditional lines of authority and encouraged Athenian political self-consciousness. By 508 B.C.E. the ordinary Athenian male was no longer a politically passive client of a great house. He had begun to view himself as a citizen rather than as a subject, and at least some part of his loyalty was owed to the abstraction "Athens."[11] Cleisthenes played to the demotic desire for recognition, and he gained the trust of the demos by promising (perhaps actually proposing) legislative initiatives that would place decisions about citizenship in the hands of the people themselves, and would broaden the scope of non-elite political participation.

In 508 Athenian political institutions were rudimentary and dominated by the elite. We may suppose there were occasional meetings of a political assembly that citizens (even subhoplites) had the right to attend. But it is unlikely that those outside the aristocratic elite could addresss the assembly; nor could a non-elite Athenian hope to serve as a magistrate, or on the Areopagus council.[12] Cleisthenes, as a leading member of a prominent family and as an Areopagite, surely did have both the right and the power to address the assembly. It seems a reasonable guess that he cemented his alliance with the demos by proposing in the assembly changes in the structure and duties of the tribes and the council that prepared the assembly's agenda (hence called probouleutic). The subelite (and especially the subhoplite) Athenians saw that these reforms would reduce their vulnerability by guaranteeing their standing as citizens, and might allow them to express more fully their emerging sense of themselves *as citizens*. With his new mass *hetaireia,* Cleisthenes surged past his aristocratic rival in the struggle for power and influence.[13] Our sources are silent on the matter of just how Cleisthenes' new influence was made manifest, but we may guess that it was signalled by victories in the assembly, possibly even by demonstrations in the streets.

Isagoras was, however, still archon, and any proposed constitutional changes would remain mere words until and unless the citizen assembly's expressed will actually decided the course of events. To prevent that outcome, Isagoras called upon his guest-friend (*xenos*) and ally, the Spartan king Cleomenes, who ordered the expulsion of Cleisthenes and many others on the "standard archaic" assumption that eliminating aristocratic leadership would solve the problem. Cleisthenes had no interest in heroism or martyrdom; he duly snuck out of town. Yet even after Cleisthenes' departure, Isagoras remained uneasy about the Athenian situation. A mixed-nationality military force, featuring a core of Spartans and led by Cleomenes, soon arrived in the city. On Isagoras's recommendation, Cleomenes proclaimed some seven hundred families "religiously polluted," on the grounds of blood spilled by Cleisthenes' Alcmaeonid ancestors, and drove them from the polis. Presumably this mass purge served to eliminate the deeper "second tier" of Cleisthenes' supporters.[14] With Cleisthenes and other prominent Athenians who had opposed Isagoras in exile, the archon Isagoras and his

Spartan allies now seemed to be securely in control of Athens. That might have been the end of Cleisthenes' experiment in "mass politics." Athens seemed fated to become a second Argos—an occasionally restive but ultimately impotent state within Sparta's zone of control, unhappy with Spartan dominance but incapable of becoming a serious rival.

What happened next was completely outside of any Athenian's prior experience. It was the moment of popular revolution I alluded to above. Cleomenes attempted to abolish the existing council in favor of a body of three hundred supporters of Isagoras. But the councilmen refused to obey the dissolution order. Their resistance would have been futile in the face of Cleomenes' soldiers, except that "the rest of the Athenians, being of one mind" now rose up in arms. Caught by surprise by this dangerous expression of popular solidarity, Cleomenes, Isagoras, and their supporters quickly withdrew to the stronghold on the Acropolis. But the problem did not go away. The armed multitude besieged them on the Acropolis for two days, and they surrendered on the third. Cleomenes and his Spartans were expelled from Athenian territory. In the aftermath of the expulsion of the Spartans, some non-Spartan members of Cleomenes' force (including Timesitheus of Delphi) and perhaps some supporters of Isagoras (although not Isagoras himself: Hdt. 5.74.1) were arrested and subsequently executed. It was after these events that the Athenians recalled Cleisthenes and the seven hundred families (Hdt. 5.73.1). Cleisthenes had retained the people's trust through his short period of exile, and he immediately set about instituting the promised changes in the constitutional order, presumably by proposing a series of decrees that were passed by the citizen assembly.[15]

EXPLAINING A REVOLUTION

The retelling of the story I offer above attempts to make sense of our two surviving ancient accounts. I have tried to show that Herodotus and the *Athēnaiōn Politeia* described a truly remarkable but perfectly possible chain of events, albeit in light of their own interpretive principles and in the political vocabulary of their own eras. The alternative to trying to make sense of what our primary sources tell us happened is to assume (as do some historians studying this period) that the ancient accounts must be rejected out of hand on the grounds of their putative incompatibility with the conditions of archaic Greek society and the sociology of mass action. Their argument is that an essentially leaderless uprising by "the demos" *did not* take place because such an event *could not* take place in Athens in that period. This approach seems to me flawed for two reasons: (1) it rests on an a priori denial of the possibility of exactly the sort of historical rupture that I suppose is necessary for Athenian democracy to come into being; (2) it leaves the field of interpretation more confused than need be: having rejected the stories offered by the ancient sources, the historian must either make up his own account of 508/7, on the basis of an elaborate theory of "human behavior under the conditions of archaic society," or remain completely agnostic about what took place. Neither approach seems to me to be a desirable interpretive stance for Greek historians. I hope to have shown that we can make good sense of the evidence without resorting to either one.[16]

My goal in retelling the story was to draw attention to the revolution of 508/7 as a historically significant event. I do not offer here anything like a full and satisfactory account for the classical democracy of the fifth or fourth century. The revolution was, I believe, a necessary condition for the emergence of democracy in that it made the overt rule of the people possible. The energy released by the revolution was a key factor in Athens' subsequent political evolution: in the short term in the "Cleisthenic" innovations affecting citizenship, local authority, the advisory council, the army, and control over leaders; in the longer term in the panoply of democratic institutions that developed over the course of the fifth and fourth centuries. I do not, however, claim that the revolution of 508/7 *caused* democracy in the strong sense of being its *sufficient* condition. In and of itself, the revolutionary event would not have been sufficient to bring about the complex and sophisticated body of institutions associated with classical Athenian democracy. Any full explanation for Athenian democracy must make room for the influence of individual initiative, for external developments, for contingency, and so on.

Moreover, a full and satisfactory account of classical democracy would have to take into account a long prerevolutionary history. The transgressive (Wolin 1996), episteme-shattering-and-creating moment of revolution certainly could not have come about accidentally or by magic; it required a prior history of volatile mass/elite relations and the emergence of demotic self-consciousness (see, in general, Ober 1989: chap. 2). The prior conditions that enabled the revolution of 508/7 certainly include the much earlier Greek embrace of what Robert Dahl calls the "Strong Principle of Equality" (Dahl 1989; Morris 1996); the archaic coevolution of Greek agriculture, land warfare, and "republican" political organization (Hanson 1995, 1996); Solon's reforms and the beginnings of citizenship as defined by specific legal immunities (Manville 1990; Wallace 1998, and chapter 3 above); the development of "civilian self-consciousness" under the Peisistratid tyranny (Eder 1988); as well as Cleisthenes' promise to institute a political program emphasizing guarantees of citizenship and enhanced participation.

Proper attention to the prerevolutionary background can help us understand why the Athenian demos was ready and willing to act as a collectivity in response to the offensive actions of Isagoras and Cleomenes, on the one hand, and to the resistance offered by the Athenian councilmen, on the other. And yet deep background can take us only so far. There must be a

moment when potential energy is released as kinetic energy—when political possibilities become realities. In the history of Athenian democracy that
moment occurs while Cleisthenes and his close supporters are in exile and
when the demos steps out onto the historical stage to besiege Isagoras and
his Spartan minions on the Acropolis. Revolutionary action is important in
my story because (whether or not the term *dēmokratia* was used in 508/7) it
made democracy possible by changing the terms of discussion, by enlarging
the bounds of the thinkable, and by altering the way citizens treated one
another.

Our two surviving ancient historical accounts of the actual moment of
revolution are clear in assigning collective agency to the demos, but they are
frustratingly compressed. We will presumably never know the details of what
actually happened between Cleomenes' attempt to dissolve the council and
his surrender on terms. The material specificity of the events of the
Athenian revolution still exist for us only at the level of imagination. But we
can at least attempt to define the limits of reasonable speculation by speci-
fying what did *not* happen. First, and perhaps foremost, we should not imagine the siege of the Spartans on the Acropolis as a leader-organized military
campaign. My retelling of the events of 508/7 foregrounds what is perhaps
the most striking element in the story: the absence of organized leadership.
The uprising was in favor of a program of constitutional changes, yet it
occurred when the proposer of those changes was in exile, along with all of
his most prominent (primary- and secondary-tier) supporters.

There is no mention of military leaders in Herodotus's or the *Athēnaiōn
Politeia*'s description of the siege. Nor is there in the only other classical
source for the revolution: Aristophanes' comedy *Lysistrata* (lines 273–82).
Here the chorus of old Athenian men, girding themselves for an assault on
the Acropolis (held by a mixed-nationality force of women), urge each
other on, "since when Cleomenes seized it previously, he did not get away
unpunished, for despite his Laconian spirit he departed giving over to me
his arms, wearing only a little cloak, hungry, dirty, hairy-faced . . . that's how
ferociously I besieged that man, keeping constant guard, drawn up seventeen ranks deep at the gates." The "I" in question, the agent of Cleomenes'
humiliation, is a collectivity: the Athenian demos here represented by its
patriotic old men. This is not, of course, history, but a poetic and comic
description. Nevertheless, the Aristophanes passage probably does represent a living popular tradition about the siege (Thomas 1989: 245–47).
And that tradition apparently focused on the military action of the people
as a collectivity rather than on any doings of their leaders.[17] By contrast,
institutionalized leadership is a prominent feature of the surviving historical accounts of a prior siege by Athenians of political revolutionaries on the
Acropolis: the result of Cylon's attempt to seize a tyranny in 636 or 632
(Ober 1998b: 74 with details).

The ascription of the leading role in the drama of 508/7 to the Athenian people as a collectivity, rather than to individual leaders, is reiterated later in Herodotus's text (5.91.2): when the Spartans reconsider the wisdom of having deposed Hippias in 510, they complain to their allies that at that time they had handed over the polis of Athens to "an ungrateful demos," which, "having just recently been freed by us, reared up (*anekupse*) and, in an act of exceptional arrogance (*periubrisas*), drove out [from Athens] both us and our king." This is, of course, Herodotus speaking and not the "real" Spartans, but it confirms that the historian regarded the Athenian demos as the primary revolutionary actor. The absence of leaders in his earlier account is no casual lapse. There is, of course, no way of countering the argument that there still "might have been" prominent leaders who were subsequently mysteriously or maliciously neglected by the Athenian histor-ical and oral traditions. But the only reason to invent such leaders is an a pri-ori assumption that a coherent and plausible story cannot be told without them. My point is that a coherent and plausible story *can* be constructed on the basis of the sources that we do have. Those sources focus on a demos that was both revolutionary actor and direct beneficiary of the reforms that followed the uprising.

Those who prefer to seek prominent men as leaders for the uprising can point to that fact that leaderless revolts are extremely rare in human history. But the appearance of democracy is *also* a historical rarity. The problem with a purely "longue durée," evolutionary, "business as usual" approach to his-tory, an approach that rejects the unique significance of remarkable events, is that it cannot allow for sudden and dramatic changes in what is possible; it cannot accommodate the conundrum that revolutionary action (and thus democracy) is impossible until the moment of its occurrence. Explaining the sudden appearance of the possible through (formerly) impossible action is the point of focusing on radical disruption and trans-formation. This does not happen often in history, but we should pay careful attention when it does (see, further, Kuran 1991).

If my retelling is not leader centered, neither is it hoplite centered. Again, I appeal to the sources. Neither Herodotus nor the Aristotelian *Athēnaiōn Politeia* depicts the siege of the Acropolis as undertaken by an army of hoplites, as opposed to a socially diverse body that included both men of hoplite status and thetes (free subhoplites). According to Herodotus it is *Athēnaiōn hoi loipoi* (the rest of the Athenians) who, united in their view of the situation, do the besieging. The *Athēnaiōn Politeia* (20.3) mentions *to plēthos* and *ho dēmos*, two words designating "the people." The fact that no "regular army" appears in our sources might best be explained by the hypothesis that no "national" army existed in the era before the carrying out of Cleisthenes' constitutional reforms. If there was no national army, then we must suppose that archaic Athenian military actions were ordinarily carried out by aristocratic leaders, men who were able to muster substantial bodies of armed followers (Frost 1984). If this is right, the mass expulsion recommended by Isagoras and carried out by Cleomenes would have thoroughly disrupted the traditional means of mustering the Athenian army—and this may well have been among their motives for undertaking large-scale expulsions of their opponents. It is not modern scholars alone who doubt the ability of the masses to act without orders from their superiors.

The action that forced the surrender of the Spartans was evidently carried out in the absence of traditional military leaders and without a regular army. It is thus best understood as a riot—a violent uprising by large numbers of armed and semi-armed Athenian citizens—perhaps somewhat akin to the surprising mass uprising that led to the siege and capture of the Bastille in Paris in 1789 and thus precipitated the French Revolution (see Ober 1996: 46–49 for details of the comparison). In order to explain Cleomenes' quick surrender, we must assume that the riot was sudden, large-scale, and intense.[18]

The rioters were also disciplined enough to sustain their action over a period of days. Having occupied the Acropolis, Cleomenes and his warriors were barricaded on a natural fortress, a stronghold that had frustrated the regular Spartan army during the campaign against the tyrant Hippias in 510. Herodotus (5.65.1) claims that if Hippias's sons had not fortuitously fallen into their hands, the Spartans would never have succeeded in dislodging Hippias, who had supplied himself with adequate provisions. Rather, "they would only have besieged the place for a few days and then returned to Sparta." Yet in 508/7 the royal Spartan commander agreed to a humiliating conditional surrender on only the third day of the siege—a surrender that entailed sacrificing certain of his comrades. Cleomenes' agreement to these harsh terms suggests that the forces arrayed against him were too numerous for a sortie and that he had not laid in enough supplies to wait out a siege. Apparently Cleomenes had occupied the Acropolis in haste, which in turn suggests that the popular uprising occurred quite suddenly. What was the factor that sparked the demos's unexpected action?

Herodotus's account describes the relevant events in the following stages:

1. Cleomenes attempts to dissolve the council.
2. The council resists.
3. Cleomenes and his force, along with Isagoras and his supporters, occupy the Acropolis.
4. The rest of the Athenians are united in their views.
5. They besiege the Spartan force.
6. Cleomenes surrenders on the third day of the siege.

If we are to follow Herodotus, we must suppose that steps 1, 2, 3, 5, and 6 are chronologically discrete and sequential events. Step 4 cannot, on the other hand, be regarded as a chronological moment. Herodotus's language (*ta auta phronēsantes*—"all of one mind") supports the idea of a highly developed civic consciousness among the Athenian masses—a generalized ability to formulate a popular consensus and act upon common knowledge. Of course popular unity of purpose would not have been instantaneous. Word of events 1-3 would have spread through Athens through the piecemeal word-of-mouth operations typical of a largely oral society. Presumably those living in the city learned what was going on first, and the news then quickly spread to the rural citizenry.[19]

It we take our lead from Herodotus's account, two precipitating factors could explain the crystallization of opinion and the outbreak of violent anti-Spartan action on the part of the Athenian demos. First, the riot may have been sparked by the Spartan attempt to dissolve the council and the councilmen's resistance (thus the demos's action would be a consequence of steps 1 and 2, but before step 3). According to this scenario, Cleomenes and Isagoras responded to the sudden uprising by making a defensive retreat to the nearby stronghold of the Acropolis. Alternatively, the riot might have broken out only after the Spartan occupation of the Acropolis (thus after step 3). On this reading, the riot would be precipitated by the Spartans' offensive (in both senses of the term) takeover of the sacred Acropolis. This second hypothesis fits with Herodotus's story of Cleomenes' disrespectful behavior at the temple of Athena on the Acropolis (5.72.3-4; cf. 5.90.2). Yet it does not explain why Cleomenes brought his entire force up to the Acropolis or why Isagoras and his partisans (Hdt. 5.72.2) were with Cleomenes on the Acropolis during the siege.[20]

It is certain that the author of the *Athēnaiōn Politeia* (20.3) saw Cleomenes' and Isagoras's move to the Acropolis as a defensive response to the threat posed by a mass action on the part of the Athenians: he claims that when "the *boulē* resisted and the multitude gathered itself together, the supporters of Cleomenes and Isagoras *fled for refuge* (*katephugon*) to the Acropolis." *Athēnaiōn Politeia*'s ascription of motive has independent evidentiary value only if its author had access to evidence (whether in the form of written or oral traditions) other than Herodotus's account. That issue of source criticism is contested and cannot be resolved here. But if (per above) Aristophanes relied on Athenian oral tradition in his comic restaging of the siege, it is not de facto unlikely that the author of *Athēnaiōn Politeia*, who certainly had independent information on Cleisthenes' actual reforms, might have read or heard that Cleomenes and Isagoras fled to the Acropolis when a mob formed subsequent to their unsuccessful attempt to dissolve the council. Even if we were to regard the account of the siege in the *Athēnaiōn Politeia* as completely derived from Herodotus's account, it would remain the case that the author of the *Athēnaiōn Politeia* *interpreted* Herodotus's account as describing a flight rather than a planned act of aggression.[21]

Although certainty cannot be achieved in the face of our limited sources, I think it is easiest to suppose that the riot initially broke out when Isagoras and Cleomenes sought to dissolve the council and the councilmen resisted. Once again, the French Revolution provides an illuminating parallel: the mass uprising that led to the capture of the Bastille was sparked by an attempt by King Louis XVI to dissolve the National Assembly (Ober 1996: 46–49 with details). Caught off guard by the uprising, Cleomenes and Isagoras retreated with their forces to the Acropolis stronghold to regroup. They must have hoped and expected that the riot would subside overnight. Yet rapidly spreading news of the occupation of the Acropolis further inflamed "the rest of the Athenians," and so the ranks of the rioters were continually augmented as rural residents took up arms (regular or makeshift) and streamed into the town. From Cleomenes' perspective, the bad situation, which had begun with the resistance of the councilmen, quickly degenerated into a crisis. Stranded on the barren hill without adequate food or water, and with the ranks of his opponents increasing hourly, Cleomenes saw that his position was hopeless, and he negotiated a surrender that saved himself and his Spartan countrymen. With the successful completion of the siege by the Athenian demos, democracy became possible.

THE ORIGINS OF DEMOCRACY

To say that an event made democracy possible requires us to define what we mean by democracy. If we define democracy as the institutional practices prevalent in 461–411 (or subsequently) we will of course have aprioristically eliminated any era before that period as "democratic." My preferred alternative is to look at the root meaning of the compound word *dēmokratia* and the ideals that are exemplified in philodemocratic writing (and parodied by democracy's critics) from the fifth through the fourth century. *Dēmokratia* means, imprimis, "the power—in the sense of effective capacity—of the people": the publicly manifested ability of the demos to make things happen. Its ability to *do* things is what brings about the authority or dominance of the demos in the polis. That demos includes as full "sharers" in the *politeia* not only the "middling" hoplites but the common (working, sub-hoplite) people who make up the clear majority of the adult native male population. The distinction between "demos = all native males, irrespective of class" and "demos = lower classes only" is one drawn by critics or opponents of democracy, not by democrats themselves.

I have suggested that the inauguration of democracy is attendant upon an "epistemic shift"—one with profound implications for speech, thought, and action. But the shift that occurred in 508/7 did not lead to the sudden end of leadership by members of the Athenian elite. Even those (like myself) who regard collective actions without formal leadership as possible must grant that such actions are historical rarities. Indeed, as noted above, it is their rarity that makes them important. Building a complex society on the basis of an ongoing sequence of "genuinely leaderless actions"—on "revolution, revolution, and more revolution"—remains in the realm of naïve anarchist fantasy or cynical political mystification. Nor is it necessary to assume that the profundity of the epistemic shift was universally recognized or acknowledged at the time. In his 1835 introduction to *Democracy in America*, Alexis de Tocqueville chided his aristocratic French contemporaries for their failure to grasp the scope of democratic change in the early nineteenth century. As Tocqueville pointed out fifteen years later, in the introduction to his twelfth edition, it was not until the revolutions of 1848 that many aristocrats finally woke up to the new order of things. So, too, it may not have been until the mid-fifth century—by which time the political options for each elite Athenian had been reduced to asserting himself within the democratic order (by seeking to become a popular orator), working at overthrowing the democracy (per the oligarchic revolutionaries of 411), or criticizing democracy from the sidelines (per Pseudo-Xenophon's *Athēnaiōn Politeia*) —that the full extent of the epistemic shift was manifest. But, remembering Tocqueville's impatience with his contemporaries, we should not allow some Athenians' delayed "uptake" to blind us to the substance of the epistemic shift itself.

As both Athenian democratic orators and critics of democracy such as Aristotle (among others) pointed out, *dēmokratia* is the celebration by the demos of a way of life centered on the freedom of the citizen and political equality. Clearly the content and application of both *eleuth*-root and *iso*-root terms (such as *eleutheria*, freedom, or *isonomia*, equal participation, equality before the law) evolved dramatically in the course of the fifth century, in part as a result of political debates between democrats and their critics (Raaflaub 1983, 1985, 1989b, 2004). Yet I would say that any time that a demos that included subhoplites (1) possessed and employed the power to make things happen and (2) used that power to establish or further practices predicated upon and productive of freedom and equality among the members of that broad-based citizen body, then *dēmokratia* in a classical Greek sense also pertained. Under this definition, democracy became at once a possibility and a reality only when the demos became at once a self-conscious and willful actor in its own right, a grammatical subject rather than an object of someone else's verb, when that which "seemed right to the people" (*edoxe tōi demōi*) determined policy. Once again, that moment occurs in 508/7.[22]

In sum, the narrative I have offered above, based on close reading of Herodotus and the Aristotelian *Ath. Pol.*, is quite different from what some classical scholars suppose "must have been" the case, based on the presumption that the story of democracy's origins should focus primarily on the ordinary conditions of archaic society, on aristocratic leaders, and on the "hoplite class." Yet this presumption requires slighting our closest contemporary accounts, which indicate that (1) the demos did act, and (2) that it acted in the absence of organized leadership. In addition (3) the action of the siege was sustained, and (4) it was carried through to its conclusion (the surrender of Cleomenes). Finally (5) it had profound implications for the future of the polis. It is to a consideration of a few of those implications that we may now turn.

One immediate consequence of the revolution was actualization of the package of "Cleisthenic" reforms. The relationship between those reforms and the promises Cleisthenes made to the demos in order to bring them into his *hetaireia* remains unclear; the reform package might best be thought of simply as prerevolutionary promises reviewed and reinterpreted in the new light of postrevolutionary social realities.[23] Below, I sketch a few of the changes that were put into place during the immediate postrevolutionary generation (the thirty-year period 507–478). In my introduction, I rejected the "institutionalist" explanation for the origins of democracy as putting the cart before the horse. But without the structure provided by subsequent institutional changes, the energies of the revolution of 508/7 would have dissipated. The revolutionary event might have proved to be no more than an archaic Greek Jacquerie—a moment that scared entrenched elites and riffled the surface of society yet failed to disrupt the deep structures of elite control. The essential series of "first (postrevolutionary) generation" institutional changes marks a break with past (predemocratic) practice, a break that is arguably more radical than anything that happened subsequently in the long and eventful history of Athenian democratic development. Inter alia, these early changes promoted the rise of the polis of Athens from the middle ranks of regionally significant towns to the status of a great Mediterranean power.[24]

First and foremost, the reform of the system of Athenian tribes and demes, as described by the Aristotelian *Ath. Pol.*, and elucidated by the work of several generations of Greek historians, is truly remarkable. As Pierre Lévêque and Pierre Vidal-Naquet (1996; orig. French ed., 1964) argued in detail (one need not accept all of their ideas to take the basic point), the reform was sweeping, amounting to a rupture in the way that public space and time were imagined. The new system of local authority at the level of the demes enforced a startlingly new conception of each man's claim to citizenship as directly dependent upon a decision of his fellow citizens as a voting group: one's claim to merit citizenship, based on one's legitimate birth, was now to be a matter judged by one's fellow demesmen. Thus, by making "the inhabitants in each of the demes fellow demesmen of one another" (*Ath. Pol.* 21.4), the new constitution placed directly in the hands of ordinary men the power to decide the momentous question "Who is fit to be one of us?" From that moment on, at the highly charged moment at which he sought to have his son recognized by the community as an adult Athenian, and thus regarded as worthy of all the immunities and all the participation rights of the citizen, the wealthy aristocrat and the landless laborer alike were dependent upon the vote of their fellow Athenians.

The new system had an immediate and measurable effect upon Athens' capacity to compete militarily with neighboring powers. In 506 B.C.E., barely a year after the tribe/deme reform, Athens celebrated its first really significant foreign policy/military success, against a dangerous coalition of Spartans, Boeotians, and Chalcidians. The four-horse bronze monument erected on the Acropolis with its cocky inscription commemorating the victory over the Chalcidians, along with the establishment of a cleruchy at Chalcis, sums up the new Athenian military self-confidence (Hdt. 5.74–78).[25]

Given that there was little time to train a new army, we may guess that the Athenian victories were largely due to the great size and high morale of their field armies: I imagine something like the "levée en masse" of revolutionary France, the hastily assembled but massive armed force that scored dramatic victories over regional rivals in the years after 1789. The postrevolutionary Athenian land army was clearly an artifact of the new postrevolutionary political order. The victories of 506 immediately changed Athens' status within the Greek world. As Herodotus notes, "the Athenians at this point became much stronger. So it is clear how worthy an object of attention is equality of public speech (*isēgoria*), not just in one respect but in every sense. Since when they were ruled by tyrants, the Athenians did not stand out from their neighbors in military capability, but after deposing the tyrants, they became overwhelmingly superior" (5.78).

We need not necessarily imagine the victories of 506 as the work of a clearly articulated hoplite class within the Athenian state. Pericles Georges (1993) makes the compelling suggestion that the Cleisthenic reforms, which put the Athenian citizen body in control of its own membership, may have been more radically egalitarian in their effects than is often supposed. Georges points out that most elements of the hoplite panoply could be quite cheaply "home made" and that the true worth of the warrior was tested in battle. A man's hoplite (zeugite) status was self-asserted and confirmed by those of his demesmen and tribesmen with whom he fought. It was not tested by some government functionary on the basis of "objective" wealth criteria. And so there was much room for slippage between the categories of subhoplites and hoplites, between thetes and zeugites. This sort of slippage would surely have been encouraged in the aftermath of the military success of the siege of 508/7, which, if we are to believe our ancient sources, must have included Athenians of "subhoplite" status.

In the years following the revolution the Athenians adopted a bold new plan for a probouleutic council, which would now be selected according to the new system of tribes and demes. The organization of the new council of 500 allowed "local knowledge," gained through face-to-face interactions, to be "networked" and thereby made available at the national level. The new system also proved to be an extremely effective "learning by doing" form of civic education. It promoted polis-level patriotism and a conviction that personal sacrifices for the common good benefited each Athenian, rather than serving the interests of a narrow elite. The organization of the new council of 500 was based directly on the new system of tribes: much of the work of the council was done by tribal teams of fifty. The experience of working closely with (indeed, for part of the year living with) a team of men from all across Attica, addressing the vital matter of designing the agenda for the citizen assembly (and much routine administration as well), constituted a deep education in the value of "equality of public speech" and in the habits of group-based decision making. Upon his return home, the former councilman brought back to his fellow demesmen a deeper understanding of how the new system worked in practice.[26] Moreover, his term of service was annual, and so the council's membership changed every year. As A. W. Gomme pointed out long ago, the principle of rotation meant that the new council of 500 (unlike the Areopagus council, with its life membership of former archons) could never develop a cohesive "corporate identity." And this meant that the extraordinary power associated with "agenda setting" was annually redistributed among a broad spectrum of the citizenry, rather than being monopolized by a small and cohesive elite.[27]

The newly established probouleutic council points to the consolidation of the postrevolutionary assembly as a deliberative decision-making body and is a clear sign that postrevolutionary Athenian decision making would not return to prerevolutionary "business as usual." A purpose-built council building was, according to the most likely chronology, part of an ambitious Athenian public building program inaugurated around 500 B.C.E. (Shear 1994). The new building program established the central, open area below the Acropolis, Pnyx, and Areopagus as the center of Athenian civic life.

Among the dramatic series of "first generation" institutional innovations, the introduction of ostracism is especially notable, in that it is a frank assertion of the power of the demos as a political collectivity to judge the public behavior of each prominent member of the community, and to gather for the express purpose of voting to expel an individual from the community. Ostracism procedure began with a decision by the assembly. Next came the preparation of makeshift (metaphorical) weapons, to be aimed at a dangerous man. The metaphorical weapons were deployed at a mass gathering in the Agora. The end product was the expulsion of a designated public enemy. The entire process could be seen as a political ritual that allows for (although does not mandate) the annual reperformance of the revolutionary moment itself. Here a strong distinction can be drawn between the Athenian revolution of 508/7 B.C.E. and the French Revolution that began in 1789. Whereas both the Athenian and the French revolutions featured the execution of persons judged "public enemies," the Athenian revolutionary moment did not devolve into organized terror against aristocratic "counterrevolutionaries." Ostracism channeled what could have become a nasty habit of venting demotic ire in acts of mass violence into a carefully delimited institutional exertion of the "power to exile." The object of that power was limited to one prominent individual each year, and punishment was limited to temporary banishment (Forsdyke 2000, 2005).

The longer-term effect of the revolution was evident in the next generation. About twenty-five years after the revolution, in 483/2, the Athenians made the remarkable decision to build the greatest single-polis naval force the Greek world had ever seen. Once again, similar stories are told by Herodotus (7.144.1–2) and the Aristotelian *Ath. Pol.* (22.7): on the motion of Themistocles the Athenians decided not to distribute the revenues from a providential silver strike to the individual citizens, but to devote the funds to the construction of a gigantic number of triremes (the *Ath. Pol.* mentions 100, Herodotus 200). The fleet was built very quickly; by 480, Athens was able to contribute 180 ships for the battle of Salamis.[28] The conditions necessary for a big polis-fleet included not only a certain amount of usable capital (the silver) but also the capacity to train a large body of shipbuilders and a very large pool of trustworthy manpower to man the ships themselves.

The providential silver surplus provided only partial means to the goal of building a navy; it was certainly insufficient to pay a full complement of mercenaries to man the great fleet. Athens in the 480s did not enjoy the reliable income that control of the Isthmus provided Corinth, the other major sea power on the Greek mainland before the Persian Wars (40 ships contributed in 480). If the key to Corinthian sea power was great wealth, which meant that reliable oarsmen could be hired, the key to Athens' navy was the utilization of Athens' relatively vast subhoplite citizen manpower reserve. But this reserve could not be tapped until the thetes were "militarized," until they, like hoplites, were ready and willing to defend the state with their bodies. Nor could it be tapped until the hoplites, in their turn, were ready to depend for their salvation on the bodies of thetes.

The full militarization of the thetes must be intimately related to the revolution of 508/7 and its immediate aftermath. The great Athenian fleet of 480 B.C.E. is the naval counterpart to the Athenian land army that succeeded against the Peloponnesians, Boeotians, and Chalcidians in 506. Both army and navy were unexpectedly successful, and each was made possible by the faith that Athenian citizen society had in itself—a generalized faith in "polis qua demos" that blurred the lines between the roles appropriate to hoplites and thetes. Because the Athenians could now trust their fellow citizens (including thetes) with military power, Athens as a polis was able to translate the potential power latent in its demography and mineral wealth into actual, deployable military force. It is the new sense that *all* citizens can now be asked to guard the polis that leads to the radical decision to abandon Attica in 480 and to depend on the fleet for the preservation of the polis.[29] That momentous decision, as Herodotus is at pains to explain (7.142), was made in the open assembly, after vigorous debate ("many opinions" [*gnōmai . . . pollai*] were aired in the assembly). In the course of the debate the traditional authority of "elders" and "religious experts" (*chrēsmologoi*) was decisively rejected, and a bold plan, which depended directly upon the recently militarized thetes, was adopted. Once again, this points to a radical break with the prerevolutionary political and social order.

If the project of building and manning a huge navy is inconceivable before the democratic revolution, then, a fortiori, so, too, is the creation of an Athenian empire. After the Persian Wars, and with the Spartans quickly bowing out of any continued leadership role, the Athenians willingly took on the task of Hellenic leadership, at a moment when just rebuilding the sacked city and its economy might have seemed more than enough.[30] The first postrevolutionary (thirty-year) generation comes to an end just as Athens launched upon the confederation/empire-building mission that other scholars have seen as the necessary precondition for "true" democracy. But the Delian League and, eventually, the empire became possible only because Athens (unlike nondemocratic poleis) could ideologically tolerate the presence of a huge and permanent armed force of subhoplite citizens. In this sense, the navy and thus the empire can be understood as artifacts of democracy, rather than its necessary preconditions.

Permanent armed forces in poleis were typically associated by the Greeks with the rule of tyrants who required mercenaries to secure their control of affairs (e.g., Xenophon *Hiero* 5.3, 6.4–5, 6.11, 10.3–8). Aside from Sparta, with its special condition of a massive helot population, the Greek moderately oligarchic "hoplite republic" is defined by the amateur and occasional nature of its politics and its armed forces (Hanson 1995, 1996). In what Victor Hanson has called the "normative polis" the demos of warriors (qua political assembly), like the army (qua phalanx of hoplites), exists only in emergencies: at and for those moments of crisis when it calls itself into being. By contrast, the democratic Athenian demos met frequently and regularly to transact all manner of business. And, as a corollary, Athens could afford (politically and ideologically as well as materially) to create and maintain (as a navy) a permanent and institutionalized military apparatus. Athens could afford to build and maintain the military force that made empire possible *because of* democratic social relations—because of the generalized feelings of trust and good faith between social classes, between mass and elite, between hoplites and thetes.

Democracy (as a state of mind, an ideology) was the enabling condition of the Athenian empire, even as that empire was itself the enabling condition of the full panoply of legislative, judicial, and magisterial institutions developed in the middle decades of the fifth century. My point is that the Athenian empire, like the navy, is a product of the origins of democracy, not vice versa. The empire certainly did indeed make possible the further articulation of the democratic institutional order. And that further articulation arguably enabled the Athenians to survive the crises of the late fifth century and rebuild a vibrant democracy in the fourth century. That is an important and exciting story, without which Greek democracy cannot be truly understood. But it is a story about democracy's long-term resilience, not about its origins.

NOTES

1. This chapter borrows freely from Ober 1996 (originally published in Dougherty and Kurke 1993: 215–32) and Ober 1998b; I have attempted to streamline the arguments made there, and to add some new points. At the same time, much that I wrote previously has necessarily been left out here. I will refer the reader to more detailed discussions in those earlier pieces on various matters of fact and interpretation. Translations of Herodotus and *Ath. Pol.*: Stanton 1990 with my modifications.

2. Of course, the process is complex, since the experience of using institutions will affect people's attitudes. The priority of sociocultural norms over institutional structure is the central conclusion of Putnam 1993. His long-term (twenty-year) study of regional differentiation in Italian politics is especially impressive in that it is based on a massive collection of empirical evidence. The bottom line of Putnam's study is that even very profound "top down" institutional changes will have very little practical impact on the process of democratization when the underlying attitudes of the populace are stable and predicated on fundamentally undemocratic assumptions (e.g., about patron-client relations). On the other hand, Putnam's study tends to assume that regional Italian sociocultural attitudes are historically conditioned and deeply entrenched. It does not envisage the sort of epistemic shift I propose for Athens in 508/7.

3. The implied subject of the verb *epeirato* is either Cleomenes or Isagoras. The grammar seems to point to Cleomenes, although presumably it was Isagoras (as archon [chief official]) who gave the official order to the *boulē*. The point is in any case merely procedural: Herodotus's narrative demonstrates that Cleomenes and Isagoras were working hand in glove throughout.

4. Stanton (1990: 142, 144 n. 6) translates *sunathroisthentos tou plēthous* as "the common people had been assembled," on the grounds that "the verb 'had been assembled' is definitely passive." But I take the (morphologically) passive participle as having a reflexive rather than a passive meaning; on the distinction see Rijksbaron 1984: 126-48. Reflexive meaning for the passive participle of *sunathroizō:* Xen. *An.* 6.5.30; of *athroizō:* Thuc. 1.50.4, 6.70.4; and esp. Arist. *Pol.* 1304b33.

5. Altruistic vs. self-interested analyses: see, for example, Lewis 1963; Ehrenberg 1973.

6. Cleisthenes' decision to "bring the demos into his *hetaireia*" was, of course, one of the factors that led to the revolution, but it should not be confused with the moment of uprising itself.

7. Here, I am borrowing concepts and imagery from Hannah Arendt (1958, 1963) and Sheldon Wolin (1994, 1996).

8. *Diapsēphismos* (civic scrutiny, i.e., a vote on the justification of claims to citizenship): *Ath. Pol.* 13.5 and 21.2, with detailed discussion by Manville 1990: 173–91.

9. Accommodation and resistance of the Alcmaeonids to the tyranny: Lewis 1988: 288, 299-301. But cf. the skepticism of Thomas (1989: 263-64), who argues that the Alcmaeonids may have made up the tradition of their antityrannical activity and the story of their exile under the Peisistratids from whole cloth.

10. Isagoras as archon: *Ath. Pol.* 21.1. *Ath. Pol.* 22.5 claims that after the institution of the tyranny, and until 487/6, all archons were elected (*hairetoi*). The tyrants had manipulated the elections to ensure that their own supporters were in office (see Rhodes 1981: 272-73); exactly how the elections would have been carried out in 509/8 (and thus what Isagoras's support consisted of) is unclear. We need not, anyway, suppose that Isagoras's election was indicative of a broad base of popular support; more likely his support was centered in the (non-Alcmaeonid) nobility. On the power of the archaic archon, see *Ath. Pol.* 3.3 and 13.2 with comments of Rhodes (1981: ad loc.).

11. See Ober 1989: 60-68; Manville 1990: 124-209; Meier 1990: 53-81. On the lack of formal patronage structures in classical Athens, see Millett 1989.

12. Solonian constitution: Ober 1989: 60-65, with references cited. For the Areopagus from the time of Solon to Cleisthenes, see Wallace 1989: 48-76.

13. Cleisthenes' connection with the demos is underlined by Hdt. 5.69.2: see Wade-Gery's seminal article (1933: 19-25). It has been widely accepted that the assembly was the arena in which Cleisthenes won the favor of the people; cf. discussion in Ostwald 1969: 149-60.

14. On mass purges as a tool of aristocratic politics in archaic Greece, see now Forsdyke 2000, 2005.

15. Herodotus (5.66.2) implies that at least some of the reforms were put into place before Cleomenes' arrival; *Ath. Pol.* 20-21 discusses the reforms after giving the history of the revolution proper. I think it is most likely that some reforms were proposed and perhaps actually enacted by the assembly before Cleomenes' arrival, but presumably there would not have been time for all the details of the new constitution to have been put into place. See below for the question of when the council of 500 was established. For a review of the chronological issue, see Hignett 1952: 331-36; Rhodes 1981: 244-45, 249; Chambers 1990: 221-22; Badian 2000.

16. Raaflaub 1998b with my detailed response in Ober 1998b; see also Raaflaub, chapter 5 below. Note that the first explanation is based on a strong version of "longue durée" historiography, which now seems pretty much passé, and that the second gives too much scope for historiography that is utterly theory driven (as opposed to theory influenced—cf. Ober 1996: 13–17).

17. Saying that the uprising occurred without institutionalized leadership does not eliminate the likelihood that there were historiographically invisible "leaders of

the moment." My "essentially leaderless revolt" allows for the likelihood that some men (who had not been especially prominent before and were not especially prominent afterwards) assumed local and tactical leadership roles during the original uprising and the three-day siege.

18. I am assuming throughout that Cleomenes was an experienced and sane military commander, and that his decisions were made accordingly. On the dubious tradition of the madness of Cleomenes, see Griffiths 1989. It is interesting to note how the demos's action simply disappears in some respectable scholarly accounts (e.g., Ehrenberg 1973: 90: "Cleomenes and Isagoras met, however, with the resistance of the council . . . which they had tried to disband and which was most likely the Areopagus. . . . The Spartans withdrew, Isagoras was powerless, and many of his followers were executed"). Kuran (1991) explains how sudden revolutionary cascades can take place.

19. On how information was disseminated in Athens, see Hunter 1994. On the role of common knowledge in coordinating mass action, see Chwe 2001.

20. Herodotus's statement that Cleomenes seized the Acropolis and was subsequently thrown out along with the Lacedaemonians (*exepipte meta tōn Lakedaimoniōn*, 5.72.4) makes it appear likely that the whole force had gone up to the Acropolis together, had been besieged together, and had surrendered together. It is unlikely that a significant part of Cleomenes' forces joined him on the hill after the commencement of the siege, and Herodotus says nothing about any of his men being captured in the lower city before the surrender. It is worth noting that Cylon (Hdt. 5.71; Thuc. 1.126.5-11) and Peisistratus (twice: Hdt. 1.59.6, 60.5) had earlier seized the Acropolis, each time as the first stage in an attempt to establish a tyranny. Cleomenes' case is different in that his move came *after* he had established control of the city.

21. For a discussion of the relationship between Herodotus's narrative and *Ath. Pol.* 20-21, see Wade-Gery 1933: 17-19; Rhodes 1981: 240-41, 244; Rhodes argues that Herodotus was *Ath. Pol.*'s sole authority for 20.1-3. For general discussions of *Ath. Pol.*'s use of sources, see Chambers 1990: 84-91.

22. The Salamis decree (*IG* I³ 1), which Meiggs and Lewis (1988) date to shortly after 510 (although by letterforms it could go as late as 480 or so), is the first attested use of the *edoxe tōi demōi* formula. It provides clear evidence for actual enactments by the demos gathered in assembly. Whatever is going on in this difficult inscription, it is clear that the demos is taking for itself the authority to regulate the conditions under which certain people in Salamis (whether Athenians or Salaminians) would be allowed to hold land and what their military obligations would be. In sum, the demos is making state policy in its own name and, what is more, has probably taken for itself the power to decide about the conditions of citizenship.

23. Herodotus (5.69–72), who is confused about the substance of some of the reforms, puts the enactment of the reforms *before* Cleomenes' arrival. The author of *Ath. Pol.* (20.1), in an apparent attempt to square his account with that of Herodotus while retaining chronological sense (see Rhodes 1981: ad loc.), says that Cleisthenes gained the advantage over Isagoras "by proposing to hand over" (*apodidous*: trans. Rhodes) the *politeia* to the *plēthos*. Then (20.2–21) comes Cleomenes' intervention and the uprising, in the course of which the people got control of affairs. Cleisthenes then became leader and hegemon. The demos

placed its trust in Cleisthenes, who then, still in the archonship of Isagoras (i.e., 508/7), undertook the reforms.

24. The precise dating of these reforms is a matter of intense scholarly debate; for my present purposes precise dating is less important than the (generally accepted) fact that they all took place within the first generation after the revolution. Cf. Badian 2000: 455–56; Badian notes that the entire implementation period of the postrevolutionary reforms was characterized by an ongoing military crisis. For more detailed discussion of these reforms, see, for example, Ostwald 1988; Manville 1990: chap. 7; Anderson 2003.

25. An as-yet-unpublished archaic inscription from Boeotia referring to the "liberation" of Chalcis may suggest that the Athenian cleruchy was short-lived (my thanks to John Ma for alerting me to this document), but it thereby offers further confirmation of Athenian success in 506.

26. The functioning of the deme/tribe system in terms of networking knowledge, civic education, and convictions about the common good is sketched in Manville and Ober 2003b: 63–76.

27. Early history of the council of 500: Rhodes 1985. Lack of corporate identity: Gomme 1951. Significance of the power of agenda setting: Dahl 1989: 112–14.

28. We may compare other mainland poleis, which contributed relatively tiny naval forces to the Hellenic navy in 480: Sparta 16 ships, Megara 20, Sikyon 15, Epidauros 10, Troizen 5; the island polis of Aigina contributed 30 (Hdt 8.1, 43–48). On Athenian shipbuilding in the late 480s, see Labarbe 1957 and Wallinga 1993.

29. On the radical newness of the form of polis power that is thereby made possible, and attempts to understand it in terms of Persian models, see Crane 1992a, 1992b; Georges 1993, 1994.

30. Rosenbloom 1995 on the early turn to imperialism. Cf. Starr 1970 for the slow pace of postwar Athenian coinage.

Chapter 5

The Breakthrough of *Dēmokratia* in Mid-Fifth-Century Athens

Kurt A. Raaflaub

EVENTS, QUESTIONS, APPROACHES

In the years around 462 B.C.E., Athens was rocked by political turmoil. Members of the venerable Areopagus council were brought to trial, as was Cimon, after Aristides architect of the Athenian empire and long-dominant general and leader. Some politicians, led by Ephialtes, persuaded the assembly to pass measures, often called the reforms of Ephialtes, that shifted certain powers from the Areopagus to institutions perceived as more representative of the demos. Many Athenians did not welcome these innovations. Tensions escalated. Within a short time, both Cimon and Ephialtes disappeared from the political scene. For several years, Athens was deeply divided and gripped by fears of a coup aiming at restoring the old system.

Despite these dramatic circumstances, the reforms of 462/1 have often been judged much less significant and incisive than those connected with the names of Solon and Cleisthenes. True, the extant evidence is sadly deficient about the cause and content of the changes involved. Yet the reforms were preceded by an important innovation in political terminology that attests to a marked shift in political awareness, and by intense public debates that left their imprint in one of Aeschylus's tragedies. They took place in a period when the Athenians experienced profound, broad, and rapid changes in every aspect of their lives, and in connection with a radical realignment in foreign relations. They were violently contested. And they were continued by a series of further reforms that culminated in Pericles' citizenship law of 451/0.

Obviously, the Athenians themselves considered these changes very important. I shall argue that they were indeed of great and lasting significance, for two main reasons. One is that with few and mostly procedural exceptions (such as the "accusation of proposing an unconstitutional decree," *graphē paranomōn*), these reforms mark the last major institutional innovations known to us before the constitutional crisis following the Sicilian disaster of 413 and the oligarchic coup of 411. Hence they must have laid or completed the foundations for the political system the Athenians called *dēmokratia* and that is well known from a broad range of evidence in the last third of the fifth century. In this system (described briefly in the introduction to this volume), "rule by the *dēmos*" was as fully realized as was possible under the conditions prevailing in antiquity: the Athenian demos (understood as the sum of *all* male adult citizens) was, as Euripides says, "lord," even "monarch" (*Suppliants* 352, 406), and "power had become a people's matter" (*kratos dedēmeutai, Cyclops* 119). Even those who claim that democracy was established ed in Athens much earlier agree that the principles that constituted *dēmokratia* after 462 or 450 went considerably beyond those established by earlier reforms.

The second argument for the reforms' significance is that they not only empowered the Athenian demos to assume full control over politics but enabled the thetes (*thētes,* forming the lowest census class) to achieve, with very few exceptions, civic equality as active participants in politics and government. That the thetes reached such equality only at that time, I add immediately, is not attested explicitly but based on circumstantial evidence and on the assumption that their political role was considerably more limited before 462; the latter, however, is contested elsewhere in this volume.

It is the purpose of this chapter to determine what exactly the reforms of 462–450 entailed and achieved. Why were they important? What were their immediate and long-term causes? Why were they so contested? In what respects did they go beyond what had been accomplished earlier, and why was this significant specifically for realizing democracy? I will first survey the extant evidence and discuss possible interpretations, then place the events in their political context and seek explanations for what happened. This will force us to reexamine in detail some of the evidence and some recent scholarly controversies before we are able to reconstruct the reforms and their meaning. Only then will it be useful to compare them with earlier ones.

First, however, a few comments on some of my presuppositions. I have discussed the problem of the definition of democracy briefly in the introduction to this volume. The two decisive characteristics of the Athenian political system at the time when it was explicitly called *dēmokratia* were that (a) regardless of property, political equality among all citizens was realized to the fullest extent possible, and (b) in the assembly and related institutions the demos not only made final decisions but was fully in charge, representing the actual government of the polis and controlling the entire political process. My question in this chapter is when and why this system originated. I shall argue that before 462 neither of these two characteristics was fully realized and that only the exceptional conditions developing in their polis after the Persian Wars enabled the Athenians to realize them both.

My discussion will show that crucial military, social, economic, and political factors combined to make *dēmokratia* possible, perhaps even necessary. Ancient historians, writing on this period, had little interest in those impersonal "factors" and "forces" that dominate modern works of history. Their perspective, focusing heavily on the leading personalities, was too narrow, but far from entirely wrong. Even if, as we must assume, the Athenian demos made their preferences known loudly and clearly, politics in ancient societies were always strongly personal. A politician made a proposal, advocated it with his associates in council and assembly, canvassed the voters for support, and then in many cases was responsible as well for executing it. Men *did* "make history" in ancient Greece, but none, of course, could do it alone. They all needed to organize their power and support, and the best of them succeeded because they were in tune with the trends of the time, capable of perceiving the will of the people, and able to translate it into creative political programs and actions. A leaderless uprising may result in victory in a particular political crisis, but it cannot resolve a crisis or transform victory into lasting political change. Creative leadership is always decisive. Hence we should not hesitate to give the leaders their due. Even so, I use "Cleisthenes' system" or "Ephialtes' reform" primarily as practical labels.

I have also said something in the introduction about "founders" and the long process, punctuated by "breakthroughs," that resulted in democracy. My task here is to analyze the breakthrough of the mid-fifth century. It was necessarily and crucially based on the achievements of earlier ones but went substantially beyond them. To gain an accurate understanding of what each of these developmental stages achieved and how they related to each other seems to me more important than to play the Greeks' favorite game: to decide who *the* "inventor" (*prōtos heuretēs*) was. If democracy was essentially realized already in the early sixth century, each of the later breakthroughs made Athens even more democratic. If this stage was fully reached only in the mid-fifth (or even early fourth) century, the earlier ones established crucial and indispensable forms of "pre- and protodemocracy." I for one find the latter historically more plausible, but this is precisely what our discussion in this volume is about.[1]

TESTIMONIA

T1: The poet Pindar says: "In every sphere, the just and well-spoken man wins respect, whether in a tyranny, or where the noisy crowd (*labros stratos*) hold sway, or the wise keep watch" (*Pythian* 2.86–88, trans. F. J.

Nisetich).[2] Probably performed around 470, this ode offers the earliest testimony for the distinction between three different constitutions, based on the number and type of persons holding power. Monarchy is here represented by *turannis,* aristocracy by "the wise men," and democracy by the army (*stratos;* see also *Olympian* 9.95; Aeschylus *Eumenides* 683, 762).

T2:   The word *dēmokratia* is explicitly attested only several decades later, in Herodotus, the anonymous treatise on the *Constitution of the Athenians* (popularly attributed to the "Old Oligarch"),[3] and Democritus (Sealey 1974; Orsi and Cagnazzi 1980)—not surprisingly, since prose texts are rare before about 430, and the word does not fit easily into poetry, which, except for comedy, avoids it altogether. In the 460s, however, two pieces of evidence indirectly attest to its emergence.

T2a: We know of two Athenians, born roughly in the decade before Ephialtes' reform, who were named Demokrates: like Isagoras (Cleisthenes' opponent), this is a political name, reflecting a surge in prominence of the political idea it expresses.[4]

T2b: In *Suppliants,* performed most likely in 463, Aeschylus uses formulations (such as "the demos's ruling hand" [*dēmou kratousa cheir,* 604] or "the people who rule the polis" [*to damion to ptolin kratunei,* 699]; cf. 607–8) that paraphrase *dēmokratia* as closely as seems possible in poetry (Ehrenberg 1950: 516–24, accepted by Cartledge, chapter 6 in this volume).[5]

T3:   The *Ath. Pol.* provides the most detailed report, as follows.

T3a: After the Persian Wars, the Areopagus council was politically dominant (25.1).[6]

T3b: "Then, with the increase of the power of the masses, Ephialtes . . . became champion of the people; he had a reputation for incorruptibility and justice in public life. He launched an attack on the Areopagus. First, he removed many of its members on charges of administrative misconduct. Then [in 462/1] he stripped it of all its additional powers through which it exercised the guardianship of the constitution; he distributed them among the council, the assembly, and the *dikastēria*" (25.1–2). The accusations against members of the Areopagus, and the latter's loss of power, are repeated in a confused section (25.3–4).

T3c: "Ephialtes . . . died shortly afterwards, murdered by Aristodikos of Tanagra" (25.4).

T3d: After another confused section blaming demagogues for "an increasing absence of control in political life" (26.1) and criticizing Athenian neglect of laws, the author states: "In the sixth year after the death of Ephialtes they decided to admit *zeugitai* [members of the third census class] to the preliminary selection of those from whom the nine archons would be selected by lot. . . . [Previously,] the *zeugitai* had held only the ordinary offices, unless any of the legal restrictions had been disregarded" (26.2).[7]

T3e: "Four years later . . . the thirty justices were re-established who were known as the magistrates of the demes" (26.3).

T3f: "Two years later [in 451/0] . . . it was enacted, on the proposal of Pericles, that those whose parents were not both citizens should not themselves be citizens" (26.4).

T3g: At least the laws of Ephialtes concerning the members of the Areopagus council were recorded on the Areopagus and removed from there in 404 by the "Thirty" who pretended "to be aiming at the ancestral constitution" and "correcting the constitution" (35.2).

T4: In *Politics* 1274a, Aristotle maintains that, as the law courts, installed by Solon, "grew in strength, they [presumably the political leaders or demagogues mentioned below], seeking to flatter the people in the way that men flatter a tyrant, transformed the constitution into its present form of democracy. Ephialtes and Pericles curtailed [the power of] the Council of the Areopagus; Pericles introduced the system of paying the members of the law-courts; and thus each demagogue, in his turn, increased the power of the people until the constitution assumed its present form."

T5: In the *Life of Cimon* (Carena et al. 1990), although confusing the chronology of events, Plutarch describes the rivalry between Cimon and Ephialtes.

T5a: In a trial for bribery, instigated by Pericles, among others, Cimon was acquitted (14.3–5). "During the rest of his political career, he succeeded in arresting and even reducing the encroachments of the people upon the prerogatives of the aristocracy, and in foiling their attempts to concentrate office and power in their own hands, but only for as long as he was at Athens" (15.1).

T5b: When Cimon was absent [in 462/1], "the people broke loose from all control. . . . Following Ephialtes' lead they deprived the Council of the Areopagus of all but a few of the issues which had been under its jurisdiction. They took control of the courts of justice and transformed the city into a thorough-going democracy with the help of Pericles, who had now risen to power and committed himself to the cause of the people" (15.2).

T5c: When Cimon returned and tried to restore the Areopagus's "judicial powers and revive the aristocratic regime of Cleisthenes," the democratic leaders stirred up the people against him, bringing up old scandals and denouncing him as a Spartan sympathizer (15.3).

T5d: [Earlier,] Sparta, hit by an earthquake and a helot revolt, had asked Athens for assistance (16.4–7). Ephialtes opposed the request, hoping that Athens would profit from Sparta's predicament, while Cimon "persuaded the Athenians to send a large force of hoplites to her aid," advocating the continuation of the existing alliance (16.8–10). This expedition returned after a while (17.1–2).

T5e: Later, when the Spartans besieged the rebels at Ithome, the Athenians received a second request for help. "The Athenians once more came to their support, but their boldness and enterprise frightened the Spartans, who singled them out from among all the allies as dangerous revolutionaries and sent them away. They returned home in a fury and proceeded to take public revenge upon the friends of Sparta in general and Cimon in particular." The latter was ostracized (17.3).

T5f: During his exile, Cimon was prevented from participating in a battle of the Athenians with a Spartan army at Tanagra in Boeotia (in 457), because he and his friends were suspected of pro-Spartan sympathies, intending "to create confusion in the army and then lead the Spartans against the city"—a suspicion that his friends dispelled by fighting heroically (17.4–7).

T6: In the *Life of Pericles* (Stadter 1989), Plutarch describes the beginning of Pericles' career.

T6a: Fearing to be accused of tyrannical aspirations and ambitious to build his own power base against a rival who was popular among the elite, Pericles joined those who favored the people and took up "the cause of the poor and the many" (7.3–4). One of his collaborators "was Ephialtes, who destroyed the power of the Council of the Areopagus" (7.8).

T6b: In later chapters, Plutarch attributes to Pericles a series of popular measures, including pay for public service, that corrupted the demos (9.1). He explains these measures with Pericles' need to compete with Cimon, whose wealth and private generosity to the people he could not match; hence he began to distribute public wealth, "and soon, introducing allowances for public festivals, pay for jury service, and other grants and gratuities, he succeeded in bribing the masses wholesale" (9.2–3).

T6c: Pericles then "enlisted their support in his attack on the Council of the Areopagus," succeeding so well that it was "deprived of most of its judicial powers through a bill brought forward by Ephialtes" (9.3–5).

T6d: "Cimon himself was ostracized on the charge of being a friend of Sparta and an enemy of the people's interests" (9.5).

T6e: Here follows the account of the battle of Tanagra and the honorable death of Cimon's friends; Pericles' friends are blamed for excluding Cimon, which prompts Pericles to fight with special distinction (10.1–3).

T6f: Out of context, presumably because he did not connect it to the power struggles in which Pericles was involved, Plutarch refers to Pericles' citizenship law (37.3; Stadter 1989: 333–36).

T7: Thucydides comments only on the foreign policy aspects, which are mentioned by Plutarch but omitted by the *Ath. Pol.*

T7a: The Athenians sent a force under Cimon's command to assist the Spartans besieging the rebels at Ithome. Soon, however, "the Spartans grew afraid of the enterprise and the unorthodoxy of the Athenians." Fearing that "they might listen to the people in Ithome and become the sponsors of some revolutionary policy," they dismissed the Athenians alone from among the allies, without sufficient explanation. The Athenians, however, realizing that their dismissal was due to suspicion, felt humiliated, took offense, and, upon returning, cancelled the treaty of alliance dating from the Persian Wars and allied themselves with Sparta's enemy, Argos (1.102).

T7b: A few years later, the Spartans intervened in a war in central Greece. They stayed in Boeotia, among other reasons, because "there was a party in Athens who were secretly negotiating with them in the hope of putting an end to democratic government" (1.107.4). This is the Spartan force the Athenians attacked at Tanagra, not least "because they had some suspicions of the plot to overthrow the democracy" (107.6–108.1).

T8: The specter of civil strife (*stasis*) is also reflected in Aeschylus's *Eumenides* of 458, discussed below.

INTERPRETATION

The fact that we owe most of the extant evidence to Aristotle and Plutarch complicates our task. As explained in the introduction to this volume, their reports are often marred by lack of reliable information (Rhodes 1993) and influenced by later experiences (especially the "radical democracy" of the late fifth century), resulting criticism of and prejudices against democracy and demagogues (Roberts 1994; Ober 1998a), interpretive schemes imposed on the narrative (such as Aristotle's pairing of aristocratic leaders and democratic demagogues), and Plutarch's moralizing perspective and focus on class struggle. Efforts beginning in 411, in a period of violent polarization between democrats and oligarchs, to (re)invent an "ancestral constitution," uncontaminated by later excesses (Fuks 1953), reflect tendencies to think of Cleisthenes' system as the ideal of an "aristocratic democracy" (T5c; cf. *Ath. Pol.* 29.3) and of the reforms of 462–450 as the beginning of a disastrous decline into political corruption and irresponsibility. Moreover, the chronology of events is badly confused in the sources and intensely debated among scholars.[8] Still, if we try to ignore such dis-

tortions the extant evidence reveals important basic information that suffices for our present purposes.

Dēmokratia

The creation of the word *dēmokratia* (T2) indicates a shift of awareness
among the Athenians (Meier 1990: chap. 7). *Isonomia* (political equality),
the word perhaps used to characterize Cleisthenes' system (Raaflaub 1996b:
143–45), modified a traditional ideal of "good order" (*eunomia*) by the criterion of equality. By contrast, *dēmokratia* and related terms defined a constitution by the criterion of who (how many and what kinds of persons) ruled
or held power (*kratos* or *archē*). The earliest document reflecting this new distinction (T1) dates to ca. 470 and, significantly, takes a popular alternative to
monarchy and aristocracy for granted. Here the equivalent of democracy is
the "fierce army" (*labros stratos*). Perhaps words like *dēmos* or *plēthos* served the
same purpose (Meier 1968), but such simple words were replaced in the
460s by *dēmokratia* (T2), indicating that in this system the *dēmos* really held
(or should hold) power. This most likely happened when the underlying
idea was new, interpreted in new ways, or much contested or debated.

Aeschylus's Suppliants *and Democracy in Action*

It is thus important that Aeschylus's *Suppliants,* performed in 463, offers
much more than tantalizing allusions to this new terminology (T2b) by
emphasizing essential constitutional characteristics of democracy (Meier
1993: 84–97; Raaflaub 1988b: 286–88). The play dramatizes the plight of
a community that faces an excruciatingly difficult decision. If it grants asy-
lum to a group of women, refugees from Egypt, it may be forced to fight a
war for their protection and suffer the harm war inevitably causes; if it turns
them away it may suffer divine retribution. The mythical king does not dare
to decide by himself (*Supp.* 407–17, 468–79). If the community is threatened by lethal danger all citizens must help ward it off and participate in the
decision: "Therefore I will undertake no pledge till I have shared this issue
with all citizens" (366–69). The suppliants, used to an authoritarian monarchy, do not understand: "*You* are the polis and the people (*dēmion*). . . . *You
alone* control the vote; merely nodding, *you, sole* holder of the scepter on the
throne, decide all that is necessary" (370–75). This is the exact opposite of
a free and democratic polis, where officials are accountable and not one but
all make the decisions.[9] That all citizens in common decision must bear
responsibility for the common good is repeated several times (398–401,
483–85). In the assembly, the demos's "ruling hand" expresses its will and
passes "with full authority" the decree to accept the suppliants; the air bris-
tles with the right hands of the entire demos, swayed by the "persuasive

turns" of the king's "people-leading" rhetoric. And the decision is binding for all, under threat of exile and loss of civic rights (600–624). Gratefully, the suppliants ask for the gods' blessing: "May the people who hold the power in the polis maintain their office without trembling: a rule that looks ahead and is well concerned with the common weal" (698–700).

Whatever Aeschylus's motives and sympathies, the unusual emphasis he places on the need for all citizens to participate in decisions that affect the community's welfare suggests that these issues were highly prominent and intensely debated at the time. Yet what exactly were the issues? The poet's emphasis could in principle concern either the type of decision involved or the number and range of citizens participating in it, or both. Since the assembly had long been voting on issues of war and communal defense (we need think only of the debate about the "wooden walls" oracle before Xerxes' invasion: Hdt. 7.140–43; see also Cartledge, chapter 6 in this volume), in this case only the second alternative fits the situation. By implication, it was previously not the entire city or citizen body (*pasa polis*) that shared such decisions. Hence the lower classes were not yet fully integrated—which is suggested as well by the choice of *stratos* (army) for demos in T1.[10]

A Political "Change of Guard"

The reform of 462/1 was preceded by a series of attacks, in courts and assemblies, against individual members of the Areopagus and Cimon himself (T3b, 5a). Such attacks probably reflect efforts by younger and ambitious politicians to replace an older generation of leaders who had long dominated Athenian politics.

Domestic and Foreign Policy Intertwined

In 462/1 the reform bill was passed in the assembly while Cimon was absent with a large hoplite contingent, helping the Spartans suppress a helot revolt (T5b–c). That the absence of these hoplites was crucial for the vote in the assembly is unverifiable and debated in scholarship (Rhodes 1992: 69; Badian 1993: 96); the absence of Cimon himself was perhaps more crucial—if we can trust Plutarch (T5d) that the decision to assist Sparta was hotly contested by the same men who advocated the reforms, and hinged on Cimon's power of persuasion. Details about this expedition are contradictory but do not concern us here. Thucydides (T7a) crucially corroborates Plutarch (T5e), that the Spartans, for whatever reasons, grew suspicious of the Athenians and dismissed them under less than honorable circumstances. The results were disastrous both for Cimon and for the alliance with Sparta. The Athenians broke with Sparta and completely reoriented their foreign policy. Although less than ten years earlier they had ostracized Themistocles and apparently sided with Cimon, and although we have no evidence to illuminate the immediate background of the turn-around of 462/1, the latter is not likely to have happened on the spur of the moment (Fornara and Samons 1991: 126–29). Apparently Athens had reached a point at which the direction of its foreign policy (whether to pursue a soft or hard line in dealing with Sparta) needed to be decided in principle. The two options were represented by rival leaders and strong factions in elite and citizen body; this was precisely the situation in which an ostracism was called for (Eder 1998: 118–21). Cimon lost and went into exile (T5e, 6d); his opponents came to dominate Athenian politics for a long time. Overall, then, the reform of 462/1 perhaps needs to be interpreted in its connection with a serious conflict about a major shift in foreign policy.

Purpose of the Reforms

What was this reform about?[11] What did it achieve? The sources are vague but agree that the Areopagus council lost certain powers that were transferred to the assembly, the council of 500, and the law courts (T3b, 4, 5b, 6a). Many scholars think these powers concerned at least the scrutiny and control of officeholders and perhaps other judicial functions, especially in trials against officials.[12] These changes may seem minor, but they should not be underestimated. As Charles Fornara and L. J. Samons emphasize, "Ephialtes' transferal of jurisdiction to the generality of Athenians . . . was an extraordinary and unpredictable political act, which presupposes, by its novelty and daring departure from tacitly accepted premises, the adumbration of a new theory of citizenship or, rather, a new theory of popular sovereignty." The result of this reform "leaves no room for doubt that its purpose was to convey power (*kratos*) to the *demos* and to eviscerate the aristocratic establishment" (1991: 64, 66; cf. Bleicken 1994: 45). The Areopagus council, very influential (T3a) and, despite the introduction of the lot in the selection of archons in 487/6 (*Ath. Pol.* 22.5; Badian 1971), probably still largely composed of members of elite families, lost its most important instruments to influence the shaping and execution of policies. Its prestige and authority, already weakened by the trials instigated against some of its members (T3b, 5a), suffered a heavy blow. True, it retained some important functions and an honorable position, and the leading officials (especially the *stratēgoi*) continued for several decades to be furnished by the aristocracy. But overall the Areopagus as the last bastion of institutionalized aristocratic predominance ceased to play a significant political role (Davies 1993: 54–59). By contrast, the institutions that represented the entire demos benefited from the reform: they gained prestige and power and, by controlling the officeholders, took a big step toward effectively controlling politics and policies.

Other Changes

Some additional changes in administrative structures should probably be placed here, necessitated by the massively increased business of the council and law courts (on which see below): the system of executive committees (prytanies) of the council of 500, rotating among the ten tribes, was perhaps not introduced at this time but refined and expanded to the form known from later sources (Rhodes 1972: 16–21; Ostwald 1988: 329; Ryan 1994a). The *ēliaia* or, conventionally, heliaia (Ostwald 1986: 10 n. 27), the Solonian appeals court (whether or not it was identical with the assembly [Hansen 1989b: 237–49]), was replaced by the system of multiple *dikastēria* so characteristic of classical democracy (Ostwald 1986: 62–77). The appointment of thirty judges, circulating among the demes (T3c), points in the same direction (Rhodes 1981: 331).

Other measures, introduced in subsequent years, are less controversial, although details remain disputed. The archonship was opened to the third census class of the *zeugitai* in 457 if not 462 (T3d; see note 7 above). By around the mid-fifth century, most of the increasingly numerous offices (except for the archons, *stratēgoi*, and treasurers), the juries in the law courts (*dikastai*, counting in the hundreds if not thousands), and perhaps the seats in the council of 500 (*boulē*) were open to all citizens, including those in the lowest census class (thetes), and mostly filled by lot.[13] Especially for the poor among the thetes, such involvement posed economic difficulties, prompting the introduction of pay for some of these functions (T4, 6b; Markle 1985; Hansen 1999: 38). All this made it important to determine precisely who was entitled to participate and share the citizens' privileges. Massive demographic changes in recent decades added urgency (see below). Hence in the citizenship law of 451/0, introduced by Pericles, the demos tightened the criteria of citizenship, demanding descent from citizen parents on both sides (T3f, 6f; Patterson 1981; Boegehold 1994). All these measures make most sense if they were intended to supplement and complete the initial reforms of 462/1. If so, the intention of the latter must have been to root power and government in the demos and its institutions and to enable all citizens, including those who could ill afford it economically, to share such power (Fornara and Samons 1991: 66, 73). Thus for the first time the lower-class citizens were fully enabled to enjoy political equality and participation.[14]

Violent Reactions

Echoes survive of the debates and polemics surrounding the political changes realized in 462. The reform itself apparently was bitterly contested. When Cimon tried to reverse it, he was ostracized (T5e, 6d). Ephialtes was

assassinated (T3c). A deep rift opened up in the community. Rumors cir-
culated, fueling fears of a "fifth column" that might betray the city to the
Spartans in order to reverse the hated innovation (T5f, 6e, 7b). The most
impressive document attesting to these tensions again stems from the pen
of Aeschylus.

In 458, only four years after the reforms, Aeschylus staged his masterpiece, the *Oresteia*. By choosing, in *Eumenides*, to "reenact" the establishment, by Athens' protectress Athena herself, of the Areopagus council—the
very institution that had just been deprived of much of its traditional
power—the poet clearly intended this play to convey a significant message
to his fellow citizens (Meier 1990: chap. 5; 1993: 102–37). Orestes, killer of
his mother in revenge for her murder of his father, is hunted by the Furies,
chthonian deities of retribution for blood guilt especially among kin. They
are characterized as representatives of a primeval order that is sanctioned by
tradition and divine providence; it is their holy obligation and right to punish Orestes (*Eum.* 171–72, 208–10, 227, 307–96, 419–21). Apollo, the
prophet god of Delphi who has commanded Orestes to avenge his father's
murder, cleansed him of blood guilt, and promised to protect him, despises
these "old gods" (67–73, 179–97). They in turn see in him the representative of a new and radically different world order. In their view, Zeus and his
"young gods" have arbitrarily introduced new laws and, by ignoring old customs, established a violent, tyrannical form of rule (148–54, 162–72, 490–
524, 778–79).

These two orders, Christian Meier suggests, stand for the old and new
political orders of Athens (a more aristocratic and a more democratic one)
that confront each other as a result of Ephialtes' reforms. From the perspective of the old order, the victorious new order appears as an arbitrary
form of government that, like a tyranny, despises and violates traditional
rights and customs. What happened on stage through Orestes' act of
revenge and the counterrevenge intended by the Furies corresponded to a
serious threat to Athens in reality as well, given the violent reactions of certain circles and the deep split among the citizens (echoed in the play by a
warning against *stasis*, 976–87). Apparently considering the reform, as
enacted, inadequate to defuse the real problems, Aeschylus represents the
conflict between the old and new gods as a clash between two opposing
principles, both of which are justified and can be reconciled only with great
difficulties. Hence the acquittal of Orestes by the Areopagus resolves the
legal issue but not the underlying conflict, for the court's decision does not
appease the losers, who interpret it as a partisan victory of their opponents,
achieved against their justified resistance. Since they keep aiming at
revenge, the conflict continues and threatens the survival of the entire community (477–79, 780–86). The threats of the Furies must therefore be
taken seriously; reconciliation is indispensable. Peace and unity can be

restored only if *both* orders are given (and agree to assume) a function that allows them to contribute to the common good, each according to its nature and capability. Hence it is significant that Athena, although leaving no doubt that she has the power to thwart any resistance (826–29, a point strongly emphasized in Cohen 1986: 138–39), tries to achieve her goal primarily through patient persuasion (*peithō*, a crucial concept in democracy: 885, 969–74, 988–89; see Buxton 1982) and by offering the Furies a constructive compromise (794–807, 824–36, 847–69, 881–902): the former opponents, transformed into "Eumenides," well-meaning deities, are integrated into the new order (892ff.).

Just as the poet had argued in *Suppliants* that the democratic participation of all citizens, even the lowly ones, was based on just claims and could benefit the polis, so he now emphasized that the aristocratic element too had its justified claims and must be given a responsible function. This was the only way to endow the new order with stability and permanence. Reconciliation, unity, and collaboration for the common good—this was Aeschylus's message, formulated from a position in the middle: "Not a life of anarchy nor the rule of tyranny: take the middle way endowed by gods!" (526–30; cf. 696–99).

BACKGROUND AND EXPLANATIONS

The Transformation of Athens

In the generation after the Persian Wars Athens was profoundly transformed in every respect (Raaflaub 1998c). In warfare, the confrontation with the Persians represented a watershed. Previously, wars had mostly been fought on land, in long intervals, and between neighboring communities; they consisted of brief and violent clashes between heavily armed infantry militias (hoplite phalanxes), consisting of the landowning farmers (Hanson 1995: pt. 2). The trireme, though invented earlier, was an expensive luxury few poleis could afford in sufficient numbers (Wallinga 1993). Naval warfare had thus been waged mostly on a relatively small scale and with ships requisitioned for the purpose. It entered a completely new dimension in the wars against the Persians and became a permanent feature when the Delian League, formed in 478/7 under Athens' leadership, continued this war intermittently over almost three decades. This changed the experience of war fundamentally (Raaflaub 1999: 141–47; Hanson 2001). Naval campaigns lasted much longer. The crews needed intensive training. The manpower requirements were enormous (up to 200 men per trireme, hence up to 20,000 for a fleet of 100 ships; 9,000 Athenian hoplites fought at Marathon, 180 Athenian triremes at Salamis). To build and maintain a fleet of triremes and to pay its crews was very costly (Gabrielsen 1994, 2001). The crews consisted of lower-class citizens, mercenaries, and slaves; over time, the proportion of the latter two categories may have increased but even so every year many thousand citizens were involved regularly in rowing the fleet and thus in paid work for the community (Gabrielsen 1994; see Rosivach 1985). Finally, although the hoplite army continued to play a significant role (Hanson 1996), reliance on the fleet changed the community's outlook on war. The Piraeus had been fortified earlier; in the mid-450s the Athenians built the Long Walls connecting the city with its harbor and turning both into one impregnable fortress. They abandoned the traditional ideology of defensive hoplite warfare and assigned the fleet permanently a vital role.

In this period, Athens developed into a large, economically and demographically diverse community that became the economic center of the Greek world. A vast infrastructure and a whole industry, encompassing many trades, was created to build and maintain three hundred ships and to support the required personnel (Gabrielsen 1994: chaps. 6–7). Public and private construction proliferated, especially in Athens and the Piraeus, which became a city in its own right, planned by the famous architect Hippodamus of Miletus (Boersma 1970; Hoepfner and Schwandner 1994: 22–50). Booty from wars against barbarians and recalcitrant Greek cities, tribute from the subjects in the empire, and other revenues brought unprecedented material profits to Attica.[15] Trade and other business activities increased rapidly along with the consolidation of the Athenian sphere of domination: the Piraeus became the hub of trade in the Aegean and far beyond, and Athens experienced an unprecedented influx of goods from all over the world (Garland 1987).

The manpower required especially for the naval yards was huge: perhaps 15,000, based on Robert Garland's estimates for the fourth century (1987: 68); many of these will have served as rowers in the summer months. The labor force was probably mixed; the influx of metics and slaves was considerable, but by far the largest component must have come from the farming population of rural Attica (Frost 1976: 70–71). Thousands of Athenians thus changed their work habits and ways of life; even if not all of them migrated permanently to the metropolitan area, their outlook and loyalty shifted from rural village mentality and local dependencies to the polis and its policies (Frost 1976: 72; Davies 1992: 291–302). By the mid- to late 460s this process had been going on long enough to change the political outlook of vast numbers of Athenians who had been marginalized before. The impact on Athenian society of these military, economic, and social changes—massive, accelerating, and interacting with each other—must have been enormous.

Nor did the political sphere remain unaffected. By the 450s, if not the late 460s, the Delian League had been transformed into an Athenian empire (Meiggs 1972; Fornara and Samons 1991: chap. 3; Rhodes 1992:

49–61). Naval power and empire were interconnected. The empire consisted mostly of coastal communities in the Aegean and Black Sea areas. Their financial contributions largely provided the resources needed to maintain and operate the fleet, they formed the support network that made it possible for this fleet to move around freely, and the fleet's control of the seas and capacity to transport troops quickly usually sufficed to keep the subjects at bay. Imperial rule required an unprecedented level of administrative, political, and military centralization and extraordinary personal involvement on the part of the Athenian citizens. Eventually, hundreds served abroad as officials in various administrative and military capacities (*Ath. Pol.* 24.3). Thousands of lower-class Athenians received land allocations on territory confiscated from rebellious allies, and thus moved upward socially (Jones 1957: 7, 167–77). In Athens itself, council, assembly, and law courts experienced a massive increase of business generated by or connected with the empire, which necessitated the structural adjustments mentioned earlier (prytanies and *dikastēria;* Schuller 1984).

All this could not but have a serious impact on the way the Athenians perceived, performed, and structured politics. To understand this, we need to look at the function of the assembly and the connection between military capacity and political duties and privileges.

Assembly, Military Capacity, and Political Participation

In a Greek polis, normally the function of the assembly was more passive than active: it listened to proposals and debates among the leaders and expressed its approval or disapproval by shouting or voting; it elected officials and made communal decisions. In this sense, it was sovereign, but it lacked initiative, and its decisions could be vetoed by the authorities in charge; initiative and control lay with the council, which was usually dominated by the elite.[16] Nowhere but in Athens and probably in other democracies (though perhaps, as we shall see, to a lesser degree) did the assembly (whatever its composition) with its related popular institutions become the governing body that controlled the entire political process. Seeing democracy as the normal form of government (although our modern versions are barely comparable to theirs: Cartledge, chapter 6 in this volume), we moderns tend to underestimate seriously the massive difference between the innovations introduced by democracy and what was traditional, normal, and generally accepted in most Greek communities.

Active participation with the capacity not only to vote but also to speak in the assembly and other political institutions usually was restricted to those who were of sufficient social standing, determined sometimes by birth, but mostly by property and military capacity.[17] The institutions were set up to make sure that a person's political influence corresponded to these criteria.

The "timocratic system" introduced by Solon (*Ath. Pol.* 7.3–4) and perhaps elaborated much later (see below) and the Roman centuriate assembly (*comitia centuriata*), based initially on military units (Taylor 1966: chap. 5; Lintott 1999: 55–61), offer good though very different examples. In a widely consistent pattern, the citizen classes that ranked higher in military and/or property qualification enjoyed certain political privileges the lower ones lacked. The virtually complete abolition of such discrepancies by the Athenian democracy represents a radical break with age-old and deeply ingrained traditions and is, overall, a rare exception.

The reason is that, generally speaking, at least in the Greek and Roman worlds, political rights and military capacity were connected, based on social and economic status, which, in the archaic period, was linked with ownership of land. Tilling the land and fighting for the community were the most honorable pursuits, typical of the free and noble man (Vernant 1965). They also formed the base of what Ian Morris (1996; see also 2000: chaps. 5–6; Hanson 1995: chap. 5) calls the "middling ideology," which can be traced back far into the archaic period (Raaflaub 1996b: 150–53) and included the farmers fighting in the hoplite phalanx (Hanson 1995). The modalities of the political participation of these farmers were *formally fixed*, through legislation and institutional changes, between the late seventh and late sixth century in many poleis, though not everywhere in the same forms (Robinson 1997), when it became indispensable, for the sake of communal unity and survival, to base the polis on this class and to engage its members fully in communal responsibility (Raaflaub 1999: 139–40). Hence by the late sixth century egalitarian *politeiai* (constitutions based on some form of *isonomia*, that is, equal political participation and equality before the law) were fairly widespread. Ancient historians and theoreticians (Herodotus and Aristotle, among others), partly ignoring the differences, partly for ideological reasons, called this type of constitution democracy, as do many modern historians (e.g., Robinson 1997; Wallace and Ober, in this volume). For reasons explained in this chapter, I prefer to reserve this term for a later stage in constitutional development.

The Athenians began this process under the leadership of Solon and completed it under that of Cleisthenes. It was facilitated, despite differences in lifestyle and outlook between elite and non-elite farmers, by the shared values of those who owned and worked the land and fought in the army to defend this land. Those who did not fit this pattern or fit it only partially were part of the community but on an inferior level: they were tolerated but not respected by those holding power. The assembly in the *Iliad*, of course, consists only of soldiers; even unruly Thersites (2.211–70; see chapter 2 above) is a member of the army. The *Odyssey* that, perhaps typically, lets Telemachus take his spear along when he goes to the assembly (2.10; cf. van Wees 1998), vividly illustrates the low and vulnerable status of the *thes* in early Greek society (11.489–91, 18.356–75; cf. Raaflaub 1997a: 638). Although evidence is lacking, we have no reason to think that this changed substantially in the centuries to come. Even if sometimes they may have been needed (if they had special skills or contributed in some important way to the communal well-being: see below) it is plausible to assume that they usually remained excluded from sharing power and privileges.

Thus throughout the fifth and fourth centuries, in many, if not most, poleis various forms of constitutions prevailed that extended full citizenship to the hoplite-farmers but excluded the nonhoplite lower classes and, in this sense, were aristocracies or oligarchies rather than democracies (Whibley 1896; Ostwald 2000). From a late-sixth-century perspective, this was nothing but normal. It is obscured only from a late-fifth- or fourth-century and Athenian perspective, which emphasized a stark contrast between democracy and oligarchy. In the case of Athens, this certainly corresponded to reality. Otherwise, as Aristotle demonstrates in *Politics* (Mulgan 1991; see Robinson 1997: 35–44; Cartledge, chapter 6, note 4 below), both democracy and oligarchy existed in many varieties, there was a great deal of overlap between the moderate forms of both, and often "democrats" and "oligarchs" were hardly more than labels in struggles between similarly composed factions (Ruschenbusch 1978: 24–54). In fact, as we shall see, there are good reasons to think that, even when democracies had become more frequent in the course of the fifth century, the Athenian version was extreme and unparalleled. The *full* political integration of the thetes, unlikely under normal circumstances, remained an exception. It required as a precondition some massive and lasting change in their economic or social status and/or communal function.

Naval Warfare, Empire, and Democracy

The victory of Salamis in 480 was a triumph of the fleet—even if prevailing ideologies and prejudices tried to salvage much of it for the hoplites (van Wees 1995: 158–59 with bibliog.); those of Marathon in 490 and Plataea in 479 certainly were not. Had the Athenians after 479 ceased operations against the Persians, not assumed hegemony in a new alliance that soon became an empire, and mothballed their fleet, their constitution, I suggest, would have progressed only minimally beyond Cleisthenes' *isonomia*—even in a world undergoing widespread social and economic changes (Davies 1992). After all, several allies contributed major fleets to the common war effort; none of them became a democracy. True, given their rivalry with Aegina, the Athenians might have maintained a substantial fleet anyway. But, as the examples of other naval powers indicate (see below), this alone did not necessitate democracy.

The decisive difference, in the case of Athens, was precisely the continuation of the war against the Persians, the Delian League, and the empire. More specifically, it was, in this context, the function assigned to the fleet and the composition of the crews rowing it. Under the special conditions prevailing in Athens in the 470s and 460s, the fleet emerged as a crucial instrument for the city's security, prosperity, and power, and the Athenian lower-class citizens (thetes), who furnished most of the crews, as decisive contributors to their city's might. Moreover, this new role of fleet and thetes turned out to be not an exception but the rule. Accordingly, a large class of citizens who traditionally and everywhere else did not count for much became permanently indispensable to their community; through their firmly established and undeniable military role the thetes acquired the necessary minimum of social prestige and self-confidence that made their political integration possible and, I think, even necessary (Bleicken 1994: 52; see also Strauss 1996; Pritchard 1999). Even opponents of democracy, such as the "Old Oligarch" (Pseudo-Xenophon *Ath. Pol.* 1.2, quoted below), eventually came to recognize that.

Since many thetes were not economically independent, however, unlike previously the propertied classes, they could not afford to contribute without compensation the considerable amounts of time to be spent in politics. Their paid employment by the state as rowers on the fleet had already introduced compensation into military service—also an innovation in Greece. This must have facilitated the introduction of pay for political service. The availability of vast financial resources accumulated through the imperial tribute must have helped overcome deeply ingrained prejudices against this change. Financially, too, democracy thus depended on the empire, even if much later it was able to persist without it (Kallet 1998).

The Historical Plausibility of Connecting Military and Political Change

Recent scholarship has yielded a number of important new insights that have considerably advanced our understanding of some of the processes involved. As a result, some potentially serious objections to the thesis and argument I am proposing in this chapter need to be addressed. These concern (1) the Athenians' own awareness of the connection between the role of the navy and the evolution of democracy, (2) the historical plausibility of such a connection in general, and (3) the hoplites' and thetes' social standing, economic capacity, and political role as determined by the Solonian census classes. I will address these issues in turn, although I can do this here only briefly, discussing the first two problems in this section, the third in the next.

Athenian Awareness of Connections between Naval Power and Democracy. The "Old Oligarch" famously comments on this connection:

It is right that the poor and the ordinary people there [in Athens] should have more power than the noble and rich, because it is the ordinary people who man the fleet and bring the city her power; they provide the helmsmen, the boatswains, the junior officers, the look-outs and the shipwrights; it is [all] these people who make the city powerful much more than the hoplites and the noble and respectable citizens. This being so, it seems just that all should share in public office by lot and by election, and that any citizen who wishes should be able to speak in the assembly. (Ps.-Xen. *Ath. Pol.* 1.2)

The author understands the rationale of this system without approving of its political implications (1.4–9 and passim). In an equally famous passage, Plato makes a similar observation, though condemning democracy much more harshly on moral terms (*Laws* 706c–707a). On the factual level, the connection between naval power and democracy in its fully developed form was thus established by the mid- to late fifth century.[18] On the causal level (establishing that democracy was made possible or necessary by the emergence of the fleet as the main support of Athenian power, or that the developments of naval power and democracy were interlinked), this connection apparently was made later, perhaps not before Aristotle.[19] In a thorough discussion of this issue, Paola Ceccarelli (1993) concludes that this causal connection was nothing but a theoretical and ideological construct. This may be correct, but it does not invalidate the explanation: modern historians constantly propose explanations of which contemporaneous or near-contemporaneous ancient observers did not think, or, if they did, did so only from a limited perspective. All that matters is whether such a connection or explanation can be justified with plausible arguments.

Historical Parallels. Robert Wallace (1998: 27) and Walter Eder (1998: 135–36) find the particular connection I am proposing here implausible. To the extent that ancient authors were commenting on it, Wallace considers it "abstract, theoretical, and probably also a *post hoc, propter hoc*. History offers plenty of contrary examples of people's armies in nondemocratic states—beginning with the massed popular armies in Homer." In the Greek world, I would respond, beginning with Homer, these armies usually consisted of free farmers and not of mass levies of lower-class citizens. Moreover, Wallace points out (written communication), "other Greek cities were becoming democracies at this time [in the second quarter or so of the fifth century] but did not possess Athens' empire or thetic fleet." He attributes this to "the power of an idea, of democratic ideology" and to "the basic Greek mentality of egalitarianism." Other factors may have contributed as well (Robinson forthcoming). Wallace admits that he does not know (and, I suspect, the extant evidence in most cases does not permit us to know) "whether these democracies were open to even the lowest classes" but insists that "they were still democracies." His objection thus misses the point, because I am concerned here precisely with the emergence of a democracy that did fully include the lower-class citizens.

Eder does not see why rowing should have raised the self-confidence of the thetes or why they should have been paid by the ruling classes "with political money for their military successes." He mentions slaves and metics, who fought in Athens' wars but were not rewarded with political advancement, and lists several historical counterexamples (including the Persian, Carthaginian, and Roman fleets, and the Athenian metics, Spartan *perioikoi*, and Roman farmers manning some of the most powerful armies and fleets of the ancient world); I can think of others. This objection goes back at least to Julius Beloch, who wrote in the second edition of his famed *Greek History:*

> If Themistocles acquired the reputation of having been a leader, even the real founder, of radical democracy, this is a result of the view that dominated among elite circles in Athens in the time of the Peloponnesian War, and which particularly Plato and after him Aristotle expressed, as if the rise of Athens to great sea power had elevated the rabble to ruler in the state. The moderns tend to copy this; yet it is nothing but a completely wrong conclusion that confuses chronological sequence with cause (*post hoc ergo propter hoc*). Aegina, Corinth, Carthage, Rome, Venice, Holland were great sea powers but oligarchies. . . . In fact, one could say that Athens is the only example known in history of a democracy that was a naval power and thalassocracy. Very understandably: on a warship ironclad discipline must rule . . . , which certainly is no environment favorable to breeding democracy. (1922: 135; my trans.)

This obviously would need to be discussed in some detail; I can offer here merely a few suggestions, confined to antiquity and based on two assumptions: each case needs to be analyzed separately before we can proceed to make generalizations, and it is useful to include in such an examination land as well as naval forces.

Aegina (until 457), Corinth, and among the Athenian allies (before their revolts) Samos, Lesbos, and Chios had strong navies. We do not know how these were operated; presumably they were manned at least partly by citizens. Aegina's fleet, perceived as a threat by Athens before the Persian Wars and contributing substantially to the allied fleet at Salamis (Hdt. 8.46.1), is not heard of between 479 and c. 459, when it lost a major sea battle that sealed Athens' hegemony over the island (Figueira 1991: 104–13). Before the Peloponnesian War, the navy of Corinth seems to have been active only on a few occasions. The fleets of the Athenian allies were used more often but in wars of Athens or the Delian League rather than their own communities. All these fleets and the citizens rowing them therefore failed to play the same crucial communal role that those of Athens assumed year-in and year-out.

The Athenian metics (resident aliens) served both in the hoplite army and in the navy (Whitehead 1977), fulfilling an obligation incurred by settling permanently in Attica. They were attracted by economic opportunities and remained a minority, despite their sizable numbers. Their exclusion from political life was due to the narrow interpretation of the concept of citizenship and restrictive enfranchisement policies typical of Greek communities in general and especially of Athens (Whitehead 1991; Patterson 1981). Their status entailed advantages but was precarious, and they might have jeopardized these advantages by raising political demands.

Slaves served in the Athenian land army (certainly at Marathon [Hunt 1998: 26–27] and probably more often) and in the navy, often together with their masters (Welwei 1974: 96–107; Rosivach 1985). In times of emergency, larger numbers were enlisted. They were often freed before they went into action and, very exceptionally, enfranchised collectively without, however, being endowed with the active citizen capacities typical of the "true" Athenians (Hunt 2001). They, too, always remained a minority, and the reward they received for their military service was seen as congruent with their merits. The discomfort the Athenians (and other Greeks) felt about relying on slaves in warfare is mirrored in the historians' obvious efforts to play down their presence and contribution (Hunt 1998).

The Spartan *perioikoi* (those dwelling round about) formed their own communities and were part, but not citizens, of the large Spartan polis. They served in the Spartan hoplite army and perhaps paid taxes but enjoyed local autonomy and considerable economic opportunities (Cartledge 1979: esp. 178–85; Shipley 1997; Hall 2000). Paul Cartledge sees analogies with Sparta's Peloponnesian allies (1987: 16); I find significant parallels in the status of the Roman allies. Even if both these groups presumably would have preferred complete freedom, if given a choice, we know that they found their situation quite satisfactory, even advantageous—until their hegemonic leaders began to infringe upon their vital interests (Cartledge 1987: chap. 13; Raaflaub 2004: 122–26, 198–99; Keaveney 1987). The *perioikoi* may have felt the same way, at least before pressures and dissatisfaction increased in the fourth century (Xenophon *Hellenica* 3.3.6; Cartledge 1987: 177–78); it seems symptomatic, for example, that to our knowledge only two of the perhaps eighty perioikic communities supported the great helot revolt of the 460s (Luraghi 2001a: 290–92, 298–99).

The Spartan slave population (helots) that supplied the workforce, enabling the citizens (Spartiates) to devote themselves to their duties and privileges as professional citizen-soldiers, offers a particularly interesting case (Cartledge 1979: 160–77; Ducat 1990). Large numbers served in some capacity or other in the Spartan army (although the ratio of seven helots for each Spartiate attested for the battle of Plataea was probably exceptional [Hunt 1997; 1998: 31–39, 53–82]). They were usually freed, and the survivors were settled in marginal areas. In several cases we learn of extraordinary measures the Spartan authorities took to neutralize the potential sociopolitical impact of the helots' military service (Cartledge 1987: 170–77). Even so, it is quite possible that the many thousand helots returning from the victory of Plataea played a crucial role in the massive helot revolt that broke out little more than a decade after that battle (Luraghi 2001a: 301).

Well into the third century B.C.E., Rome had a coast guard but not its own war fleet. For the first time, Roman citizens rowing a Roman navy played a major role during the First Punic War. Most likely, the crews were composed of proletarians (citizens listed in the lowest census class), naval allies and citizens from maritime colonies (who traditionally had provided the coast guard), and freedmen (Lazenby 1996: 65–66). Yet at least two factors blunted any potential sociopolitical impact the proletarians' and freedmen's service might have had. One is that their military significance was not maintained. The Romans fought few wars that depended so heavily on the performance of the navy as the first war against Carthage.[20] Rather, it was their infantry legions that won their wars and conquered their empire. The other factor is that by the time of the First Punic War the social and political structures of Rome were firmly established. The rule of the senatorial oligarchy was sanctioned by the long string of military successes that had sealed the conquest of Italy and the victories over Pyrrhus. The large-scale conquests of the next hundred years would cement these structures further, until only a century of domestic violence and civil wars was able to shake and destroy them.

Already in the early republic, vast numbers of non-elite (plebeian) landowning citizens (*assidui*), serving as infantry soldiers, played an indispensable role almost every year in the defense of their community as well as the expansion of its sphere of power (Harris 1979: 41–53; Raaflaub 1996a). This was one of the decisive factors that eventually secured the plebeians' successes in their intermittent but long-lasting social and political struggles with the patrician aristocracy (Raaflaub 2005: 196–97). In the crisis of the late republic (the so-called Roman Revolution), lower-class citizen (*proletarii*), volunteering for service in the armies of Marius and other "warlords," provided the bulk of the "client armies" that decided the power struggles among Roman senators and eventually propelled Caesar and Augustus to sole power (Gabba 1976; Brunt 1988: chap. 5). They were rewarded with booty, land, and eventually (in Augustus's principate) with the establishment of a professional army with regulated conditions of service and discharge (Keppie 1984; Raaflaub 1987). Nor was the Roman Senate able, in the long run, to ignore or suppress the political consequences arising from the constant military involvement of the Italian allies (Keaveney 1987; see below). In fact, the Roman republic offers important support for my thesis that I will now define more precisely.

Three Decisive Factors. As my brief survey shows, the military engagement of lower social classes (whether in the navy or infantry, whether, in Greek terms, hoplite-farmers or thetes or, in Roman terms, *assidui* or *proletarii,* or even resident aliens, freedmen, slaves, or other noncitizens) in the wars of states governed by an elite of higher classes (whether an aristocracy or an oligarchy of elite and non-elite hoplite-farmers) did not automatically and necessarily trigger social and political change. Nor was military success per se sufficient. Rather, as I suggested above (cf. Raaflaub 1999: 139–40, 145, 147), a decisive factor was that the military involvement of these lower classes, for whatever reason and in whatever form, became permanently and indispensably significant to the community. This is what secured for the Spartan hoplites the status of *homoioi* (peers, Cartledge 1996a), when they became their polis's mainstay in controlling the large helot population. For the same reason, in Rome the early republican patrician aristocracy eventually had to yield to plebeian demands and to accept their political integration. The constant dependence of the Roman state on the allies' military contribution was a necessary condition for their enfranchisement in the first century B.C.E., and their indispensable military role enabled the late republican proletarian citizen volunteers to gain recognition as professional soldiers with corresponding benefits of service.

Yet these Roman examples indicate that a second factor was equally decisive. The early republican plebeians fought a long struggle to achieve their goals, combining confrontation with compromise and creating their own institutions to advance their cause. The late republican allies demanded an improvement of their status and eventually Roman citizenship, and they risked war to gain it. The proletarian armies of the first century learned to exploit their leaders' power struggles to their own advantage and eventually imposed their will on their generals. The decisive second factor thus was the will of the soldiers to achieve an improvement of their condition, whether socially, economically, or politically, and to use their military leverage to this end.

On the Greek side, it is more difficult to document expressions of such will. In the second half of the seventh century, Sparta suffered through a severe crisis that was triggered or aggravated by a defeat against Argos and a Messenian revolt (Cartledge 1979: 127–28, 131–35; Meier 1998). Hints in extant traditions suggest demands for redistribution of land (Tyrtaeus 1 West 1992 [henceforth W]) and civil strife preceding a state of good order (*eunomia:* Hdt. 1.65.2; Thuc. 1.18.1; cf. Plutarch *Life of Lycurgus* 5.4–5). Pressure from below thus is likely to have played an important role in creating the community of *homoioi* and in bringing about the "Great Rhetra" that institutionalized, among other issues, the process of decision making among the Spartiates (see chapter 2 in this volume).[21] Civil strife and the call for redistribution of land are attested for early-sixth-century Athens as well (fr. 34 W), and Solon says explicitly that he yielded (though only partially) to the demands raised by those who were ready to revolt against both those in power and the established order (Wallace, chapter 3 above). Popular sentiments or demands certainly played an important role in determining the outcome of dramatic developments at the end of the sixth century (strongly emphasized by Ober, chapter 4 above). Hence, even if we cannot prove it, it is likely that popular demands helped bring about the reforms of 462–50 as well (see below).

As we shall see, a third factor also played a crucial role in translating military into political importance: the availability of aristocratic leaders who, for whatever reasons, were willing to lend their support to popular causes or to demands voiced by specific groups (Eder 1998). Before we look more closely at this factor, we need to ask what might have prompted the Athenian thetes to raise political demands in the period before 462—if their rise in military importance is not accepted as a sufficient explanation. At this point we need to digress and reconsider the social and political status of the Athenian hoplites and thetes and its relation both to the institutional recognition of military functions in Solon's timocratic system and to the reality of warfare at the time.[22]

Hoplites, Thetes, Timocracy, and Changes in Warfare

Problems with the "Solonian" Census Classes. The notion that citizens qualifying as hoplites were privileged politically over those who did not is based on Solon's "timocratic" constitution. According to *Ath. Pol.* 7.3–4, Solon established census classes (*telē*) that tied political privileges to the citizens' economic capacity, measured in units (*medimnoi*) of agricultural produce yielded by their landed property. The "500-measure men" (*pentakosiomedimnoi*), the "horsemen" (*hippeis*, 300 measures), and the "yoke men" (*zeugitai*, 200 measures) were entitled to hold office, while the *thētes* ("hired laborers," below 200 measures) could only attend the assembly and the law courts. As the *Ath. Pol.* suggests (7.3), it is likely that Solon modified an already existing system by correlating military and political capacity (Rhodes 1981: 137).

Hippeis, zeugitai, and *thētes* correspond to the horsemen (*equites*), the "class" (*classis*) and those "below the class" (*infra classem*) of the "centuriate organization" instituted in sixth-century Rome (supposedly by King Servius Tullius), and thus to a division of the citizens into horsemen, hoplites, and all the rest who did not qualify for hoplite service. In Rome, too, military capacity was linked to political privileges, here concerning not access to office but priority and numerical preponderance in voting. The numbers of voting units (centuries) were distributed in such a way that the *equites* and hoplites were guaranteed a majority. This remained true even much later, when the military system had become more differentiated, additional classes (with lesser equipment) had been added, and membership in these classes was defined by a fixed property census (Livy 1.43). The Roman system of census classes thus developed from a simple one, based on military capacity, to a more complex one, based on military capacity and a fixed assessment (Ogilvie 1965: 166–76; Cornell 1995: chap. 7; Forsythe 2005: 111–14).

Upon closer inspection, Solon's timocratic system is riddled with problems. References in the extant sources to the census classes are late and rare; information on the nature of the fixed assessment is confused and full of errors (de Ste. Croix 2004: 5–71). Even the author of the *Ath. Pol.* (7.4) was unclear about whether a *hippeus* needed to meet an assessment or simply own a horse. Whether the zeugites designate hoplites, "yoked together" in their tight formation, or farmers owning a yoke of oxen is much debated (Rhodes 1981: 138; Whitehead 1981; Hanson 1995: 111). The Roman analogy suggests the former, and G. E. M. de Ste. Croix now supports this with compelling arguments (2004: 49–51). If so, the zeugite census of 200 *medimnoi* is remarkably high. It is only 100 measures lower than that of the *hippeis*, who, as horse breeders, must have been well-to-do aristocrats with large estates. Moreover, the size of farms required to produce 200 *medimnoi* (at least 25 acres) is much larger than the generally assumed size of the average family or hoplite farm (9–13 acres; Hanson 1995: 181–201; Ruschenbusch 1995: 440–43; Foxhall 1997: 130–31). The zeugites thus must have been wealthy farmers whose agricultural income permitted them to live much more comfortably than one would expect of those simply able to afford a hoplite panoply (Foxhall 1997: 129–32; van Wees 2001: 47–51). Moreover, given these figures, it seems impossible to fit the 9,000 Athenian hoplites attested for the battle of Marathon or the 8,000 at Plataea (Beloch 1886: 60; van Wees 2001: 71 n. 75), let alone the much higher numbers mentioned by Thucydides (2.13.6–7) for 431, into the cultivable territory of Attica (Raaflaub 1999: 138 with n. 49; van Wees 2001: 51–54).

Three attempts have been made recently to overcome these problems, one more radical than the other. I discuss these in more detail elsewhere (Raaflaub 2006) and give here only a brief summary. Hans van Wees (2001; cf. van Wees 2006) accepts the sources' testimony on the zeugite census and concludes that the hoplites did not form a "largely unified, cohesive group" (2001: 45). In Athens, "and perhaps elsewhere, hoplites were economically and politically divided right down the middle" between the wealthier ones, who met the 200 *medimnoi* requirement and had certain political privileges and duties, and the poorer ones, who had neither because they did not meet the requirement. The highest property classes, van Wees thinks, were liable to service as hoplites, while the others were not but could serve as volunteers, especially in "national emergencies." The implication is "that the structure of society and politics was shaped by the distribution of wealth, regardless of the differentiation of military functions, and that most 'democratic' rights were, officially at any rate, much less widely shared than we normally imagine" (45, 59).

In an essay written in the 1960s but published only recently, de Ste. Croix (2004: chap. 1) reexamines the evidence for the *telē*, with important and largely compelling conclusions. The three lower classes represented military categories based on economic ability and self-declaration. These military categories were primary and determined membership in the *telē*, which were thus secondary and only important as qualification for offices and a few additional purposes. There never was a fixed quantitative census assessment. The highest class of *pentakosiomedimnoi*, a Solonian addition to the system, was an exception in every respect: it lacked a specific military purpose and required, to provide surety for financial responsibilities, a fixed and very high assessment in income from agrarian property. Hence de Ste. Croix considers the notion of census classes based on a fixed assessment a late construct, probably based on a misunderstanding of information contained in a now lost law that was, rightly or wrongly, attributed to Solon.

The consequences for the issue at hand are obvious: if there were no fixed quantitative assessments, calculations, such as those of van Wees, of how many hoplite farms of the required size would have fit into the cultivable territory of Attica become unnecessary. Moreover, I suggest, to explain the large number of Athenian hoplites, we must consider, in various combinations, the mobilization of slaves, metics, and thousands of Athenian hoplites settled (or at least owning land) outside of Attica. Either way, the large hoplite figures reported for the early and mid-fifth century no longer pose a problem, and it is unnecessary to divide the hoplites into two (zeugite and thetic) categories—a division that causes its own major difficulties.[23]

On the other hand, de Ste. Croix's solution, that no quantitative assessments ever existed for *hippeis* and *zeugitae,* seems incompatible with the *Ath. Pol.*'s assumption that such assessments were still valid at the time of its composition, even if they were mostly ignored. I propose, therefore, against de Ste. Croix, that such quantitative assessments were introduced at some later date. The only period that fits such a major innovation is precisely that of Ephialtes' and Pericles' reforms of 462–450.[24] This date has the advantage of resolving as well a number of other problems raised by the traditional attribution of the quantitative *telē* to Solon. By the late 460s, Athenian financial officials, especially the treasurers of Athena, were dealing with vast amounts of funds (Samons 2000) that justified the introduction of a new census class for very wealthy citizens who were able to provide the required amounts of security. Around that time Athens created its first ever formally organized cavalry force; communal pride in this force is reflected in its prominence on the Parthenon frieze.[25] General prosperity in the decades after the Persian Wars and the assignment of land in settlements abroad (cleruchies: Schmitz 1988: 79–115; Figueira 1991: 161–225; Brunt 1993: 112–36) to thousands of lower-class citizens had increased the number of citizens qualifying as hoplites to such an extent that it now became feasible to introduce a property assessment for hoplites and to set it high. Such a move perhaps even seemed necessary in view of the predominant role the navy had assumed in imperial warfare and the navy's enormous manpower needs. Horsemen and hoplites were normally exempt from service as rowers on the fleet. The latter were recruited, apart from mercenaries, metics, and slaves, among thetic volunteers (see above), and it may have seemed best to keep the pool of such volunteers as large as possible by limiting the number of citizen hoplites.

Most importantly in our present context, the "Solonian" timocratic system explicitly assigns to the thetes "membership of the assembly and the jury-courts" (*Ath. Pol.* 7.3). Many have taken this to imply that before Solon they were excluded from any public function but now enabled to participate fully in the assembly's proceedings. P. J. Rhodes (1981: 140–41) disagrees: "It is unlikely that there was a formal distinction between full citizens, who could attend the assembly, and inferior citizens, who could not. More probably every citizen could attend, though . . . the lower-class men were expected, both before Solon's reforms and for some time after . . . to attend as 'brute votes' rather than active members." In the mid-fifth century such a regulation makes perfect sense. In fact, it fits the general thesis of this chapter rather well. We know that the rise of the navy and the thetes prompted misgivings and resistance.[26] Balancing this new regulation that favored the thetes with the introduction of a new quantitative census and political privileges for hoplites and *hippeis* might reflect an effort to diffuse their opposition—while probably prompting opposition among those no longer qualifying as hoplites.[27]

With the evidence available to us, it is impossible to prove such a late date for the fully developed timocratic system. All that speaks for it is plausibility and a Roman analogy. To most scholars, this may not seem sufficient to abandon the testimony of the *Ath. Pol.*, which, however, has been weakened decisively by recent scholarly criticism. Given how little precise and specific evidence survives about constitutional developments in the sixth and fifth centuries, it should not surprise us that the correct date was no longer remembered by the mid- to late fourth century, when the author of the *Ath. Pol.* or his source collected their information.

At any rate, and even if we retain the Solonian date, de Ste. Croix's conclusions strongly support the view that military capacity and political functions were and remained closely linked. This a priori enhances the likeli-

hood that a massive change in the distribution of military capacity among
the Athenian citizens had an impact on the distribution of political power.
In recent publications, van Wees attacked this possibility—and long-standing orthodoxy—from yet another angle.

Hoplites and Light-Armed Troops. The "pure" hoplite phalanx with its almost
ritualized mode of fighting (Connor 1988), van Wees thinks, developed not
in the seventh century but much later, perhaps only after the Persian Wars
(van Wees 1995: esp. 162–65; 2000; see also Krentz 2002). Throughout the
archaic age, despite gradual but slow changes, the formation was far less
tightly ordered and rigidly disciplined than is usually assumed. Essentially,
light-armed troops, effective even against hoplites, not only supported the
phalanx by skirmishing before the clash of the phalanxes or from behind
the formation but were actually mixed in with the hoplites. Van Wees
observes:

> The notion, propagated by ancient authors and accepted by modern scholars,
> that archaic and classical infantry battles were won and lost by hoplites alone
> thus stands in need of some revision. Hoplites reserved for themselves the
> credit derived from military success, but to achieve that success they enlisted
> the services of large numbers of disenfranchised, poor citizens or serfs. They
> managed to monopolize this source of political legitimation, in part through
> not developing the full potential of the light-armed mass, but more impor-
> tantly by simply employing these masses in battle without openly acknowledg-
> ing their military significance or entering their achievements in the historical
> record. (1995: 165)

The "hoplite ideology," cherished by the upper classes, thus was guilty of fal-
sifying history, just as demonstrably in the classical period the military contribution of slaves and other outsiders was widely passed over in silence (van
Wees 1995: passim; Hunt 1998). If, however, citizen thetes had been
involved in fighting for their community long before the post–Persian War
period, van Wees concludes, it is hard to maintain the claim that their *new*
role on the fleet raised their self-confidence and prompted them to demand
political concessions. Rather,

> we must assume that the common people at the time *already* cherished politi-
> cal ambitions, which impelled them to reject the traditional perception of
> hoplite superiority and to seize upon the successes of the fleet to justify their
> own desire for a voice in politics. . . . Serving in the fleet might not have made
> any difference to the political ambitions of the lower classes, had they not al-
> ready been seeking a greater share in government. (van Wees 1995: 161–62)

The same, van Wees thinks, happened earlier with the hoplite-farmers.
Contrary to long-held views, they played a crucial role in warfare already in

Homer's time.[28] The formalization of their political privileges in Solon's tim-ocratic system therefore was not due to their previous rise in military impor-tance. Rather, their "political ambitions . . . must have arisen indepen-dently." Most likely, it was "rising discontent with oppressive aristocratic rule which caused commoners to seek greater political power, and . . . this new political awareness made them see their own military role in a different light." Hence, van Wees concludes, "the development of the phalanx and the expansion of the Athenian fleet, although of military significance, did not have the revolutionary political impact generally attributed to them" (169–71).

I fully agree on the role of the masses in "epic warfare" and on the need to eliminate from our books the notion of a "hoplite revolution."[29] Despite a plethora of excellent observations, however, some of van Wees's conclu-sions do not seem to me fully convincing as presented. I will confine myself here to listing a few major objections.

First, I have doubts about ideologically based "conspiracy theories" on a large scale. It is one thing to suppress the contribution of slaves, another to do the same over centuries with that of citizens. One of the weaknesses of the theory of the "hoplite revolution" was precisely that it needed to assume a deliberate effort on the part of elite and hoplite farmers to keep the lower-class citizens out of the army in order to keep them out of politics (Snodgrass 1965: 114–16, 120–22; Cartledge 1977: 23–24). Even Sparta, which may have resisted change longer than others precisely in order to pre-serve its specific system (Davies 1993: 43), adapted its policies and strategies when this proved necessary to win the Peloponnesian War and maintain control over its allies. The archaic poleis were intensely competitive. Had it offered them a decisive advantage to develop an organized force of light-armed infantry they would have done so—just as the Athenians did not hes-itate to build and use large fleets when their survival and communal advan-tage recommended it. Rather than conspiring to avoid the gains offered by the systematic use of light-armed troops, the archaic poleis, I suggest, were not aware of such gains. The hoplite phalanx matched their specific needs, values, and culture (Raaflaub 1999: 135–38). Hence it was perfected and maintained, until massive outside interference (by the Persian empire) and rapidly changing conditions in the fifth century created new needs, includ-ing naval warfare and organized corps of light-armed troops and cavalry.[30]

Second, van Wees has presented compelling arguments that light-armed soldiers played a more significant role than is generally recognized in the early phases of hoplite fighting and perhaps throughout. Yet, in my opinion, fighting in somewhat compact formations was more common already in Homer's time than even van Wees allows for (Raaflaub 2005a). Moreover we do not know when the light-armed disappeared from the ranks of the hoplites. No clear evidence exists for the period between the late seventh century and the Peloponnesian War to prove the case either way. Hence the argument from silence is not of much help here. The examples of continuing anomalies van Wees cites have little to do with phalanx battle per se.[31] I consider it more decisive that the evolution and specialization of armor and weapons that were designed to increase the impact of a close formation oriented entirely to frontal fighting (especially the "Corinthian helmet," which restricted vision and hearing in exchange for full protection; the spear provided with a sharp iron butt; and the concave hoplite shield with its double grip) began in the eighth century and were essentially completed by the mid- to late seventh (Snodgrass 1964; 1967: chap. 3; Hanson 1991: 63–84). Moreover, in the second half of the seventh century evidence abounds that emphasizes the communal importance of hoplites (Snodgrass 1980: 99–106). And, again from the mid-seventh century, some communities introduced structural and organizational changes to accommodate the new realities of the hoplite army: they divided their community into districts that facilitated the registration and mustering of the army, and they kept lists of those qualified to serve in this army.[32]

All this, of course, does not prove that light-armed fighters were not involved, in some way or other, in hoplite battles even after the late seventh century. If so, however, they did it in an unorganized, haphazard way, as volunteers and as much for the sake of adventure and booty as for that of helping to win the victory. In a much later period, the battle of Delion (424/3) offers a good example for this type of involvement. Thucydides writes:

> There were no properly armed light troops present on this occasion, nor did Athens possess any. The ones who had joined in the invasion had been in much greater numbers than those on the Boeotian side [which numbered 10,000 (4.93)], but most of them had merely followed the army inadequately armed, as part of the general expedition of foreigners and citizens from Athens, and, since they started first on their way home, only a very few were still present. (4.94; cf. van Wees 1995: 163)

Overall, the impact of light-armed troops was rather negligible, some notable counterexamples notwithstanding.[33] Before the development, in the late fifth century, of special light-armed corps that were well trained and used special tactics (Ferrill 1997: 157–60), the hoplite phalanx, displayed properly and fighting on its own terrain, remained vastly superior.

Third, van Wees points out correctly (1995: 157–58) that the Athenians were engaged in military operations requiring naval support long before the Persian Wars and that they perhaps even maintained some kind of "coast guard" organization responsible for keeping ships prepared for military actions.[34] In his view, "the fleet and the military role it provided for the common people were not created from scratch by Themistokles in 483 BC; it seems likely that Themistokles did no more than double the number of ships." Most of the military actions reported before the Persian Wars, however, including Athenian support of the Ionian Revolt and Miltiades' campaign against Paros, depended on transportation capacities rather than naval fighting squadrons, and they could be executed with nonspecialized pentekontors. This is true as well for rare naval engagements (such as one against Aegina, for which the Athenians needed to borrow twenty Corinthian ships: Hdt. 6.89, 92.1). The long-standing view that these were armed merchantmen is compelling (Wallinga 1993: chap. 2); nothing requires us to assume that the Athenians maintained a sizable standing fleet of highly specialized and expensive warships (triremes) before the Persian Wars. Herodotus (7.144) explicitly connects the construction of a big war fleet in the 480s with the discovery of a new silver mine in Laurion and with a debate in the assembly that decided not to distribute the proceeds among the citizens (as was apparently customary in cases of such windfalls) but to spend them on the fleet. Even if Athens already had some triremes before then, the increase of this fleet to two hundred ships, with all the support facilities needed to maintain and repair them, was not merely a quantitative but a qualitative leap (Wallinga 1993; Gabrielsen 1994, 2001). As a consequence, before the late 480s the Athenians did not maintain a large contingent of rowers either, and the involvement of lower-class citizens in this military sphere was sporadic and relatively small. All this changed dramatically only with the Persian Wars.

Fourth, overall the evidence van Wees adduces falls far short of supporting his main conclusion:

> In reality it was by no means clear that one particular social group—now aristocratic horsemen, now well-off hoplites, now poor rowers and light-armed—contributed far more than others to the protection of the community. Most men, most of the time, played a role in war of some significance, and although changes in military practice occurred, these were not such as to confer a wholly new significance upon first the hoplites and then the lower classes. (1995: 156–57)

Whatever the role of light-armed troops and cavalry in archaic Greek warfare, and whatever the proportion of slaves, metics, and mercenaries among the crews of the Athenian fleets, in my view there can be no doubt about three essential facts. (a) Warfare in the period from the late seventh to the early fifth century was dominated by the hoplite phalanx, which developed out of earlier forms of massed combat that are visible already in the *Iliad* and continued to play an important role much longer. (b) The rise of naval warfare and its role in Athenian imperial policies brought about drastic changes in the nature of warfare and caused dramatic demographic, social, and economic changes as well (Hanson 2001; Gabrielsen 2001; Raaflaub 1999: 141–46). Although these changes did not make the hoplites obsolete, far from it (Hanson 1996), they had a marked impact on the mentality and self-perception of the military personnel involved (Strauss 1996; Pritchard 1999). Overall, many thousand thetes served as rowers over long periods of time; their numbers were probably higher than those of the hoplites, and their losses greater (Strauss 1986: 179–82). (c) The change in the thetes' contribution to their community's wars from unorganized skirmishing in occasional land battles to long-term engagement in very large numbers in large-scale naval operations is massive: it again represents not simply a quantitative leap in frequency and numbers but a qualitative leap.[35]

Fifth, and finally, because of this qualitative leap and a number of other reasons it seems to me difficult to maintain, as van Wees does (1995: 161), that the Athenian thetes would not have been fully aware of how they were affected by their community's new policies and how their new military contribution affected their community. As pointed out above, in the decades after the Persian Wars their community underwent a deep and comprehensive transformation; thousands of Athenians moved from the Attic hinterland to Athens and the Piraeus, where they found unprecedented opportunities of long-term employment. These citizens now lived and worked close to the political center; they were concentrated in one area and offered ideal targets for political agitation. Athenian politics were no secret affair; what was discussed in the assembly and *boulē* promptly became public knowledge (a fact duly noted by a critic of democracy in Hdt. 3.82.2; see Raaflaub 1989b: 42–43 and n. 25). Even if the thetes were not yet speaking and voting participants in these meetings, they were aware of and affected by such discussions. They could form their opinion, develop a collective will, and let it be known to those in power.

Still, van Wees is probably right in emphasizing that military change by itself usually did not suffice to bring about political change. I differ from him in proposing that the military changes the Athenians experienced in the post–Persian War period were of a very unusual scope in that they prompted much larger numbers of lower-class citizens than ever before to be involved much more regularly, even constantly, in operating a part of the polis's military force that was not secondary (and by a large margin) to the hoplite army but quickly reached equality with it and assumed vital importance to the community. This brings me back to the main course of my argument.

Popular Will and Political Rivalry

After a half-century of tyranny, during which the free play of forces in politics was suspended, and an even longer period, during which wars were sporadic and often private or semipublic actions rather than full-blown polis wars (Frost 1984), at the end of the sixth century the political and military spheres were reorganized and revived. Athens was in ferment. Great changes were happening in every aspect of communal organization and life, and the polis's outlook, position in the Greek world, and foreign policy were shifting rapidly as well (Anderson 2003). The demos acted decisively in averting new tyranny or narrow oligarchy and foreign domination (Ober, chapter 4 above). Determined action in foreign policy (Cartledge, chapter 6 below) and decisive military victories followed soon. At Marathon and Plataea, all hoplites were involved; at Salamis every able-bodied Athenian manned the ships; subsequently, in the actions of the Delian League, year after year thousands of thetes served on the Athenian fleet. In other words, within fifty years after the fall of tyranny demotic revolt, political reform, a series of national emergencies that necessitated the involvement of all citizens in efforts to save their country, and the new role and power of Athens in international politics must have changed the political consciousness of all citizens, including especially the thetes. Under these new conditions, the traditional monopolization of the political sphere by elite and hoplites, cemented in Solon's timocracy and Cleisthenes' reforms, clashed with powerful new realities.

But there was more. The massive shipbuilding and maintenance program, the switch to naval policies, and related comprehensive economic changes not only affected the Athenians themselves in numerous ways; they also caused a massive influx of foreigners into Attica. We saw above how this in turn prompted the Athenians to define the status of the metics and by contrast to become more consciously aware of their status as citizens and the privileges connected with it. This is most conspicuous in the citizenship law of 450 and a "purging" of citizen lists a few years later (Philochorus, *FGrHist* 328 F119; Plut. *Pericles* 37.4; Stadter 1989: 336–39), but the mental processes and political discussions leading up to these adaptations probably began much earlier. At any rate, there was no lack of strong reasons that could have prompted the lower-class citizens in the 470s and 460s to foster and voice political ambitions.

What probably assisted them in achieving these ambitions was the traditional rivalry among elite leaders—a factor strongly emphasized by Eder (1998). Herodotus says of Cleisthenes that he prevailed over Isagoras after joining the demos to his *hetaireia* ("club of supporters," 5.66.2, 69.2; see Cartledge, chapter 6 below). He did this by proposing substantial changes that met their needs and expectations. Josiah Ober (chapter 4 above) acknowledges Cleisthenes' genius for perceiving a ground swell of public opinion and transforming it into political program and action. This, I suggest, is precisely what Ephialtes and his friends did: involved in a power struggle with an older generation of politicians led by Cimon, they exploited two areas of popular dissatisfaction. Presenting themselves as "hawks" and promising to secure Athenian primacy in Greece, they pounced on Cimon's "dovish" policy toward Sparta. Attacking the "aristocratic regime of the Areopagus" as corrupt and passé, they promoted a major change in the structure of domestic politics and supported trends among the people that aimed at fuller participation of all citizens. In 508/7, those affected were the hoplite-farmers; now they comprised the *nautai*-thetes as well.

Again, we do not know why "the people" (and what parts of the people) supported the "reformers," and what the latter's primary intentions were: leadership for themselves, a change in foreign policy (because it was seen as necessary or opened up new opportunities, not least for themselves), or a change in institutions and the structure of politics (for the same two reasons). All may have contributed, and for the first two the last was indispensable. The question of what role the democratic reform played in the larger picture of changes enacted in 462 is debated. Yet, clearly, the democracy was neither the accidental result of measures that primarily aimed at different goals nor the intended result of efforts that were directed entirely at this goal (Raaflaub 1995: 44–46 with bibliog.). More specifically, I am not convinced by Eder's (1998) effort to explain the reforms achieved in 462, like all the earlier ones, almost exclusively as the result of rivalries among aristocrats who, in fighting for primacy, prompted changes over which they (like the sorcerer's apprentice over his ghosts) eventually lost control. At least in the stark emphasis placed on it by Eder, this thesis seems to me as one-sided as the tendency, visible in Wallace's and Ober's chapters in this volume, to attribute most of the initiative to the demos and to minimize the role of elite leaders, who, in this view, largely followed the demos's lead. Rather, I suggest, both the leaders' and the demos's contributions were necessary: as happened in the early and late sixth century, decisive political change was possible only as the result of a specific constellation in which opportunity, popular will, and the political ambition, experience, skills, and sensitivity of a leader (or leaders) produced a new system and new realities. Still, as in the cases of earlier political reforms that also consciously transcended familiar patterns (Meier 1995), the long-term consequences of the changes of 462–450 exceeded the anticipations and intentions of all involved.

RECONSTRUCTION

We are now ready to reconstruct the events of 462–50. In the aftermath of the Persian Wars, the Athenian fleet assumed a new role. While Athens developed rapidly from *hēgemōn* in the newly formed Delian League to imperial power, ruling over a far-flung thalassocracy, the fleet executed its policies and became the principal carrier of the city's security, power, and prosperity. This development, unprecedented in Greek history and beyond anybody's capacity of anticipation, swept the Athenian lower classes into a completely new position of communal importance and prominence: providing a large part of the crews rowing this fleet, they contributed decisively to their city's success, and they did so not once or twice but regularly, permanently. Militarily, therefore, the thetes achieved parity with the hoplites. The economic changes connected with empire and naval policies prompted many thousands of lower-class citizens, who had previously been marginalized at the lower end of Attica's farming population, to move to the metropolitan area. Their outlook changed, they were much closer to the political sphere where decisions about communal policies were made, and they were directly involved in executing these decisions. If I am right that their active political participation had hitherto been limited, their political status inferior to that of the hoplite-farmers, they now had every reason to demand a change, and it is plausible to assume that by the mid-460s, when this process had been going on for more than a decade, they expressed this demand vigorously. Moreover, the empire had created entirely new financial possibilities that could not but influence political decisions.

By the mid-460s, Cimon's pro-Spartan policies had lost some of their popularity. Many Athenians, led by a group of ambitious younger politicians, no longer accepted that Athens, head of a large naval alliance, commanding vast resources, and master of the seas, should yield first place in Greece to Sparta, Hellas's traditional leader. They launched a series of political attacks and criminal prosecutions against members of the venerable and influential Areopagus council and against Cimon himself. They listened to the people's opinions and demands. Probably considering institutional changes both necessary as adjustments to new conditions and desirable to create new opportunities for themselves, they helped fuel debates about political innovations that would meet such demands. In these debates, *dēmokratia,* "power in the hands of the people," coined recently or conceivably even for this very purpose, provided a succinct catchword. Aeschylus's *Suppliants* suggests as one of the main arguments in its favor that in a polis facing frequent decisions about war all citizens who were going to fight those wars—that is, under the new conditions of naval warfare: *pasa polis* (the entire city or citizen body)—should participate in such decisions. Those favoring *dēmokratia* certainly took *dēmos* here in its comprehensive, inclusive meaning of "all the people," while their opponents perhaps exploited the word's exclusive meaning ("non-elite") to give it a more radical interpretation ("lower classes, rabble") and to denounce the proposed new system as a sellout to the masses. It is thus possible that the word assumed at this very time the contrasting and ideologically loaded interpretations that were typical of the later fifth century (Donlan 1970).

An opportunity arose when Cimon persuaded the Athenians, apparently against heavy opposition, to assist Sparta with a large hoplite contingent in its fight against a helot revolt. While he was gone, Ephialtes proposed, and the assembly passed, a reform bill that, probably among other items, deprived the Areopagus of its responsibility to control and supervise officeholders and thus of its direct collective influence on Athenian policies. This proved the end of the Areopagus's political power. The competences involved were transferred to those institutions that represented the entire demos: assembly, council of 500, and law courts. These institutions gained in power and authority and were now in a position to assume control over all phases of the political process, a crucial characteristic of fully developed democracy. In addition, over time the Athenians created a large number of administrative offices with limited responsibility that were held collectively by groups of citizens (Hansen 1980; 1999: chap. 9). Through all these institutions the people exerted their rule.

If the thetes had so far not been entitled to participate actively even in the assembly (that is, if they were not expected to speak or perhaps even to vote [see below]), such long-standing disabilities, based not on law but convention, were now eliminated, informally or even formally (if my suggestion above concerning timocratic reform is valid). With few exceptions, some of which applied to other citizen classes as well, the thetes were now recognized as fully entitled, active citizens. Possibly, at this time, too, fixed assessments were introduced for the Solonian census classes of *zeugitai* and *hippeis,* and a new, even higher census class (the *pentakosiomedimnoi*) was introduced for those who were to hold important financial offices.

Administrative adjustments to the operation of the council and courts may have been instituted around the same time. The fact that the composition of the fully empowered demos changed, or at least that the political involvement expected of the lower classes increased greatly, is confirmed by the introduction, within a few years, of pay for some public functions (above all, participation in the large juries for the law courts and perhaps membership in the council) and by the increased use of the lot in assigning offices and functions (Headlam 1933; Staveley 1972: index s.v. "sortition"). Restrictions on eligibility to the archonship were lowered. Eventually, probably in reaction to the great increase in the number of full citizens as well as the massive influx of metics and problems caused by their frequent intermarriage with citizens (Boegehold 1994), membership in the ruling citizen body was restricted by introducing a narrower definition of citizenship. The institutional prerequisites needed to realize "rule by the people" were now in place. Their full impact became visible only in the decades after 450, when the new realities had sunk in and both demos and politicians had "learned their new roles" (Raaflaub 2004: 208–21).

Reactions to the reforms of 462 were intense on all sides, inflamed even more by Sparta's humiliating dismissal of the Athenian hoplite corps. Cimon tried to undo the reforms but failed and was ostracized. A murderer's dagger eliminated Ephialtes. The assembly decided on a radical turn in foreign policy: the long-standing alliance with Sparta was cancelled, a new one concluded with poleis opposed to Sparta. A deep rift split the community; violence, hatred, and fear reigned; members of the elite were suspected of conspiracy and plans to bring in Sparta to reverse recent developments; *stasis* was a real threat. The losers obviously saw in Ephialtes' reforms not a change necessary for the common good but the partisan victory of only one part of the citizen body. They felt their own vital interests violated to such an extent that they saw no choice but to resist with all means. In the 450s, however, the Athenians undertook extraordinary efforts to expand the empire further, fighting against the Persians and the Spartan alliance at the same time. Such shared focus on the outside, combined with a major crisis in the empire (Rhodes 1992: 54–61), eventually helped overcome the domestic rift.

All this confirms that the reforms of 462–450 were momentous and perceived as such. They fully realized democracy for the first time in the Greek world. To extend full political participation to all citizens, without regard to descent, wealth, landed property, and other criteria that normally determined political rights, and to endow these citizens with full control over the entire political process, was an unprecedented step into uncharted territory. It could be initiated only in Athens, made possible by the unique circumstances that prevailed there in the generation after the Persian Wars. Athenian democracy was therefore unique; the Athenian model of democracy cannot be generalized. Since it was so closely connected with Athens' naval policies, empire, and wealth, democracies in other Greek poleis can have corresponded only partly to this model, as is amply confirmed by Aristotle's distinction between various types of democracy (Robinson 1997: 35–44; forthcoming; O'Neil 1995: 32–55). In particular, the role, engagement, and self-consciousness of the demos could not reach the level typical of Athens if the demos was not directly responsible for the power and prosperity of the community, and the character of elite leadership must have differed significantly if the entire sphere of foreign policy was as insignificant as it was to most poleis in the fifth century (Ruschenbusch 1978: 68–71).

If, then, the reforms of 462 were so important, why are they recorded so poorly and late in ancient historiography? Several answers are possible. That laws were passed that defined the new powers and procedures seems certain, even if few traces of them survive. At least by the late fifth century, some laws of Ephialtes were still preserved (T3g), although we do not know what exactly they contained; the removal of these documents from the Areopagus probably caused their destruction. Like Cleisthenes, Ephialtes had a brief and somewhat obscure career, was not the subject of one of Plutarch's *Lives,* and did not leave writings of his own or a large law code. Unlike Cleisthenes, he did not reorganize the entire political and much of the social structure of the polis. Neither in Solon's nor in Cleisthenes' case are any laws concerning political institutions preserved. What we know about the changes Cleisthenes introduced to the functions of the new council, assembly or law courts is no less vague than in Ephialtes' case (see also Anderson 2006). Even so, in 411 it did not seem hopeless to recover the "ancestral laws" and constitution enacted by Cleisthenes that supposedly was "not democratic but similar to that of Solon," but this may be an ideological rather than a realistic claim (*Ath. Pol.* 29.3; Rhodes 1981: 375–77). Oral traditions focused on action, drama, and anecdotes, not on constitutional details (Raaflaub 1988a: esp. 211–14). Herodotus ended his *Histories* long before 462—and what he says about the events of 508/7 does not explain at all why it might be justified to say that Cleisthenes together with the tribes or through the tribes "established democracy for the Athenians" (6.131.1). Thucydides, our main surviving source for this period, was interested in the buildup of power and empire, not in domestic affairs and constitutional developments. Finally, the overpowering personality and career of Pericles may soon have overshadowed the achievement of Ephialtes (as is the case in Plutarch's *Pericles*)—and there could hardly be more uncertainty about domestic policies and institutional changes even during his time. The scarcity and lateness of the evidence, therefore, should not encourage us to belittle the significance of the reforms enacted between 462 and 450.

COMPARISON: EARLIER BREAKTHROUGHS

I have argued that it was only by the mid-fifth century that all Athenian citizens were fully empowered politically and that the assembly (assisted by the other institutions representing the entire demos) was placed in charge not only of making final decisions but of devising and shaping policies and controlling the entire political process. In order to buttress this conclusion, we now need to examine the political role of citizens and assembly before 462. In keeping with this volume's intention to emphasize controversial aspects and facilitate discussion, I shall present forcefully especially the arguments that seem to me to counter some of Wallace's and Ober's views on these issues.

Solon

In his poems, Solon claims that he established equality before the law for low and high (*kakos, agathos*) and "straight justice for each man" (36.18–20 W).[36] He did not take away any honor (*timē*) from the demos, but the extent of the esteem or privilege (*geras*) he gave the demos was limited to what he considered "sufficient" (*hoson aparkei:* 5.1–2 W). He intended the elite, though checked in their tendency to abuse power and seek unjust gain

(4.5–14, 4c, 5.3–4 W), to remain in a position of political leadership and the demos to follow their lead, "neither oppressed nor let loose too much," for, as he puts it, "excess breeds insolence, when great prosperity comes to men who are not sound of mind" (6 W).

These and other statements leave no doubt that Solon did not consider the demos fit to rule and thus did not think of placing the demos in a position of power or control. Accordingly, one important purpose of his institutional innovations, as Aristotle (*Ath. Pol.* 5–12) and Plutarch (*Life of Solon*) describe them, was to establish balance and protection: to install checks on the elite's power in order to prevent the recurrence of earlier abuses, and to protect the demos from such abuses. Measures serving this purpose included a ban on loans against personal security, which was tantamount to abolishing debt bondage and guaranteeing the citizen's personal freedom (Raaflaub 2004: 45–53), the enhancement of equality before the law by comprehensive legislation, the possibility of appealing to the people (heliaia), and a law that allowed any citizen (*ho boulomenos*) to seek redress on behalf of another who had been wronged ("Popularklage"). Innovations that affected the citizens' political awareness, sense of responsibility, and involvement include the last two just mentioned, the creation of a new "council of 400" (if authentic) and the *stasis* law (if authentic) that compelled every citizen to take sides in cases of civic conflict. In addition, as we saw earlier, in his "timocratic system" Solon linked the citizens' political and military capacities.[37]

What about the demos's participation in politics? If Solon indeed created a new council, independent of the Areopagus, its members were probably elected and served for a limited time only; it presumably prepared the agenda and recommendations for the assembly. Most likely, as happened in Sparta (Raaflaub and Wallace, chapter 2 above), Solon would also have enacted a minimal set of regulations for the assembly, including schedule, agenda, and powers. According to the timocratic scheme reported in *Ath. Pol.* 7.3–4, the thetes were entitled to attend the assembly but barred from office. Although this has been accepted by most scholars, we have seen above that the questions raised in recent scholarship about the authenticity of many details of the Solonian timocracy shed doubts on this particular regulation as well. At any rate, Solon's distinctly aristocratic outlook makes it seem doubtful indeed that he would have invested much political capital in the lower classes (see also below).

Aristotle believed that Solon's reforms represented the beginning of democracy (*Ath. Pol.* 41.2; cf. 22.1); accordingly, he lists three measures he considers "most democratic" or "friendly to the demos" (*dēmotikōtata*): the ban of loans on personal security and, probably because of the entitlement of *ho boulomenos*, the "Popularklage" and the law courts: "for when the people are masters of the vote they are masters of the state" (9.1; cf. Arist. *Pol.* 1274a). This statement clearly reflects fourth-century views (Rhodes 1981:

159; Hansen 1989d). Other, even later sources share Aristotle's assessment. Tending to accept most of these late statements, although they were written by authors who had no real understanding of how much even conditions in the late fifth and fourth centuries differed from those in the early sixth, some modern scholars (including Wallace, chapter 3 in this volume) follow Aristotle's lead. I prefer to trust Solon's own words, which tell a different story. However, to conclude that Solon, and the majority of Athenians who approved of his reforms, did not consider the lower classes worthy of equal political participation does not imply, as Wallace suggests, that non-elite Athenians must then have been universally "downtrodden" and contemptible, by their own judgment or that of others—although, if the views attested in the *Odyssey* (see above) were still shared among the elite, to some of them the nonfarming day laborers among the lower classes may have been. It only means that by tradition and prevailing sentiment full political participation was tied to certain economic, social, and military capacities and status expectations. As Rome's example demonstrates, it might take centuries for such expectations to change and eventually disappear.

I have no doubt that, overall, Solon's reforms were crucial in enhancing popular involvement and responsibility and in making the political process more transparent, public, and regulated (Raaflaub 1996c: 1067–71). Yet the political system Solon instituted was far from *dēmokratia* in its fifth-century meaning. Perhaps a generation earlier, the Spartan poet Tyrtaeus described the assembly's power to make decisions with the formula "to the mass of the demos belong victory and power (*kratos*)"—although the Spartan assembly lacked initiative, and its vote could be rejected by the council (4.9 W; Plut. *Lyc.* 6.8; Raaflaub and Wallace, chapter 2 in this volume). The Spartan demos, of course, was composed only of landowners serving in the hoplite army. Solon's Athens did not share Sparta's militaristic ethos, but there too, I suggest, those who really counted in the assembly were the hoplite-farmers. After all, Solon's ideal (4.30–39 W), like that of Tyrtaeus's Sparta (4 W), was *eunomia,* the traditional, aristocratic "good order." And when he describes his efforts to improve equality of law, he uses the term *homoiōs,* not *isōs: homoiotēs* (relative equality, similarity) was the Spartan ideal, while democratic equality later was characterized by *isotēs,* absolute equality (Cartledge 1996a).[38]

Cleisthenes

Several decades of tyranny weakened the elite's social and economic power, curtailed their political dominance and traditional rivalries, helped the community prosper, and gave the citizens a new communal focus, although they were kept inactive politically and militarily. Overall, this period was important in unifying the polis and creating the potential for independent communal action.[39] Hence, after the fall of tyranny, the resumption of factional strife between groups of aristocratic families was anything but popular among most Athenians. Cleisthenes' reform proposals were welcomed precisely because they promised to reduce the potential for such detrimental rivalries by advancing the political integration of polis and citizen body, increasing equality, and fostering more participation by more citizens.

The events of 508/7 are reported and discussed in detail by Ober (1993, 1998b, and chapter 4 in this volume).[40] The ancient authorities believed that Cleisthenes had been the founder of democracy—or at least the second founder, after Solon (Hdt. 6.131.1; *Ath. Pol.* 20.4, 22.1), although doubts were possible (T5c; *Ath. Pol.* 29.3). Was he really? And in what ways? I agree with large parts of Ober's analysis but differ on some important aspects. I have space here only to summarize my arguments briefly (for further details, see Raaflaub 1995; 1998b: 39–44, 91–95).

Lack of Partisanship. Cleisthenes' proposals must have been attractive because they did not pursue partisan purposes but offered all or most Athenians substantial individual and collective advantages. The citizens' favorable disposition was enhanced decisively when Isagoras resorted to a time-honored device in aristocratic power struggles and enlisted the support of an outside ally. Thus Cleisthenes became the defender of Athenian unity and patriotism against Spartan intervention. Still, it is remarkable (and not explained sufficiently by the elimination of Isagoras and some of his followers) that, after the departure of the Spartans and Isagoras, we hear of no opposition against the implementation of the reforms nor of any later effort to repeal them. This must indicate that Cleisthenes' program met with broad support in the citizen body and the elite (Kinzl 1977: 202). All this differs strikingly from the reactions we observe in 462/1 (see above); it suggests that the reforms did not change the power balance in a way that the elite perceived as threatening. Hence what was especially offensive to many Athenians in 462/1 (the full political empowerment of the lowest citizen class, and the dominant political role of the assembly) can hardly have been intended or anticipated as the result of the earlier reforms.[41]

The Principle of Civic Equality. Cleisthenes' system undoubtedly contained strong elements of civic equality, visible especially in the central role assigned to the demes with their self-administration (often called grassroots democracy), in the ten new tribes, each designed to unite ("mix") different segments of the citizen body in common events (festivals) and shared service in the army and in the new "council of 500." The latter was based on an exceptionally dense quota of representation (Meier 1990: 73–78) that made it impossible to restrict membership to the elite. This system indeed was based on massively increased political participation by large segments of the demos on all levels, from deme to polis. It would thus make sense, although it cannot be proved, that the terminology of political equality (*isonomia, isēgoria*) was applied to this new system (Raaflaub 1996b: 143–45).

The Extent of Equality. We still need to ask how far such equality reached. Were all citizens entitled to participate equally? Ober sees the significance of the "Athenian revolution" of 508/7 "in a violent and more or less spontaneous uprising by large numbers of Athenian citizens," which in turn was the result "of a highly developed civic consciousness among the Athenian masses—a generalized ability to formulate a popular consensus and act upon it" (chapter 4 in this volume). No doubt, this was a momentous turning point in Athenian history: the demos acted with unexpected self-confidence, and its actions indeed prompted the creation of new realities. But crucial doubts remain.

a. The extant reports are largely based on oral traditions that had been transmitted over several generations. Inevitably, they are fraught with uncertainties and distortions. Moreover, ancient historians tended to "flesh out" the reports they received, to judge and interpret past events on the basis of the experiences of their own time, and to describe them in the language and terminology they were familiar with (Stahl 1987: pt. I; Thomas 1989). We should therefore be cautious in drawing conclusions that rely heavily and literally on every word in Herodotus's narrative (5.72.1–2).

b. More than a century earlier, a comparable event took place in Athens that is reported with striking similarity of detail and narrative pattern (esp. by Thuc. 1.126.3–12; cf. Hdt. 5.71; *Ath. Pol.* 1; Plut. *Sol.* 12.1–9): a spontaneous uprising by all Athenians, without a named leader, against a coup attempt undertaken by an aristocratic faction under Cylon's leadership and supported by foreign contingents sent in by the tyrant Theagenes of Megara on the basis of private obligations. True, there are important differences, too (emphasized by Ober)—especially the subsequent leading role of magistrates and the Alcmaeonid family in Cylon's case, as opposed to the enforced absence of Cleisthenes and his supporters, as well as the previous announcement and widespread endorsement of popular reform plans in Cleisthenes' case—but the similarities in the narrative should still discourage us from drawing far-reaching historical conclusions based on details.[42]

c. What exactly does *dēmos* mean in Cleisthenes' context? Even more than Meier (1990: 64–70) and Eder (1988: 465–75), who had already emphasized the significance of the popular revolt, Ober assumes that the uprising that in his view resulted in democracy was spontaneous, leaderless, and staged by the masses, including the lower classes. In fact, we simply do not know. Herodotus's text assigns an important role to the resistance of the council that Isagoras and Cleomenes wanted to dissolve. It is reasonable, therefore, to assume that council members acted as catalysts and leaders in the resistance movement.[43] Moreover, while elite families decades later boasted the merits of their ancestors (Thomas 1989), popular traditions in post–Persian War Athens emphasized the demos's collective achievement, starkly repressing the leaders' role in military victories. This may largely account for the specific way the story was remembered not only in Herodotus but also, for example, in Aristophanes' *Lysistrata*.[44]

d. The reform was comprehensively based on the new demes. In an overwhelmingly agrarian society with as yet little urbanization and no "urban masses," those who dominated the political will of the demes were the farmers, including many members of the elite. Presumably it was these farmers who were most interested in Cleisthenes' reform plans and particularly incensed by Cleomenes' and Isagoras's attempt to wipe them out. To them domestic peace and stability, a curb on violent and destructive rivalries among the leading families, the continuation of political developments begun under the tyrants, and a proposal greatly enhancing the role of the demes must have been most welcome.

e. Militarily, these same farmers formed Athens' hoplite army. As said earlier, the creation or reorganization of this army on a new social and organizational basis was another major component of the reform (van Effenterre 1970; Siewert 1982: pts. 3–4). In 506 and 490, the community relied entirely on the strength of this army to ward off serious external threats. The fleet was no factor (Wallinga 1993: esp. 140–48); militarily, the thetes, though perhaps not negligible (van Wees 1995 and see above), were clearly inferior in status. Why, then, would they have been counted as equals politically?

f. Quite likely, many thetes participated in the forceful uprising of the Athenian demos and helped expel Isagoras and his Spartan supporters. But this was a short, one-time effort.[45] I doubt whether it sufficed to change permanently the status of the thetes and the distribution of participatory power in the community; for the reforms were proposed at a time—before the demos's revolt of 508/7—when there was little reason to take note of the thetes, and while the reforms were being implemented the Athenian hoplites in 506 won their glorious triple victory over the Spartans, Thebans, and Chalcidians, commemorated splendidly on the Acropolis (Hdt. 5.74–78; ML 15A). For another generation—until the battle of Salamis—those who really mattered for the security and well-being of the community still were the hoplite-farmers. In my view, their formal political integration was one of the reform's chief purposes.

g. According to Ober, the manpower pool of the thetic class could not be
tapped militarily before they were politically involved and ready to
defend their country or before the hoplite-farmers in turn were ready to
entrust their salvation to these thetes. This, in my view, reflects abstract
thinking. The threat posed by Xerxes' invasion represented a communal
emergency of the highest degree. Once the assembly decided to entrust
the polis's survival to the fleet, every able-bodied man from highest aristocrat to lowest thete (and probably metic as well as slave) was needed
and called upon to man this fleet. The victory of Salamis was the triumph
of this desperate mass-levy. Until that day, the Athenians hardly considered the "arming of the thetes" anything but an exceptional emergency
measure without long-term implications. Even the fleet's other use that
could be anticipated, against Aegina, need not have required more than
an occasional appeal to thetic volunteers. The real consequences of the
Persian victories, however, must have transcended everybody's expectations. From then on, Athens' policies, opportunities, and successes rode
on its fleet and thus on the thetes, and this development could neither
be anticipated nor reversed, whatever people had thought previously—
and perhaps continued to think—about their lower-class fellow citizens.

Hence, although the late-sixth-century reforms greatly enhanced political equality and encouraged and institutionalized active participation by
large segments of the citizen body, we should not take it for granted that
such equality extended fully to all citizens. With few exceptions (such as the
provisions in Solon's constitution), political participation probably was not
regulated by law; rather, it was determined by social status and prestige. As
mentioned above, Rhodes suggests that customary restrictions still applied
in Solon's time and beyond. Thus in Cleisthenes' time it was perhaps still
considered normal that only those were entitled to participate actively in
politics (by holding office and speaking in council and assembly, if not by
voting) who could boast sufficient social prestige—which was determined
by (at least) hoplite status based on landed property. The thetes were not
excluded but considered "lesser citizens"; they were not expected to speak,
perhaps not even to vote; they expressed their sentiments only collectively
by heckling and shouting.

This view is supported by the fact that even decades later democracy
could be characterized as a system in which the "fierce army" prevails (T1),
reflecting a time when the assembly naturally consisted of the men who regularly served in the army.[46] Later, this was true of all citizens, and *stratos* in
the late fifth century often included the navy, just as *stratiōtēs* by then could
designate soldier as well as sailor (Strauss 1996), but earlier this was hardly
the case. Again, we do not know about Cleisthenes' time, but I am not alone
in thinking it possible that the military factor then still was decisive in

excluding the thetes from active political participation (Ostwald 1986: 23; Whitehead 1986: 23 n. 78). Moreover, why would Aeschylus in his *Suppliants* of 463 have placed such heavy emphasis on the participation of all citizens in crucial communal decisions if they had been involved in such decisions all along?

The Institutions. How powerful were the institutions in which the citizens entitled to do so participated on equal terms? The significance and political role of both assembly and council were probably enhanced, but how much? Clearly, the reformers spent much thought on the composition of the new council—which helps explain the overall purpose of the reform. But, apart from its probouleutic function, we know next to nothing about its powers and how they affected those of assembly and Areopagus. Despite the lack of evidence, some scholars (Larsen 1966: 13–21; Woodhead 1967: 135–40) assume that this council played a powerful role from the beginning; others disagree (Rhodes 1972: 209–10). It is perhaps best to assume (with Ostwald 1986: 19, 26–27; Meier 1990: 71, 77) that council and assembly were intended to assume the function of an institutionalized check or counterweight, balancing the power of the archons and the Areopagus council, which represented aristocratic leadership and authority and, most importantly, continued to scrutinize and supervise the holders of public office. Nor should we overstress the notion of "popular sovereignty" (Fornara and Samons 1991: 52–56): the assembled demos could have the final decision in all important matters without being fully in charge of politics. Cartledge (chapter 6 below) rightly stresses Athens' increasingly active role in foreign policy after 508/7. This must somehow be connected with the new political system. Still, I find a world of difference between this system and the way the demos in the assembly after the reforms of 462 controlled the entire political process, from setting policies and supervising their execution to controlling the magistrates. Overall, it seems all too obvious that at the end of the sixth century assembly, council, and law courts were far from assuming the dominant role characteristic of them later in the fifth century.

From an institutional perspective, then, I conclude that the Cleisthenic system was not democratic in the full sense of the word, because (a) it did not take *dēmos* in its comprehensive meaning, and (b) it did not assign to the institutions of the demos a sufficiently powerful role to enable them to exert full control over the government. Even if it were possible to demonstrate that I am wrong on the first aspect (a), which may well be the case, the second aspect (b) suffices to support my point. None of this, however, reduces the historical significance of this system—nor that of the "Athenian revolution of 508/7." The structural reforms enacted in those years in the social and political realms and the long-term changes they set in motion, not least in political consciousness, were of truly monumental importance.

By decisively advancing the integration and unity of the polis, the reforms strengthened solidarity among the citizens—a crucial precondition for success in war, especially against the Persians.[47] By enhancing equality and participation, they made it possible for large numbers of non-elite Athenians to grow into their new political responsibility and gain self-confidence—thus paving the way for later and even more momentous developments. By changing the conditions for political competition and decision-making, they eventually caused the focus of politics to shift de facto to the assembly. As a result, over time it became obvious that a new constitutional alternative had emerged, in which neither one man nor the elite but the demos or *stratos* held power. Under the unique conditions prevailing in Athens after the Persian Wars, this alternative was finally developed to a logical but unprecedented, previously unthinkable, and profoundly controversial extreme, in which the demos, fully including all citizens, controlled government and politics: here lies the significance of the breakthrough of *dēmokratia* in the reforms of 462–50.[48]

NOTES

1. The former is the perspective of the *Constitution of the Athenians* (*Athēnaiōn Politeia,*henceforth cited, without author, as *Ath. Pol.*), produced in the late fourth century in Aristotle's school: 9.1, 22.1, 23.1, 27.1. For introduction and commentary, and on authorship, see Rhodes 1981; Chambers 1990; Whitehead 1993; on the composition and structure, Keaney 1992; Wallace 1999. Flaig (2004: 38) characterizes the "Cleisthenic" order as "half-democratic" and, referring to Martin 1974, emphasizes that according to criteria of political science democracy was realized only in 462/1.

2. Translations used (often modified): Barker 1946; Warner 1954; Scott-Kilvert 1960; Vellacott 1961; Moore 1975; Rhodes 1984.

3. This pamphlet is preserved among Xenophon's works and thus cited as Ps.-Xen. *Ath. Pol.*, to be distinguished from the work with the same title mentioned in note 1.

4. Hansen 1986; 1991: 69–71. Breuil (1995: 81) observes rightly that, in analogy to other aristocratic names, Demokrates designates one who has power either through the people or over the people (cf. next note). Leppin (1999: 24) concludes that the name therefore does not need to be connected with democracy. Though theoretically correct, I consider this highly implausible. The two men in question are the first attested with this name; they belonged to prominent Athenian families and received this name when the issue of *dēmokratia* was hotly debated in Athens: reason enough to choose this name either as an expression of support for the current populist agenda or (in my view less probably) as a sign of defiance, signalling determination to resist it. It is notoriously difficult to pin down the exact meaning of compound names. In this case, I think, in expressing a sentiment or tendency, the associations triggered by the politically loaded compound would have prevailed over the literal meaning of the parts.

5. Debrunner (1947: 13; cf. Breuil 1995: 81; Eder 1998: 113) interprets *dēmokratia* as "to be master over the people," "to be in power with the help of the people." Leppin (1999: 24) accordingly takes *dēmou kratousa cheir* to mean the "hand that rules over the people." In *Suppliants*, this interpretation of line 604 is ruled out by line 699, where the meaning is unmistakable; even in the context of line 604 Leppin's interpretation makes no sense.

6. On the Areopagus in *Ath. Pol.*, see Wallace 1989: 77–93; Ostwald 1993; Saïd 1993; Ryan 1994a.

7. Ryan (2002) argues plausibly that this change should be dated to 462, not 457.

8. E.g., Badian 1993: 92–96, 100–101; Fornara and Samons 1991: 133–35; and the commentaries on individual authors.

9. Aeschylus stresses accountability implicitly in *Persians* 213–14 (performed in 472) as characteristic of the free Greek polis, in contrast to tyranny or the absolute Persian monarchy. Decision by all citizens is first emphasized in *Suppliants*.

10. Interestingly, issues concerning resident aliens or metics receive attention in this play as well: Bakewell 1997. Such concerns must have helped trigger legislation defining the metics' status (Whitehead 1977) and eventually the citizenship law of 451/0 (below).

11. See Rhodes 1981; Chambers 1990 (both at *Ath. Pol.* 25–27); Ostwald 1986: 28–83; Meier 1987; Jones 1987; Cawkwell 1988; Wallace 1989: chaps. 3–4; Ober 1989: 71–81; Hall 1990; Fornara and Samons 1991: 58–75; Rhodes 1992: 67–77; Bloedow 1992; Davies 1993: chap. 4; Bleicken 1994: 44–46.

12. Wallace (chapter 3 above at note 17) contests this view, following Isocrates and Aristotle in attributing the scrutiny of officeholders by the demos already to Solon's reforms.

13. Emphasized as typical of democracy by Hdt. 3.80.6; see Headlam 1933; P. J. Rhodes, *DNP* 7 (1999) 443 with sources and bibliog. No evidence exists for the *boulē*; Rhodes (1972: 2–3) thinks that membership was limited to the three highest census classes, but see Hansen 1999: 248–49.

14. Elsewhere (Raaflaub 2006, summarized briefly below) I suggest that the elaborated "timocratic constitution" attributed to Solon (in *Ath. Pol.* 7.3–4; Plut. *Sol.* 18.1–2) might for several reasons be dated to this very period. In this view, Solon would have linked political functions to three census classes defined only by military capacity (for the latter, see de Ste. Croix 2004: chap. 1). My argument in the present chapter does not depend on this hypothetical suggestion.

15. Booty: Jackson 1969; Kallet-Marx 1993a: 52–53. Tribute and other revenues: Meritt et al. 1950; Meiggs 1972: 234–54; Schmitz 1988: 8–78; Kallet-Marx 1993a; Kallet 1998, 2001; Samons 2000.

16. Sparta (discussed briefly in chapter 2 above) and Rome (Lintott 1999: esp. chaps. 5 and 11) offer good examples.

17. On the origins of the counting of votes, see Larsen 1949; Staveley 1972: chap. 1.

18. This depends on the date of the "Old Oligarch's" pamphlet. Suggestions range from the late 440s to about 415; for a thorough discussion, see M. Treu, *RE* 9A.2 (1967) 1928–82; briefly, Moore 1975: 20, 60. We simply do not know how representative this author's thinking was at the time. But see Hdt. 5.78 on the connec-

tion between freedom and democracy (roughly contemporaneous with the "Old Oligarch"), and the anecdote in Plut. *Them.* 19.4 about the change in the orientation of the Pnyx under the "Thirty."

19. See, for example, *Ath. Pol.* 22.3, 24, 27.1; Arist. *Pol.* 1274a12–15, 1304a21–22, and the generalization in 1297b16–28; cf. 1289b34–41; Plut. *Arist.* 22.1; *Them.* 19.4. In his discussion of this issue, van Wees (1995: 153–56) points out that Aristotle himself does not consider this connection necessary in every case (*Pol.* 1327b4–9) and is, for ideological reasons, strongly opposed to the lower classes' share in power.

20. It seems symptomatic that we know very little about the Roman navies of the republican period and that bibliography is hard to find; see, for instance, *DNP* 4 (1998) 570.

21. Van Wees (1999) contests the connection between the Rhetra, Tyrtaeus, and *eunomia;* for a critique of his argument, see Meier 2002 (with van Wees's response [2002]); Link 2003; Raaflaub 2006: 394–98.

22. The main line of my argument will continue in the section entitled "Popular Will and Political Rivalry." I thank the anonymous readers for encouraging me to elaborate the section that follows here.

23. Suffice it to say here that the existence of a very large thetic class, many of whom were economically quite affluent and most of whom were capable of contributing usefully or even decisively to the polis's security, would have created a different political dynamic than we see it in the late sixth and early fifth centuries. Moreover, part of Cleisthenes' structural reorganization of the polis concerned the hoplite army, including its mobilization and the registration of hoplites in the demes (van Effenterre 1976; Siewert 1982). Such measures, enacted in a time of continuous outside pressure (Badian 2000), made sense only if they encompassed the polis's entire hoplite force. See van Wees 2006 for a defense of his views.

24. The economic prosperity and imperial control that were, in my view, required for the introduction of high assessment levels fit only the period between c. 470 and 432. It seems logical to attach such an innovation to a well-attested major reform effort. De Ste. Croix (2004: 27) argues plausibly that the 400 in 411/10 ignored any fixed assessment; hence they certainly did not introduce one. A terminus ante quem is perhaps provided by Hdt. 2.177.2, a reference to an Athenian law requiring the citizens to declare their income annually; see Ruschenbusch 1966b: no. 78a and comm. on p. 100.

25. The terminus ante is a dedication on the Acropolis by the *hippeis: IG* I^3 511; Raubitschek 1949: 135–135b; de Ste. Croix 2004: 15. Frieze: Jenkins 1994.

26. On the emphasis Aeschylus places in the *Persians* on the role of hoplites at Salamis, see Fornara 1966; van Wees 1995: 158–59; see above on violent reactions to Ephialtes' reforms.

27. This would help explain the violence of such opposition. Opening the archonship to the zeugites (T3d) might be seen, then, as another concession to the *zeugitai,* and all the more feasible at the point when a high census was imposed on them. See Raaflaub 2006: 419 on reasons that may have mitigated loss of zeugite status.

28. Van Wees 1995: 165–70; cf. van Wees 1994, 1997, and 2004: chap.11; cf. Raaflaub 1997c, 2005a, and Raaflaub and Wallace, chapter 2 in this volume.

29. Raaflaub 1997c; 1999: 132–34; 2005a; *contra:* Cartledge 2001a.

30. As they are reflected in Thucydides and Xenophon. See, for example, Anderson 1970; Roisman 1993.

31. Van Wees 1995: 169 with n. 41. Elite warriors, represented on vases, rode to the battlefield, accompanied by mounted squires; what matters is that they left their horses behind, as the Homeric heroes did their chariots, and fought on foot like every other hoplite. The examples of single combat, in which the Argive Eurybates and the Athenian Sophanes excelled, took place in the context not of a hoplite battle but of an Athenian siege of Aegina (Hdt. 6.92.3; 9.75), and nothing is known of the actual conditions under which these duels were possible. Herodotus mentions prizes awarded for outstanding bravery even in hoplite battles: why should this not be compatible with phalanx fighting? The "mix of warriors and weapons" in representations of warriors on vases, mentioned in Krentz 2002: 29–30, needs to be analyzed in the broader context of artistic traditions and conventions influencing the painters' choices and images; the best, but only partial, discussion is Lissarrague 1990.

32. Examples include the *phulai* and *obai* mentioned in Sparta's "Great Rhetra"; the territorial organization of Attica, introduced by Cleisthenes in the late sixth century, that served military as well as political purposes (Siewert 1972); and the organization of tribes (*tribus*) by Servius Tullius in the mid-sixth century, as well as the introduction of the office of censor in the mid-fifth century in Rome (Cornell 1995: 173–79, 190–94; Lintott 1999: 115–20). The division of a citizen body into such local districts or census classes (such as those of Solon or the Roman centuriate system) reflects, I suggest, structures necessitated by a community's military organization rather than, in a premonetary period, the collection of taxes. See generally Davies 1996. On the Athenian hoplite *katalogos*, see Andrewes 1981.

33. Esp. the invasions of Megara and Boeotia during the Peloponnesian War (van Wees 1995: 163). The battle of Delion (mentioned above) is a special case because of the terrain, as is the success of the Aetolians over Athenian hoplites (Thuc. 3.97–98).

34. The forty-eight *naukrariae* (ship districts) mentioned in *Ath. Pol.* 8.3.

35. Van Wees (1995: 159–60) mentions the crucial role of trierarchs and marines (*epibatai*) and refers to Arist. *Pol.* 1327b9–11 and Hdt. 8.83.1. Aristotle's ideologically tainted statement that favors the marines over the rowers is countered decisively by Ps.-Xen. (*Ath. Pol.* 1.2, quoted above), who is decidedly not a friend of democracy. Herodotus's report that Themistocles addressed the *epibatai* before the battle of Salamis reveals not prejudice but practical necessities: the battle was about to begin (8.83.2), the rowers were already on board, the marines could board quickly, and this was the last "pep talk" the gist of which the marines would convey to the rowers; it was possible to address a few thousand marines but impossible to do so with tens of thousands of rowers. My student Kimberly M. Henoch has illuminated this in her senior thesis, *The History and Historiography of Ancient Battle Speeches* (2002).

36. For Solon, see, for example, Rhodes 1981 and Chambers 1990 on *Ath. Pol.* 5–12; Manfredini and Piccirilli 1977 on Plut. *Sol.;* Sealey 1976: chap. 5; Andrewes 1982a: 375–91; Manville 1990: chaps. 5–6; Welwei 1992: 161–206; Eder 1992; Murray 1993: chap. 11; Bleicken 1994: 18–27; Raaflaub 1996c; Wallace, chapter 3 in this volume.

37. For details and sources see Wallace, chapter 3 in this volume. Virtually none of these laws are preserved in their Solonian formulation, and their interpretation by later authors may or may not correspond to the lawgiver's intention (see below).

38. For detailed discussion of these issues, see Raaflaub 2006.

39. Berve 1967: 1.41–77, 2.539–63; and recently the commentaries by Rhodes 1981 and Chambers 1990 on Arist. *Ath. Pol.* 13–19; Asheri 1988 on Hdt. 1.59–64; Andrewes 1982b; Stahl 1987; Lewis 1988; Eder 1988, 1992; Shapiro 1989; Stein-Hölkeskamp 1989; Manville 1990: chap. 7; Welwei 1992: 206–65; Murray 1993: chap. 15; Lavelle 1993, 2005; McGlew 1993; Bleicken 1994: 27–35.

40. Hdt. 5.66, 69–73.1 (with comments by Asheri 1988); *Ath. Pol.* 20.1–4 (with Rhodes 1981 and Chambers 1990). For discussion, see, recently, Ostwald 1969: pt. 3; 1986: 15–28; 1988; Traill 1975, 1986; Sealey 1976: chap. 6; Whitehead 1986: chap. 1; Meier 1990: chap. 4; Manville 1990: chap. 7; Bleicken 1994: 35–41 (with bibliog., 447–53, 605–6); Anderson 2003, 2006.

41. This is true even if we assume that some of the most determined opponents had perished in the bloody suppression of Isagoras's coup; see also note 47 below. The interpretation proposed by Cartledge (chapter 6 below) for Herodotus's formulation *proshetairizetai ton dēmon* (5.66.2) is rightly based on the assumption that Herodotus reflects words and sentiments of his own time.

42. See now Flaig 2004: 38–45 on Cylon's revolt and its suppression, and on continuing Athenian efforts to eliminate its potential for communal disruption.

43. Meier 1990: 240–41 n. 67: "Here [i.e., among the councillors] were the natural leaders of a popular rebellion." Flaig (2004: 46–53) argues strongly against the view that the people's rebellion was spontaneous or revolutionary.

44. Cited by Ober, chapter 4, at note 18. For the refusal to recognize elite leaders, see, for example, the Persian War epigrams from the Athenian Agora (ML 26; Fornara 1983: no. 51), the Eion epigrams of 476/5, also displayed in the Agora (Plut. *Cim.* 7; Aeschin. 3.184–85), or the Miltiades anecdote reported by Plut. *Cim.* 8.1. See also Aeschin. 3.182–87.

45. See here the important observations of Flaig 2004: 56–57.

46. As discussed above, in Rome's centuriate assembly the same effect was achieved by assigning the majority of voting units to the horsemen and hoplites (Livy 1.43; Taylor 1966: 85–87).

47. Flaig (2004: esp. 56–61) explores why Athenian democracy celebrated the tyrannicide of 514 rather than the popular revolt and victory over Isagoras in 508/7 as its foundation myth. The latter, he concludes, represented *stasis* and the bloody suppression of a faction in a demotic revolt, the former civic and polis unity—and aristocratic initiative—in overcoming tyranny. The political integration of the defeated part of the Athenian aristocracy demanded precisely the tabooization of *stasis.* Consequently, remembrance of the siege of the Acropolis focused primarily on the expulsion of the Spartan invaders, which again emphasized the unity of the polis. Popular memory thus suppressed *stasis* while, typically, the historians pulled it out of oblivion. See now also Anderson 2006.

48. I am most grateful to Paul Cartledge, Bob Wallace, Mark Munn, and two anonymous referees for valuable criticism and suggestions.

Chapter 6

Democracy, Origins of

Contribution to a Debate

Paul Cartledge

polis andra didaskei
SIMONIDES*

"The study of the Athenian political order is today one of the most exciting and active areas of ancient Greek history." So wrote Josh Ober fifteen years ago, reviewing Raphael Sealey's typically revisionist and iconoclastic *Athenian Republic: Democracy or the Rule of Law?*[1] In 1994 Lisa Kallet (-Marx), reviewing a number of the many works prompted by the notional 2,500th anniversary of the reforms at Athens credited (or debited) to Cleisthenes, rightly predicted: "The renewed interest in the subject will not wither soon" (1994a: 335). A decade further on, following the flawed U.S. presidential election of 2000 and the no less flawed war against the Saddam Hussein regime in Iraq in 2003, the same could be repeated with even greater confidence. A frequent lament these days concerns the democracy we have lost (Barber 2002; Skocpol 2003; Keane 2003).

Of the many recent contributions to democracy debates ancient and modern surely one of the most intriguing is Brook Manville and Josh Ober's *A Company of Citizens*—subtitled immodestly but not immoderately *What the World's First Democracy Teaches Leaders about Creating Great Organizations* (Manville and Ober 2003b; see also 2003a). Two other recent and complementary projects catch the attention in this same context: the suitably millennial publication, in 2000, of the *Cambridge History of Greek and Roman Political Thought*, edited by Christopher Rowe and Malcolm Schofield, which naturally privileged ancient democracy's ideological and conceptual dimensions;[2] and the Copenhagen Polis Project, issuing from the Copenhagen Polis Centre (CPC), directed inimitably by Mogens Herman Hansen, which

---

* "The community is teacher of the man," meaning that it teaches a man to be a (full citizen) man: Simonides, quoted in Plut. *Mor.* 784b = elg. 15, p. 517 in Campbell 1991.

emphasizes rather the practical and empirical dimensions of Greek polis life, including the workings of ancient democracy.[3]

It is therefore within a much wider framework than just the political history of Athens that the issue of the origins of democracy in ancient Greece ought now to be contemplated. For a start, Greece should at least mean Hellas, the Greek world as a whole, not just Athens (so O'Neil 1995 and Robinson 1997; cf. Robinson ed. 2004). But obvious though this may be to specialists in ancient Greek history, it is not necessarily so to nonspecialist general readers or even to most historians of modern and contemporary democratic political thought, who begin with a ritual obeisance to the ancient Greece "from where we started" (in the phrase of Crick 2002, though his little book is a shining exception to the Athenocentricity rule). I am not of course wanting to deny that the Western political tradition, in so far as it is democratic, goes back to Athens.[4] What I am emphasizing rather is that the story of ancient Greek democracy is much broader than just a story about Athens. As Aristotle (*Politics* 1296a22–23) was careful to note, in his day most Greek cities enjoyed either a form of oligarchy or a form of democracy; he did not also say that most were a form of the former only, or that democracy was somehow an anomaly.[5]

That is the first of my three preliminary points. The second is that ancient Greek democracy was a total social phenomenon, a culture and not merely a political system (as we would understand that). *Politeia,* the word we sometimes translate "constitution," could also mean, and indeed originally did mean, "citizenship," a special status of active political belonging; and even when *politeia* had come to mean also the way a city's order of self-government was arranged, that arrangement could still be referred to without strain as a *bios* (life, way of life, livelihood) or *psukhē* (soul, spirit, mind; see generally Bordes 1982). I am not of course wishing, either, to deny that institutions are important—I agree on this entirely with Mogens Hansen (1989e). Where I differ from him is in not believing that they were all-important, or all-consumingly important. Theater, the public visual arts, and the battlefield—these are only the most obvious of the other arenas where Athenian democracy happened, but not in a narrowly governmental way.[6]

My third preliminary point is that all ancient democracies, including therefore that of Athens, differed radically from all modern ones in the following six, often basic, ways:[7]

a. Theirs were direct, ours are representative. Theirs did contain some representative—or better, representational—elements, but the exercise of power (*kratos*) through decision taking was open, transparent, face-to-face, direct.[8]

b. *Kratos,* the etymology of which is connected with "grasp" and "grip," and so is a very physical sort of word, is better not translated by the abstract,

legalistic English term "sovereignty." In an ancient democracy the *dēmos*—
meaning alternatively the people as a whole or the mass/majority of the
people actually taking the decisions—had their hands on power where it
mattered, at Athens as elsewhere.[9]

c. There was no separation of powers in any ancient democracy, either in
theory (constitutional or philosophical) or in actual political practice;
the *dēmos* in principle held power and ruled equally in all the relevantly
operative spheres, legislative, executive, and judicial.

d. In ancient democracies, as indeed in all poleis of whatever constitutional
or ideological hue, citizenship was construed and constructed actively, as
a participatory sharing; as already mentioned above, it was not accidental that the same word, *politeia*, did service both for the status of citizenship and for what we call constitution.

e. The ancient Greeks, including—and perhaps especially—the democratic
Athenians, did indeed distinguish a public from a private realm, but the
rights (if "rights" talk is strictly legitimate in this context; better, I think,
duties and privileges) that they were concerned to protect or encourage
were civic/citizen rights, not human rights (regardless of gender, creed,
nationality, etc.); and they had no concern for minority rights as such,
especially not in a majoritarian democracy of the Athenian form, where
decisions, including electoral votes, were taken by plenary meetings of
the entire potential citizen body or by equipollent bodies such as the divisions of the People's Court.[10]

f. There was no concern, finally, to protect "the individual" from the State
(as we might naturally put it within the context of our tradition of
Western liberal democracy), for two very good reasons. First, individuals
were not positively evaluated as such in Greek society, where the primary
emphasis was always on the good of *to koinon*, the commonality, or
koinōnia, the commonwealth or community, so that there were no individuals in our connotation and no Greek term that might be so interpreted (the Greek *idiōtēs*, meaning often something like our "layman,"
i.e., citizen acting in an unofficial or amateur capacity, transmuted
unforcedly into our wholly pejorative word "idiot"). Second, there was
no State in a post-Hobbesian sense for the individual (citizen) to have his
rights (or rather duties and privileges) protected from.[11]

Against that background of rather dogmatically expressed preliminary
points, I proceed to comment directly and indirectly on the preceding chapters under five headings, bearing in mind that I think my fellow commentator Cynthia Farrar has done an absolutely excellent job of summarizing
them and of developing them into a highly fruitful comparison and contrast
with some modern and contemporary forms of democratic thinking and
practice, such as the promising approach often known as deliberative

democracy. I shall therefore focus rather on the more strictly ancient dimensions of our practically inexhaustible topic.

SOURCES AND METHODS

Walter Eder (1998) made some good criticisms of Ober's popular spontaneity thesis of democratic revolution in 508, but his own aristocracy thesis of democratic origins is even more vulnerable to a critique such as that developed in this volume by Bob Wallace. However, it is not so much the vulnerability of either substantive thesis to which I wish to draw attention now (see further below) as the sources and methods on which they both, inevitably to some degree, rely. My case against them is, broadly speaking, that they pay insufficient attention to situational-rhetorical context, that is, to the distinctions between description and prescription and between fact and value. All Greek political language was consciously and deliberately value-laden; there was not even a gesture made toward the probably in fact unrealizable ideal of Weberian *wertfrei* (value-free) political "science."[12] I restrict myself to just three illustrations.

First, why at Herodotus 3.80, in the so-called Persian Debate, does the pro-democracy speaker Otanes not actually use the term *dēmokratia,* when *dēmokratia,* in a pretty radical or extreme form, is clearly what he is in fact advocating, and although Herodotus does use the term elsewhere? The clue is given by Herodotus himself, when he makes Otanes assert that *isonomiē* is "the fairest of names"—*isonomiē,* that is, not *dēmokratia.* And why not? Because, regardless of whoever precisely first coined the latter term and why, and of whenever it first became common currency at Athens, *dēmokratia* always contained and actively retained the etymological potential for negative interpretation: the word *dēmos,* that is, in the eyes of one of the socially and economically elite few opinion-makers, did not mean only or merely People (all the people, the citizen body as a whole) but also—and rather—the masses, the poor, the lower-class, and often underprivileged, majority of the citizens. Coupled with *kratos,* which had the underlying physically active sense discussed above, *dēmokratia* could therefore be interpreted negatively to convey something of the flavor of the phrase "the dictatorship of the proletariat" (as not used by a committed Leninist communist). Better therefore by far for Otanes not to give a potential linguistic hostage to fortune, but to advocate—as he in fact does—a programme summed up in a single word with an intrinsically positive connotation: for all must surely agree that equality under or before the laws (see further below) was in itself a choice-worthy ideal (any disagreement would concern rather who precisely were to count as relevantly "equal," and how). Thus Otanes' nonuse of *dēmokratia* says nothing about whether or not the word was already coined, either at the dramatic date of the Debate (it could not have been, since that was c. 521) or at the time Herodotus's version of the Debate was composed (it almost certainly was, even if the prototype of Otanes' speech goes back to 450 or somewhat earlier). It says everything, on the other hand, about the context-specific resonances of key—that is, essentially contested—political terminology.

Second, at 5.66.2, where Herodotus is describing the means whereby Cleisthenes came to be in a position to introduce what he (Herodotus) later in his own person calls a *dēmokratia* (6.131.1), what exactly does he mean by saying that Cleisthenes *prosetairizetai* the *dēmos?* Here it is most important to consider the point of view from which such terminology would seem natural or usable. Formally speaking, "adding (for his own benefit) the people/masses to his *hetair(e)ia*" or "making (for his own benefit) the people/masses his *hetairoi*" is either an impossibility, a contradiction, or, at best, an oxymoron, for, by definition, a *hetair(e)ia* was a small band of *hetairoi* (intimate comrades), and in 507—or even 407, for that matter—the word *hetairos* still retained a good deal of the force of aristocratic peer-group solidarity and comradeship that it had had in Homer (eighth–seventh century B.C.E., so far as the composition of the *Iliad* and *Odyssey* is concerned). *Prosetairizetai* must therefore be being used here in a metaphorical sense, and live-metaphorical, too. Such a metaphor would, I suggest, come most easily to an aristocratic speaker, one who by no means necessarily endorsed or approved either the means that Cleisthenes so successfully employed or the goal, *dēmokratia,* he thereby (in Herodotus's view) achieved. Such a speaker, on the most economical hypothesis, would be a fellow aristocrat of Cleisthenes', better still a fellow Alcmaeonid (it is tolerably certain that Herodotus counted Alcmaeonids among his direct informants), one who thoroughly disapproved of Cleisthenes' reforms and regarded him—no less vehemently than Pericles was later regarded and for similar reasons (cf. by implication Pseudo-Xenophon *Ath. Pol.* 2.20)—as a traitor to his family and class.

In short, Herodotus's use of the formally inaccurate or misleading term *prosetairizetai* is due, in my view, to his reproduction of an aristocratic, possibly Alcmaeonid source, one who was keen to "spin" Cleisthenes' in fact revolutionary transformation of the terms of the political game as a case of "aristocratic business as usual." It is not at all surprising, either, that Herodotus should have been willing to employ such a metaphor, since he himself was by no means a wholehearted advocate of the system the Cleisthenic reforms ushered in. He may have approved of *isēgoria,* equality of free public speech, which he uses as a kind of synecdoche for *dēmokratia* at 5.78, but, on the other hand, he rather contemptuously reports (5.97) that it was easier in 500/499 to fool thirty thousand Athenians (exercising their right of democratic free public speech and equal vote) than one Spartan (a king), and it is by no means clear that he would have straightforwardly endorsed Otanes' radical-democratic reading of *isonomia.*

Cleisthenes in other words did not, in reality, either "add the people/ masses to his *hetair(e)ia*" or "make the masses/people his *hetairoi*" but rather— as Ober correctly in my view argues, though on different grounds—trans- formed the whole nature of Athenian politics, precisely by finessing or over- riding the previously taken-for-granted, aristocratic factionalism model of political infighting. By appealing to the people as a whole, or more narrowly to the effective subaristocratic majority of them, and by offering them what he was able to persuade them they wanted from political participation, namely, some sort of decisive say, he won them round to his way of thinking and for the first time incorporated them centrally in the political process (cf. 5.69.2, also biased in its expression). Although this appeal might be interpreted cyn- ically, at one level, as merely a self-serving and vote-catching political maneu- ver (though I myself would take a rather more elevated view of it), it was not at all the same thing as doing what Herodotus's anachronistic phraseology at 5.66.2 misleadingly implies, namely, winning them over, as a whole new fac- tion, within the conventional guidelines of the traditional political game.

Third, why did Aristotle (*Pol.* 1317b10–14; cf. 1319b30) identify the essence, or goal, of democratic sociability and self-government as "living as you please"? Aristotle's fundamental method of political-philosophical analysis and prescription was to proceed from the *phainomena* and *endoxa*, the reputable opinions of reputable persons, to what ideally and ideologi- cally he thought should be the case, other things being equal.[13] This method enabled him to give a much fuller and fairer appreciation of a democratic point of view than was normal among democracy's critics;[14] indeed to go so far as to concede that, in terms of a kind of social-contract idea of decision making, the opinions of the majority were likely on average and on the whole to be no worse in practice than those of an elite few.

However, Aristotle himself, like almost all known ancient Greek intellec- tuals (the known and certain exceptions can be counted on the fingers of one hand: Hippodamus, Protagoras, Democritus . . . others?),[15] was no ide- ological or intellectual democrat. Just as in his doctrine of the essence of natural slavery (Cartledge 2002: 135–41), so in his exposition of the essence of natural democracy (as it were), Aristotle allowed his prejudices to get the better of his intellect, so badly did he want and need the doctrines he was advocating—*against* democracy, *for* natural slavery—to be true. The giveaway is his overstatement of his case: for he in effect accuses all ideo- logical democrats of being anarchists, or would-be anarchists, since, he claims, so preeminently do they privilege their libertarian notion of free- dom (freedom *from,* in Isaiah Berlin's terms) that they ideally wish there to be no constraints whatsoever on their freedom of political action (freedom *to*). From there it was but a relatively small step to identifying in democracy an innate tendency to lawlessness, the overriding of the supposedly perma- nent laws by temporary decrees, and even to classifying the "last" or "ulti-

mate" democracy (by which he surely meant a democracy like that of contemporary Athens) as precisely that in which the *dēmos* does not see itself as
bound by the laws. "Foul!" a genuine ideological democrat would surely—
and legitimately—have cried on reading that.

THE INVENTION OF POLITICS AND THE POLITICAL

The distinction between politics and democratic politics has rightly been
insisted upon. The former was common to most of Hellas, by the fifth century at the latest, whereas the latter became widespread only in the fourth
century, after which it virtually disappeared once again. None of our other
contributors, however, seems to me to have taken on board fully the issue of
the (non)existence of the State and the transparency of the political under
the ancient Greek regime. Farrar, indeed, goes further and explicitly denies
the relevance to democratic Athens of the notion of face-to-face-ness that
Moses Finley (1983) borrowed originally from Peter Laslett. Against which
I would argue that all ancient Greek political communities, Athens not
excluded, were indeed relevantly face-to-face, in two different ways: first,
and more obviously, whenever it was a matter of taking binding decisions by
majority vote on behalf of the community as a whole, whether in the
Assembly or in a law court, the voters were in full view of each other—the
fact that in both types of case only a small proportion of the total citizen
body was present and voting is neither here nor there: had that been felt to
be a problem, the Athenians themselves would have done something about
it; second, in a less direct and more subtle sense, all ancient Greek communities were face-to-face and transparently so, in that there was no State
(including a government and a civil service bureaucracy) interposed
between ordinary citizens and the making of final, universally binding decisions, as there is in all our modern democracies, which are also of course—
and not coincidentally—representative, not direct, systems of government.

In an ancient Greek democratic political community "the political" (*das
Politische*), that is, the political space or political sphere, was placed *es meson*
or *en mesōi*, transparently available "in the middle" to all citizens who wished
fully to participate there (Vernant 1985: 238–60). The famous Periclean
Funeral Speech in Thucydides is actually not a simple hymn to democracy
by any means but ideologically slanted and rhetorically overdetermined in
all sorts of confusing ways (Yunis 1997; Hesk 2000). However, when
Thucydides' Pericles is made to say that Athens' *politeia* was called a *dēmokratia* because governance there was effected in the interests of the many (citizens) rather than the few (2.37.1), he was stating a fact; likewise, all
allowance made for the exaggeration of the "we alone," there is a key truth
in the claim that "we alone judge the person who has no share in those (*ta
politika*) to be not (merely) a quietist but useless" (2.40.2).

THE INVENTION OF *DĒMOKRATIA* I: THE WORD

Our term "democracy" is derived from Greek *dēmokratia,* literally "People-power," but democracy today has nothing to do with power or the People, let alone the power of (all) the people.[16] If it still retains any content what-ever, it is merely that of "free elections" and other sorts of occasional voting, a kind of placebo or Saturnalia for what is becoming an ever-smaller pro-portion of the potential electorate (Dunn 1993; Wood 1995). In Athens they did—and said—things very differently. *Dēmokratia,* at first the name for a system of governance, ultimately became sacralized—presumably in response to secular opposition both at home and abroad—as the name of a goddess. We do not know, and probably will never know, who coined the term *dēmokratia,* or how and when precisely it became accepted in the way the speech of Thucydides' Pericles (above) attests. But it is worth dwelling a little on the implications of the naming.

The speech attributed to Otanes in Herodotus's Persian Debate is, as we saw, a case of the dog that did not bark. The earliest attested usages of the term as applied to Athens are therefore either Herodotus 6.131.1 (cited above) or those in the "Old Oligarch," the Pseudo-Xenophontic *Politeia of the Athenians,* which may have been composed as early as the 430s or as late as the 410s, but in my view falls most probably in the 420s, after—I believe—the "publication" of Herodotus's *Histories.* Mogens Hansen once put forward an ingenious argument that to name an Athenian Demokrates, possibly in the 470s but certainly no later than the 460s, implied the exis-tence of the abstract noun by that date, but that's by no means probative.[17] I should myself place greater weight on the phrase *dēmou kratousa kheir* (the controlling hand of the *dēmos*) in line 604 of Aeschylus's *Suppliants,* a tragedy most plausibly dated 463, which in obedience to the rule of avoid-ing the most blatant terminological anachronism seems to use a punningly concrete poetic synecdoche implying the abstract term's existence. Regarding both those examples, I would add that the second quarter of the fifth century seems to me the "right" sort of time for the word to have been coined, for several reasons. If I am correct, this has an obvious and direct bearing on the issue to be discussed in the following section.

The earliest "buzzword" used to evoke the post-Cleisthenic political order or system was apparently *isonomia,* precisely the word employed by Herodotus's Otanes. By that seems to have been meant something like equality of active citizen privileges under the laws, combined with equality of interpersonal respect.[18] If Herodotus was right, as I am sure he was, in see-ing a direct connection between military prowess and political order or per-ception (5.78), then the battles of Marathon and Salamis in particular, together with the ostracisms of the 480s that were respectively their conse-quences and facilitators, provided the impetus for both institutional and linguistic change. *Dēmokratia,* however, could be no simple replacement or modernizing of *isonomia,* for the main reason given above for its avoidance by Otanes: it could too easily be construed negatively—and that may indeed have been how it was originally meant to be construed, if its inventor was a, literally, antidemocratic individual or group. But if that is so, why and how did *dēmokratia* become not just current but officially accepted parlance? How, in other words, are we to explain its upward mobility?

The answer, I suggest, is that it occurred as and when members of the Athenian *aristoi* opted to join rather than try to beat the ever more dominant *dēmos,* by becoming its "champions" (*prostatai*). In such a scenario the word *dēmos* would denote primarily the people as a whole, but "progressive" members of the elite would also have been endorsing an institutional system whereby the poor and humble masses enjoyed preponderant political weight, literally as well as figuratively, and seeing them no longer as the despised *kakoi* of Solon's time and later, but as equal citizens or sharers in the *politeia.* The absence of very much in the way of democratic theory properly so called, even in the fourth century no less than in the fifth, has often been noted.[19] But the coinage—or rather the reminting—of *dēmokratia* must have involved at the very least some articulate speculation as to its differences from, and alleged superiorities to, any previous system of governance (Nippel 1988, 1994).

THE INVENTION OF *DĒMOKRATIA* II: THE THING

Different, sometimes irreconcilable claims have been made for identifying the "beginning" of democracy at Athens, in this volume as elsewhere. One reason for disagreement can be failure to appreciate that democracy is not a single immutable animal. There were four main species of the genus, according to Aristotle's biopolitical classification (see note 5), and each species could undergo internally generated evolution and even mutation, or change due to external pressures. What sort, or what stage, of democracy we have in view, therefore, is a very material consideration. Part of the disagreement among the contributors to this volume is due also to their different criteria for establishing the existence of "real" or "true" or "full" democracy at Athens. Part—but not all. There are substantive disagreements, too, over how to interpret the evidence deemed usable and relevant. I shall be brief and rather dogmatic in my comments.

The Solon View

In the fourth century the Athenians themselves came to champion Solon as their ultimate Founding Father, and since they lived in a democracy, Solon had to become the Founder of Democracy (Hansen 1989c). Wallace is prepared to give some credence to the notion that the regime that Solon's reforms of 594 ushered in deserves to be called—strictly anachronistically—democratic, if only in some restricted sense and up to a limited point. It seems to me, however, to be revealing that not even Aristotle, whose ideal democracy was very much less radical and demotic than that which the Athenians of his day actually enjoyed, would have been able in conscience to classify the post-Solonian Athenian *politeia* as a *dēmokratia*. The most we can, I think, profitably do is identify certain features of Solon's reliably attributed reforms as protodemocratic, in the sense that they were found much later on to be integral components of or at least compatible with a genuinely democratic structure of governance. Of course, too, they would not have been even to that degree protodemocratic had not Peisistratus, a tyrant or absolute ruler, chosen to coexist with them, to allow them to operate more or less without interference over a long and internally stable period, such that not even the nearly twenty-year period of much more unstable tyranny that succeeded his reign could entirely dislodge them from the general Athenian consciousness.

The Cleisthenes View

The Cleisthenes view has been vigorously and articulately championed by Ober, again (cf. 1996: chap. 4), in a strong, and strongly populist, version, according to which it was not so much a Cleisthenes acting independently from above, but a Cleisthenes impelled or even compelled by popular pressure from below, who reformed the Athenian *politeia* such that it became a *dēmokratia*.[20] The extent to which a genuinely popular or populist self-consciousness can be said really to have existed by 508, and the extent to which such a self-consciousness was the principal driver of the Cleisthenic reform bill, seem to me, among others, highly dubious or problematic. On the other hand, I do agree with Ober that some theoretical or prototheoretical notion of what a *dēmokratia* (not yet so named, of course) might entail was a prerequisite of the success of the sort of mass action that occurred in and after 508. As Aristotle rightly said, one of the conditions for a *politeia* to work is that the relevant people in relevant numbers should actively want it to.[21] And, even more to the immediate point at issue, I do also agree with him—and Herodotus—that what Cleisthenes introduced for the Athenians was a form—however inchoate—of "democracy."

One critical test of an ancient democracy—that is, of whether a polity was in any useful sense democratic—is how it goes about determining foreign policy, the taking of decisions regarding "peace and war" in ancient Greek parlance. Immediately in 508/7, then again in 500/499, and most famously in 490, the Athenians in their Assembly took properly democratic decisions—respectively, to seek aid from Persia against Sparta, to aid the

Ionians in their revolt from Persia, and to resist the Persians in pitched hoplite battle. The *dēmos* of these years was mainly a hoplite (and above) *dēmos*, very different from the active post-Salamis *dēmos* no doubt; the newly introduced Council of 500 was inevitably at first filled by at least reasonably well-off farm-owning demesmen; the Archons who were to compose the Areopagus were still elected rather than selected by lot; and the Areopagus they were to compose still held a "guardianship of the laws" or ultimate veto. Yet against all that, citizenship, and so potential membership of the Assembly, were now determined at local deme level, a face-to-face institution if ever there was, as was membership of the Council, which acquired a new, more independent identity vis-à-vis the Areopagus; the new office of the Generalship, filled by open voting within the Assembly, overrode the old post of War Archon (*polemarchos*, which was remodeled to serve different, peaceable functions); and the newly galvanized *dēmos* was both politically self-confident and, at least on home soil, militarily effective. It can surely be legitimately held to have been wielding some form of *kratos*, and for that reason this "Cleisthenes view" is the view of the origins of democracy at Athens that I myself espouse. However . . .

The Ephialtes-Pericles View

The Ephialtes-Pericles view, as argued here by Kurt Raaflaub, is also mighty seductive. The reform package of Ephialtes (presumably the true protagonist, as he was the older man, and it was he, not Pericles, who was targeted for assassination on political grounds), which the Assembly passed in 462/1, removed the last formal aristocratic piece from the board, the ultimate legal veto of the Areopagus council of ex-archons (chosen by lot since 487), and replaced it with the empowerment of the People's Court (the heliaia, as instantiated by particular jury courts or *dikastēria*), while the effective power of the people in assembly was also reinforced through further administrative strengthening of the Council of 500. Pay for jurors, added on in the 450s to the use of the quintessentially democratic (cf. Hdt. 3.80.6) mode of sortition for selecting Archons and most of the other (seven hundred or so?) domestic officials, helped to ensure the practical realization of a truly democratic idea of equality of opportunity and participation. All true (in my opinion). And yet . . . see the Cleisthenes view above. For me, that is, the post-462/1 democracy is a different, more evolved democracy, but not Athens' first.

The Post-404 View

Anyone who argues that Athens did not become a *dēmokratia* in any suitable sense until after the restoration of republican government in 403 deserves in my view to have a *graphē sukophantias* (public action against quibbling) slapped on him or her forthwith (Harvey 1990). On the other hand, I do agree with Eder (1998), against, for example, Mogens Hansen, that the fourth-century democracy was not qualitatively different from that of the (later) fifth century.[22] Indeed, I would myself go further and argue that quantitatively it was actually more democratic—taken as percentages of the (smaller) total citizen body, there were more regular attenders at the Assembly, and more citizens at any one time holding an office.

REVOLUTION OR REACTION?

By way of a conclusion, I shall try to evaluate the Athenian democratic experiment within the conceptual matrix of political change (*metabolē*).[23] *Ex Africa*, it was proverbially said, *semper aliquid novum* ("Out of Africa, always something new"). *Ex Graecia*, it might have been said, *numquam* (never) *aliquid novum*. The Greek for "revolution" in the sense of dramatic, often physically violent political change was either *stasis*, a standing apart or standoff, or *neōtera pragmata*, newer, that is, too new, political affairs. Even the most ideologically motivated democrats at Athens were always terribly keen to cast even the largest innovations as a return to a universally desired world that had once been theirs but had been lost, rather than as progress toward an ideal future goal. However, in actual fact democracy ancient Greek-style was a system of majority decision-making based on conflict rather than consensus. Democratic politics was a zero-sum game, as we might put it, or an *agōn*, as they did put it.[24] In a transparent, face-to-face system such as theirs every vote on a major policy issue threatened the outbreak of *stasis* or was indeed in a sense a controlled expression of *stasis*, as the late and great Nicole Loraux so brilliantly showed.[25] Hence the universally acclaimed ancient political ideal was *homo-noia*, literally "same-mindedness" or total unanimity, precisely because it almost never was—nor could be—realized in practice.

The very fact of the instantiation of *dēmokratia* at Athens therefore implied a revolution, a fundamental transformation of political life. One final, comparative way of making that point may be essayed. Compare and contrast, on the one hand, a relatively unchanging Sparta, with its foundational *rhētra* (saying, pronouncement, law, oracle) attributing *kratos* to the *damos*, perhaps as early as the seventh century, with, on the other hand, an evolving Athens, undergoing the reforms associated successively with Solon, Cleisthenes, and Ephialtes-Pericles. Institutionally, there is no comparison. The number of ways in which Sparta could not be accounted a *dēmokratia*, even on the most generous Aristotelian definition, is legion, but I would single out especially the absence of the use of the lot for appointment to office; the absence of the notion of strict citizen equality of the one man/one vote variety, with everyone counting for one and no more than one; and the absence of a popular judiciary, coupled with the continued existence of an aristocratic council, containing ex officio the two hereditary kings, that wielded ultimate judicial powers.[26]

Only as a culture, at most, could Sparta count as a democracy, and only in the weak sense that it subjected all potential citizens (except the two heirs apparent) equally to a state-imposed educational cycle and promoted a notionally (but not in fact) egalitarian communal *diaita* (mode of life) among the adult citizen body. Yet Athens' egalitarian ethos was a match for Sparta's (see Wallace, chapter 3 above), which was severely limited by the absolute necessity for soldierly hierarchy, and Athens' democratic culture was of course far more pluralistically inclusive. Finally, if Athenian democrats were conservative in expressed outlook, they were mere children beside the Spartans, who notoriously overvalued tradition even to the—logical but ultimately self-defeating—point of fetishizing gerontocracy. That King Agesilaus II (r. c. 400–360), once the most powerful single individual in the Greek world east of the Adriatic, should have died in his mid-80s while returning from campaigning as a mere mercenary commander in north Africa (Cartledge 1987) speaks volumes—and profoundly nondemocratic volumes, at that. I rest my agonistic case.[27]

NOTES

1. *Modern Greek Studies Yearbook* 4 (1988) 312.

2. See Cartledge 2000b; I both apologize and do not apologize for repeating here matter from this article, and from my "Comparatively Equal: A Spartan Approach" (1996a) and "Democratic Politics Ancient and Modern: From Cleisthenes to Mary Robinson" (2000a) papers, where more bibliography, too, may be found cited. I apologize, that is, for telling people what they already know. But insofar as some of the other contributors to this volume do not seem to me always to have covered absolutely every vital aspect of the field in equally appropriate depth, I hope I am right in feeling an apology is not called for.

3. See, for example, Hansen 1993, 1997; and my review of three more volumes in the two CPC series, Papers 4 and Acts 4 and 5, in *Classical Review* 49 (1999) 465–69.

4. More often than not, actually, the tradition was antidemocratic; Roberts (1994) traces that from antiquity to the twentieth century.

5. Aristotle typically claims to have identified four species of each (oligarchy: 1292a40–b; democracy: 1291b31–1292a39).

6. Theater/tragedy: Cartledge 1997; Mills 1997; theater/comedy: McGlew 2003. And for democracy as culture, see Adele Scafuro's editorial introduction to Boegehold and Scafuro 1994. Public visual arts: Castriota 1992; Boedeker and Raaflaub 1998; Neils 2002. War: van Wees (2001) argues provocatively that political order shaped military organization, not vice versa. See rather Raaflaub 1997c, 1999 (as cited in chapter 2 above).

7. Hansen (1989d), paradoxically, both asks whether ancient Athens was (ever)

a democracy and answers that it was a democracy recognizably like a modern liberal democracy. I could not disagree more; see rather Finley 1983, 1985. Dunn 1992 unfortunately implies by its title that the story of democracy is single and continuous. See further below.

8. On Greek political decision-making from Mycenaean to archaic times, see Carlier 1998. See further below.

9. Aesch. *Supp.* 604 *dēmou kratousa kheir* (see Raaflaub, chapter 5 above) puns on this basic sense; on power/rule, see also Meier 1990; Eder 1991; Nippel 1993. Ostwald (1986) doubly misapplies "sovereignty" in my view.

10. Public versus private: Musti 1985; Humphreys 1993; cf. Farrar, chapter 7 below. Rights versus shares, duties, and privileges: Ostwald 1996.

11. On the *idiōtēs* see Rubinstein 1998; cf. on individuals, Strasburger 1954; Vernant 1991 (as cited at the end of chapter 2 above). On the absence of the post-Hobbesian state, see the work of Moshe Berent (1994; 1996: esp. 38–45; 2004), who persuasively in my view—despite the attempted rebuttal of Hansen 2002—prefers "stateless political community." Ehrenberg (1969) did not even address the issue. See further Cartledge 2000b.

12. On method, see further Cartledge 1996a (= 2001: chap. 6) and 1998.

13. For Aristotle's method, see briefly Cartledge 2002: index s.v. "Aristotle, method of."

14. Ober (1998a) explores the work of the contemporary critics with exemplary thoroughness; cf. also, for a longer perspective, Roberts 1994.

15. Unlike Farrar 1988, I would not myself count Thucydides as a usefully "democratic" thinker, profoundly influenced by democratic ideas and procedures though he inevitably was. The nature of his undoubted admiration for Pericles seems to me profoundly undemocratic.

16. On this section, see Brock 1991.

17. Hansen 1999: 70 (citing *Hesperia* 53 [1984] 355–60, a funerary stele); cf. 1986.

18. Ostwald 1969; cf. Vlastos 1953, 1964. See also Cartledge 1996a for discussion of the various *iso-* words used in Athenian and other Greek democratic discourse.

19. Davies 2003; cf. Raaflaub 1989b, 1992, 1993; Ober 1998a; Schuller 1998.

20. The two most important recent defenses of the position that Cleisthenes really did "establish the democracy for the Athenians," as Herodotus puts it, are Anderson 2003 and de Ste. Croix 2004: chaps. 4–5. Both appeared after this chapter was already in its near-final form. I agree with a very great deal in Anderson's outstanding monograph, including both its overall thesis and, for example, its criticisms of Ober's "populist" reading of the Cleisthenic revolution; cf. Rhodes (2003a: 80), who dismisses Ober's idea of a popular uprising to explain Cleisthenes' reforms as mere "wishful thinking." But I also have my disagreements, which are set out at some length in my review in *Classical Philology* 99 (2004). Though published finally in 2004, de Ste. Croix's remarkably powerful interpretation of Cleisthenes goes back essentially to the 1960s, when I was fortunate to be one of his undergraduate pupils. A very great debt is owed to my fellow pupils David Harvey and Robert Parker for placing this brilliant scholarship in the public domain at last.

21. "The part of the *polis* that wants the *politeia* to remain put must be stronger

than the part that does not so wish": Arist. *Pol.* 1296b15–17. Note also Aristotle's interesting view that democracies were "safer and freer from *stasis*" than oligarchies: *Pol.* 1302a8–9; cf. 1296a13–14.

22. See Hansen's review of Ober 1989, in *Classical Review* 40 (1990) 348–56.

23. In this final section I draw on an unpublished paper I gave to the distinguished Crayenborgh Seminar of the University of Leiden in 1999, entitled "Revolution and Revolt in Classical Antiquity."

24. Gouldner 1965. Honor as the (or a) political goal: Arist. *NE* 1095b19–31; *Pol.* 1302a33 (in *stasis*); cf. de Ste. Croix 1981: 80, 551 n. 30.

25. De Ste. Croix 1981; Fuks 1984; Gehrke 1985; Berger 1992; Molyneux 1993; and esp. Loraux 1987, 1997.

26. Cartledge 1996a (= 2001, chap. 6); cf. my review, in *Gnomon* 74 (2002) 143–47, of Richer 1998. See also chapter 2 in this volume.

27. For the kind invitation to contribute this comment I am extremely grateful to my friend and colleague Kurt Raaflaub, to whom I was also indebted for an invitation to participate in a conference at Brown University in April 1999 devoted to law and literature in Athens and Rome. I have drawn here, in some part, on my unpublished paper for that conference, "Polities, Politics, and Polite Letters? Some Athenian Oligarchic Pamphleteers."

Chapter 7

Power to the People

Cynthia Farrar

Why think that the "first democracy" has anything to tell us about our own? That was then and this is now; surely modern democracy has diverged from its ancient counterpart, and deliberately and rightly so?[1] As it happens, however, among people who spend their time pondering such matters, dissatisfaction with modern democracy quite often takes the form of what one wit has dubbed "polis envy."[2] We admire what we think the Athenians had, we want it, we fear it, we suspect it is unattainable, we are determined to do without it. We eventually come to the conclusion that the most mature thing to do is to recognize that our wish can never be fulfilled and to channel our thwarted desire toward aspirations that are genuinely appropriate for us.

This is, of course, precisely the question at issue: what is appropriate for us? If we turn away from the Athenian example, are we simply ignoring the possibility that a confrontation with their very different experience might enable us to identify important aspects of democracy that have been lost in the transition to the modern liberal state? But if—from the far side of that transition—we turn to their example, will we see anything other than our own reflection? It is the very strangeness of Athenian practices that underlies their potential power to alter the way we think about our own, and strangeness that may block understanding.

My contribution to this discussion is twofold: to deploy the characterizations offered in this volume to make visible the Athenian challenge to our own practices, and then (briefly) to take up that challenge. What strikes a modern as most alien and remarkable about Athenian democracy is precisely that it was a democracy: the people ruled. And it is worth considering whether it may be possible to adapt this core commitment, and the institutional contrivances that sustained it, to reorient our own rather different system of governance. The tale of the origins of Athenian democracy provides clues both to what popular rule might mean, and to how such a departure from our own tradition could possibly triumph.

WHEN DID ATHENS BECOME DEMOCRATIC, AND WHY DOES IT MATTER?

One of the charms of studying the ancient Athenians is that everyone, student and scholar alike, has relatively easy access to the limited number of literary and epigraphic sources. Disagreements about the interpretation and implications of the evidence therefore appear in sharp relief. That is especially true in this volume, which asks a group of scholars to answer the same question using the same body of evidence. Each commentator's choice of a period and context in which to locate the emergence of democracy reflects the salience he ascribes to particular elements of governance. For Robert Wallace, the key features in the creation of democracy are Solon's ascription of legal and political standing—citizenship—to the plebeian residents of Attica, the thetes, and the creation of the "basic institutions of Athens' democracy," even though the citizens did not realize the potential of those institutions for more than a century. Kurt Raaflaub agrees with Wallace that the full demos (i.e., a citizen body that included the thetes) did not exercise political control during the time of Solon or even Cleisthenes, but he interprets this fact differently. In his view, democracy properly understood requires the active involvement of the thetes.

Josiah Ober shares Raaflaub's view that the empowerment of the full demos is the defining element of the Athenian democratic achievement. He differs as to when, how, and why this came about. According to Ober, democracy was born during the popular uprising against Isagoras and Cleomenes in 508 and the subsequent ratification of the reforms proposed by Cleisthenes. This was an ideological revolution (indeed, a "rupture"), not initially an institutional one, and a necessary (though not sufficient) condition for the development of the full democracy. The groundwork for this revolution was laid during the course of the sixth century, as the legacy of Solon and the actions of the tyrants "undercut traditional lines of authority and encouraged Athenian political self-consciousness." Ober argues that reliance on the lower-class rowers as the foundation of Athenian military power was the result, not the cause, of a more inclusive political identity.

According to Raaflaub, by contrast, the birth of democracy occurred during and in the immediate aftermath of the reforms proposed by Ephialtes, from 462 through the 450s. This was an institutional revolution: legislative initiatives shifted authority from the aristocratic Areopagus to the popular assembly (among other things, the Areopagus lost the right to review and nullify decrees of the assembly). The opportunity to serve as a magistrate was explicitly extended to third-class citizens, the zeugites. The crucial social precondition for this democratic triumph (much contested before and after) was the reliance of the Athenian empire on the rowers. Raaflaub concludes that the democracy took definitive shape in the mid-fifth century as the rowers were fully integrated into the political structure.

Yet another view, not represented in this volume, maintains that even the institutions that accorded popular sovereignty to all citizens did not constitute the full realization of democracy. Walter Eder (1998) locates the fully formed democracy in the creation, in 403/2, of what he calls a constitution, which constrained popular liberty through law and thereby enabled the expanded demos to control the exercise of its own power.

Ober and Raaflaub share a definition of what counts as a democracy but differ about whether it was achieved by spontaneous action or institutional change, while Wallace (and Eder 1998) construe democracy as less (or more) than the exercise of political power by the full demos. It might be argued that each of these interpreters contributes an essential element to our understanding of the Athenian democracy, and perhaps also to democracy *tout court* (I shall have more to say about this below). One person's precondition is another's cause. Whatever element we may consider decisive, we can perhaps agree that all are relevant. Does it matter, then, to distinguish among these various aspects of democracy and to ask when and how they came into being? The answer, as the very existence of this volume presupposes, is yes, and not only to satisfy antiquarian curiosity or to pursue historical truth. If we are to apply the Athenian achievement, we need to separate out the various strands and motivations of the ancient democracy, compare and contrast them with our own, and consider how and why they emerged and flourished.

The elements stressed by Ober and Raaflaub are precisely those that set the Athenians apart from us. In democratic Athens, the people actually ruled.[3] The accounts given by these two scholars reveal the full meaning and significance of genuine popular self-government. The essential features are (1) the people's awareness of their own potential power, (2) the creation of institutions that enable them to realize that potential, and (3) the redefinition of status and power as political rather than social attributes. Only by combining the insights of Ober and Raaflaub—the popular will to power and the institutional transformation of the role and self-understanding of the demos—is it possible to bring into focus the peculiarities of Athenian democracy and the unrealized possibilities of our own.

THE ELEMENTS OF SELF-RULE

The Self-Consciousness and Drive of the Demos

Revolutionary democratizing change can occur only once the citizenry as a whole becomes aware of its own potential power and collective identity.

Raaflaub believes that participation of the thetes in the navy brought about this altered consciousness on the part both of the rowers and of those whose safety depended on them; Ober ascribes this change to the threat posed by the aristocrat Isagoras's conspiracy with the Spartan Cleomenes. According to Ober, the impromptu popular siege and expulsion of Isagoras and his Spartan allies established the demos as "a self-conscious and willful actor in its own right, a grammatical subject rather than an object of someone else's verb." Ober's argument seems to me to make better sense of the written sources that describe the crisis of 508/7 and accounts for both the passage of the Cleisthenic reforms immediately thereafter and the willingness of the Athenians to entrust not just their military might but their very existence to the navy in 480. It is highly likely, however, that the increasing reliance on the rowers during the expansion and defense of the empire helped to create the political will to pursue the further—and radical—reforms discussed by Raaflaub.[4]

Institutions of Popular Rule

The strongest argument for dating the advent of democracy to 508/7 is the character of the Cleisthenic reforms themselves. These reforms are the prototypes of the many odd contrivances devised by the Athenians to reshuffle relationships among citizens of various classes and talents and resources, in order to establish equality of political status. It is difficult to understand the sequence of democratic reforms in the absence of this initial and explicit commitment to a fundamental reordering of the Athenian polity. The character of the Cleisthenic reforms themselves argues against the notion that these institutions were devised by aristocratic families to protect their dominance. Would an aristocrat interested in cultivating long-term popular support for his clan go so far as to give ordinary Athenians in local communities the power to determine who counts as a citizen?[5] Or to create ten new and artificial "tribes" comprised of three districts, one each from the city, the coast, and the inland area, and to assign the districts to the tribes by lot?[6]

As one scholar has observed with respect to the Cleisthenic reforms, "reflection suggests that two Athenian institutions above all were intended to be put beyond the reach of the old aristocratic influences: the army and the Council" (Hansen 1999: 49). Both were now organized by (artificially constituted) tribe and therefore brought together residents from different parts of Attica (and thus from different aristocratic strongholds) to perform military and civic duties with citizens to whom they were connected solely by a political procedure. Although members of the Cleisthenic council were probably elected, they were chosen by their peers in newly formalized local units called demes, and had to exercise their power in constant collaboration with their counterparts from all over Attica, both in subgroups of fifty organized by (artificial) tribe and in the full council. The people's court was given the power to adjudicate any conflict over citizenship status. Local election and the division of councillors into groups of noncontiguous tribes, combined with the sheer number of members, made it virtually impossible for any aristocratic clique to dominate the council.[7] True, as Raaflaub notes, "we know next to nothing about the [new council's] powers." Moreover, we do not know which council resisted Cleomenes and Isagoras. However, the new council's great significance is suggested precisely by the complex and sophisticated method of putting it together and by its place at the center of the "new order."

The new council's role in setting the agenda for the people's assembly (its probouleutic function) suggests an increase in the significance of the assembly for which proposals were being prepared. As Ober argues, a more direct and powerful role for the people in assembly is also implied by the institution of ostracism. Twenty years after Cleisthenes, the Athenians introduced the use of the lot for the selection of officials, the archons—initially from an elected short list (Arist. *Ath. Pol.* 22.5 with Hansen 1999: 49–52)— a procedure that makes sustained control of the levers of power by any one faction impossible.[8] Election and traditional, hierarchical, locally rooted relationships formed the basis of aristocratic power. Competition among aristocratic clans may perhaps account for Alcmaeonid leadership in framing the reforms: Cleisthenes may well have hoped to secure popular respect and trust, and thereby some temporary influence for the Alcmaeonids within the new framework. But it cannot account for the content and consequences of the reforms. The contrivances proposed by Cleisthenes and supported by the people decisively transformed the aristocratic role from concentrated power to diffuse and contingent influence, and they make little sense unless they were explicitly intended, by both demos and leaders, to do just that.

Power of the Political Realm

The new institutions reflect a commitment to the power of the demos as a whole, not of the aristocrats or of one aristocratic family, nor indeed of a mobilized and self-conscious lower class, nor of any group that aimed to bolster its own power at the expense of others. The Cleisthenic innovations imply that the task at hand was precisely to forge a unified polis through the participation of all male citizens, of all social classes and wealth. This required significantly different kinds of institutions than had been characteristic of the traditional Greek polis. Attributing citizenship status to the thetes, as Solon did, was a critical step. But even if, as Wallace and others emphasize, the less wealthy citizens of the archaic Greek poleis were independent-minded and willing to speak up for their interests, the elite continued to govern, in Athens as elsewhere. The decisive step toward democracy, then, is the explicit affirmation and institutionalization of a system of governance that, in Plato's scornful words, "distributes a kind of equality to equal and unequal alike" (*Republic* 8.558; cf. Arist. *Pol.* 6.2). The demos was indeed in a sense "aristocratized."[9] The people as a whole assumed the privileges once accorded only to the elite. The Athenians accomplished this transformation by invoking a powerful and shared political role and identity.

Ober's insight is crucial: what made the new political system democratic was that it was the product of the will of the demos as a whole and was designed (and, over time, strengthened) to enable all members of this newly inclusive polity to enjoy freedom and exercise power. As noted earlier, Raaflaub explains the unprecedented extension of full citizenship to the propertyless in terms of the requirements of naval power; but the inclusiveness that distinguishes Athenian democracy is already implicit in the Cleisthenic reforms, which subverted the traditional role of the dominant elite by giving every citizen a political role and transforming the business of governing into an explicitly political activity defined in political—not social—terms, on the basis of "new," not "old," tribes. The reforms instituted after the expulsion of Isagoras rest on the (radical) idea that citizen status was precisely not to be defined by personal resources or social standing—that is, the very factors that enabled the prosperous individual to fight for the polis as a hoplite. In this context, the military role of the thetes is not best understood as the source of their political standing. Rather their crucial military role became possible precisely because capacity to serve the polis was now to be defined (and made possible, through pay) by the polis itself, not determined by personal resources or status.[10]

Cleisthenes apparently construed *dēmos* in its comprehensive sense, and the demos itself was an actor in the move toward democracy. This process included the creation of some institutions intended to make equality a reality. But Raaflaub is certainly justified in pointing out that full popular control of the institutions of government was not achieved until the reforms of the 460s and 450s, and even later. The practices most characteristic of the Athenian democracy, and most different from our system, were the use of the lot and rotation (which ensured access to magistracies, including the council, by all interested citizens), the power of the popular assembly and the people's courts, and payment for participation. These practices emerged and were refined over the course of the fifth century.

ATHENS THROUGH THE LOOKING GLASS

Before attempting to see these practices for what they were and what they can teach us, it is important to note that many observers have dismissed

Athenian institutions as irrelevant to modern society, and others have found in the Athenians a reflection and confirmation of our own system. Both views obscure the potential challenge to our own practices posed by the Athenian democracy. In this volume, Wallace turns to the Athenians with a definition of the essence of democracy that fits our conceptions and elides the distinctiveness of theirs. If formal citizenship status and institutions that accord a role to all citizens without the exercise of real power are the essential features of democracy, then our democracies qualify. And if the independent authority of law and a constitution is the crucial component, as Eder (1998) suggests, then many of our democracies likewise count.[11]

Moderns do not usually expect ordinary citizens to do more or other than pursue their own (often short-term) interests. In the view of many modern theorists, to secure order and the common weal, elite power and the sovereignty of law are essential. As the historian of political thought Sheldon Wolin has observed, "the twentieth-century image of the 'constitutional democracy' of the fourth century bears a striking resemblance to Madisonian democracy" (Euben et al. 1994: 43). This image obscures the most significant characteristics of the Athenian democracy and assimilates them too readily to our own, for better (Athens became more democratic, and more like us, once it had a constitution) or for worse (Athens became less democratic, and more like us, once it had a constitution).[12] In fact, the changes made in 403/2 neither fulfilled democracy nor eviscerated it. Rather, they reflect the capacity of the Athenians to address emerging political challenges through institutions that preserve popular rule.

The practice of democracy at Athens changed after 403, in the wake of the late-fifth-century oligarchic revolutions, with the introduction of the law-givers or *nomothetai* in 411 and the restored democracy's adoption of this body in 403. However, the self-control exercised by the demos was not new, and it continued in important respects to be internal and political, the rule of men through law. The (unwritten) law had always guided the actions of the people.[13] The *graphē paranomōn*, which asserted the right (and responsibility) of any citizen to challenge an illegal action by the assembly by taking the proposer of the measure to court, was regularly invoked as the safeguard of democracy and regularly suspended (as democratic in its effects) by successful oligarchs (in 411, 404, and 317; Hansen 1999: 210–11). The *graphē* induced caution, and attentiveness to the law. The juries of ordinary citizens existed alongside the assembly and had the power to curb the assembly, the council, magistrates, and leaders. The makeup and functioning of the juries suggest the perceived need to make possible more reflective and judicious deliberation, in the light of the laws of Athens, than might at times occur in the midst of a crowded assembly. The jurors were chosen by lot, but only men over thirty were eligible. And they had to swear the Heliastic Oath, which began: "I will cast my vote in consonance with the laws and with the decrees passed by the Assembly and by the Council, but, if there is no law, in consonance with my sense of what is most just, without favour or enmity" (Hansen 1999: 182, citing Frankel 1878).

The decision in 403 to distinguish laws from decrees, and to give subsets of the jury pool (*nomothetai*, still chosen by lot from among Athenians over thirty) the responsibility for lawmaking, followed a crushing military defeat. The reforms are often characterized as a response to the perceived excesses and hasty judgments of the masses during the Peloponnesian War, but they could equally be construed as a way to prevent subversion of democracy by members of the elite. In 411, and again in 404, the leaders of the oligarchical revolutions claimed that they were restoring the "ancestral constitution" and the "constitution of Cleisthenes (or even Solon)."[14] The need to specify and publicize the institutional forms of democracy must have seemed urgent. In 410, when democracy was restored (briefly), the people ruled that seats in the Bouleuterion (council chamber) were to be assigned by lot, to prevent the formation of antidemocratic cliques (Hansen 1999: 280). In 403, the people rejected a proposal to institute a property requirement for full citizenship (introduced by Phormisius, Lysias 34), which would indeed have meant a return to the real "constitution" of Solon. Instead, they added new mechanisms for promoting the consistency and reliability of the laws and public familiarity with legal requirements. The mechanisms designed to ensure equal access to decision-making power— the lot and rotation—remained in place. The people remained sovereign,[15] but the sovereignty was exercised through a new mix of institutions including a more explicit law-making process carried out by a subset of the people's court. The term "demos" continued to be reserved for the people in assembly.[16] The assembly retained significant power, especially in the realm of foreign policy. And in the fourth century, pay for office was extended from magistrates and jurors to the assembly, which further increased the ability of the poorer citizens to participate.

IS SELF-GOVERNMENT POSSIBLE?

If indeed genuine popular power (including mechanisms for self-control) was the hallmark of democratic Athens, why ascribe the realization of "democracy" to a period in which the elite still ruled (the Athens of Solon, as per Wallace) or link it to a modern-sounding "constitution" and the achievement of stability in fourth-century Athens (Eder 1998)? When considering the Athenian democratic achievement, it is understandable to feel—with many modern theorists, and indeed a number of ancient theorists and citizens—rather queasy about the power of the people. In a full democracy, citizen status and power are not dependent upon social or economic standing or education or talent or virtue;[17] why believe that the outcome of the political process will be communal order and justice? This question was posed repeatedly both by sympathetic observers and by critics of the Athenian democracy and, I believe, considered by ordinary Athenians themselves (Farrar 1988). As Raaflaub points out, anxiety about the privileging of the political realm is evident, for example, in Aeschylus's *Oresteia*. The Athenians—in the *Oresteia* and in reality—responded to such concerns by making the political realm even stronger through institutional reform.[18]

Athens offers a glimpse of a "third way" between some sort of external rule (by an elite or by an independent and entrenched constitution) and an unconstrained struggle among individuals or groups in pursuit of self-interest. We need not choose between the rule of law without popular power and the lawless exercise of popular authority. Indeed, if we believe that the legitimacy of law must ultimately be justified by popular assent to its validity—and actual assent, not merely a claim about what laws free and equal individuals would choose if they could—then the first alternative, external rule, is incoherent.[19] And the second is anarchy, not democracy.[20] Like the Athenians, modern liberal democracy seeks to reconcile human variety and the claims of equality with freedom and order—but in very different ways. The core elements of both systems are that the citizen body (demos) is not confined to an elite of aristocratic birth or wealth, and that the demos rules. In both systems, popular rule is designed to be consistent with the freedom of the individual citizen and the persistence and security of the democratic polity. Liberal democracy, however, seeks to instantiate and reconcile these principles through formal and abstract procedural means that do not influence the capacity or mobilize the power of the demos.

Diversity

The Athenians took the unprecedented step of including as full citizens individuals without property or status. Modern democracy goes further, by including women (since the early twentieth century) and "slaves" (since the late nineteenth century in principle, but in fact only since the mid-twentieth century), though not necessarily immigrant "metics." At least in the United States, the polity incorporates a wide variety of ethnicities and religions and governs an extensive territory that spans significant regional differences. The institutions of modern democracy have to stretch further, and rely on procedural mechanisms to create *e pluribus unum* and to express the will of the citizens. Procedural democracy is capable of spanning those differences only at the expense of diluting the significance of political status and the power of the political realm to "make unequals equal." However, this difference between ancient and modern is a difference of scope, not kind. Athens was not a homogeneous polity. And it was not a face-to-face society in any sense that implies the intimate personal connections characteristic of, say, a village.[21] There were at least thirty thousand Athenian citizens (adult males with two Athenian parents). They had to contrive mechanisms for achieving unity and legitimacy.

These institutional contrivances did not abstract from and neutralize popular power but rather shaped the way in which it was expressed. Athenian citizens were assigned to a tribe composed of residents of different localities. They volunteered to serve as officials but were chosen by lot; and they rotated this responsibility with their fellow citizens. In office, they experienced the need to find common ground, to consider other perspectives, to take initiative, to persuade others, to make decisions, and to assume responsibility for them. As participants in the assembly or as jurors, Athenian citizens literally confronted difference in the person of their fellow citizens, and what any individual said and did on those occasions occurred under their gaze. This kind of face-to-face relationship among "ordinary" citizens is largely missing in the modern context and may be essential to the ability of a political system to turn the many into one without compromising their individuality.

Equality

In modern democracies, individuals are presumed to be equal. All human beings by nature possess equal dignity and rights, and the state must therefore treat them equally and protect their basic freedoms. Fair procedures offer neutral, uniform treatment and formal equality of opportunity. Governance by an elite of talent is regarded not only as compatible with this view of equality but as necessary to preserve the system as a whole, because men are deemed equal in their claims but unequal in their ability to advance their own and the common good. The modern political realm is narrowly conceived and undemanding and makes limited attempts to build civic capacity. The Athenians, too, acknowledged that men are unequal by nature and by social norms; but for this very reason they constructed institutions that would render all citizens fully equal (*isoi*) politically, not just in theory but in practice.[22] The use of the lot to select magistrates (including the members of the council), rotation, pay for participation, and the open and frequent opportunity to attend the assembly meant that every citizen had an equal chance of wielding decision-making power.

Freedom

In modern democracies, freedom is most fundamentally construed as freedom from constraint by others, or "negative freedom," the liberty to do as one pleases. Individual freedoms, both political and private, are protected by identifying rights (embodied in a constitution or in the common law tradition) to be interpreted and enforced by the courts. Courts are largely run by professionals, but with ordinary citizens—a randomly selected sample of the entire citizen body—included on juries.

The freedom implicit in Athenian practice was consistent with our modern notion of "negative freedom." The freedom prized by the Athenians was not "positive freedom" in the sense suggested by Plato or Aristotle, that is, the "freedom"—and requirement—to live up to one's full potential by, for example, serving as a Platonic guardian or, in a democracy, volunteering to serve as an official or juror. Contrary to common belief, the Athenians distinguished between the public and the private realms and made room for both economic inequality and personal idiosyncrasies, including the freedom not to participate in governance. However, the Athenians believed that the preservation of freedom required the fulfillment of civic responsibilities.[23] Freedom was not god given but was preserved by the polity. Freedom was both a prerequisite and a product of citizenship. Any citizen who so desired was free to speak in the assembly, to bring a motion, to challenge or indict a fellow citizen for violating the laws. The system depended on the willingness of individual citizens to take initiative. *Ho boulomenos,* "he who wishes," is a key figure in the operation of the Athenian democracy: *ho boulomenos* stands for office, speaks in the assembly or council, and brings charges for actions he deems illegal. As Pericles' funeral oration declares, the Athenians were free to do as they pleased; but the continuation of that freedom depended on their willingness to promote and protect it, and the institutions of democracy contrived to inculcate and continually motivate that commitment.[24]

It is worth asking why the Athenians, committed as they were to popular rule, retained the principle of self-selection of candidates to stand for office. Citizens were not required to serve (compare, for example, the current requirement to perform jury duty). But a process that might otherwise have yielded an entrenched elite could not do so because of the principles of sortition and rotation. Reliance on *ho boulomenos* spoke to the Athenians' commitment to the freedom of the citizen to choose whether or not—and how—to exercise his citizenship.

Power

In modern democracies, the collective order expresses and protects the freedom of each individual member because each individual's preferences are registered through the process of voting for representatives (and, more informally, through the jockeying and bargaining of minority interests). Majority rule (and/or the serial influence of various minorities) expresses the aggregate understanding of the common good, and is open to revision by those who disagree (e.g., Dahl 1956; Cohen 1997). Popular sovereignty in the modern state is indirect, and often exercised outside the political realm; in the Athenian democracy, authority was direct, regular, and transparent. Every decision-making body was composed of ordinary citizens selected by lot, not professionals. All proposals were generated by and voted on by the citizens, in the council and the assembly, and reviewed as necessary by the popular courts. Although they often invoked the ideal of *homonoia*, or "same-mindedness," the Athenians relied on majority rule, not consensus, and decisions could be challenged.

Restraint

The political power of the Athenian people is often characterized as a threat to the human rights that we value and they did not recognize.[25] It is certainly true that for the Athenians rights (and responsibilities) were constituted politically, not simply by virtue of being born human. What does this difference mean in practice? Athenians fully recognized the importance of distinguishing the political from the economic, to prevent both leveling of economic differences and the ability of those with economic resources to subvert the will of the people. The laws specified elaborate procedures to enable any citizen to defend himself against charges of wrongdoing, and punished frivolous accusations. Institutional safeguards (rotation, scrutiny of officials, mechanisms for challenging assembly decisions) reveal that arbitrary and unrestrained power of any kind, whether tyranny or oligarchy or rule by the rabble, or indeed unchecked rule by the majority, was anathema not just to Plato's Socrates, but to the Athenian people themselves.

The American founders proposed the creation of a "filter," in the form of experienced and elite leaders, as a mechanism for reaching decisions that address all the factors affecting the well-being of the polity (Federalist Papers, no. 10). The Athenian "filter," by contrast, operated through the process of citizen participation itself. The "filtering" process included both a system of ongoing, regular exposure to different perspectives, as a temporary official and as a voter in the assembly or a juror in the law courts or scrutinizer of claims to citizenship in a deme, and also the widely shared experience of having to act on behalf of the polis. Pay for participation, selection of most decision-making roles by lot, rotation, and the artificial tribal framework limited the power of those most committed to particular goals or those with the greatest economic resources. And the system subverted and policed the possibility of corruption. Members of the council, jurors, and most officials were chosen by lot from among *hoi boulomenoi*, not from the entire citizenry—and for these roles, only from among those over thirty. They were required to pass scrutiny by their peers before and after their term and to take personal responsibility for their actions. With these constraints, not every man would choose to stand in for his fellow citizens, but any man could.[26]

Representation

The modern democratic system of governance relies upon a division of labor between ruler and ruled; the Athenians believed that citizens must and could rule themselves. The modern system of representation has resulted in specialization and professionalization of the ruling classes. Election, seen by the ancients as an aristocratic system for selecting magistrates, was likewise construed by the founders of the American republic as the appropriate method for generating a ruling elite in a democracy, because in principle any citizen could stand for office but in practice the people would choose their betters (see Manin 1997: chaps. 2–3). The system assumes that ordinary citizens are unable and/or unwilling to make substantive decisions; their role is simply to vote for one candidate (or party) or another. For theorists of the modern democratic state like Joseph Schumpeter, representative democracy is not indirect rule by the people. The people do not rule at all; there is no connection between the people's preferences and the decisions made by those in power.[27] Elections constitute merely an expression of "consent" by the people to the leadership of individuals who make decisions in their name.[28]

The doctrine of consent is a central feature of the natural rights theory that underlies liberal democracy. The grounding of legitimacy in consent is one reason why the founders of modern republics never seriously considered the use of the lot. Natural rights theorists (Locke, for example) view every man as by nature free; he gives up a measure of this freedom by entering political society, and he must therefore be seen (or plausibly assumed) to consent to rule. In Protagoras's analytic account of the foundations of political life, by contrast, man is not yet fully himself until the citizenry as a whole becomes capable of collective self-governance.[29] The process of democratization is not, in Athens, about "taking back the power" lost in the process of institutionalizing governance, but about maintaining the power men have achieved by having created law-guided polities. Those who govern can claim legitimacy not because the people have "consented" to their rule but because every citizen has an opportunity to become a ruler and to make the decisions that affect him and his fellow citizen.

The Athenian use of the lot, rotation, and the principle of *ho boulomenos* created and sustained a distinctive concept of representation and legitimacy. The Athenians, too, had to rely on representation of a kind; even the assembly tended to attract approximately six thousand of the twenty to forty thousand citizens.[30] However, individual officeholders, or members of the assembly on any given day, do not "represent" the views or the conditions of a particular constituency. Rather, the individual "stands in for" the whole. The combined effect of volunteering (for all civic roles), the use of the lot (for juries and offices), and rotation (de facto in the assembly and courts and de jure for offices) means that the decision maker on any particular occasion has to keep in mind the (unknown) citizens who will soon replace ("re-present") him. Every citizen knows that others whom he did not select will in turn be making decisions that affect him, and that they will also be scrutinizing his performance after the fact.[31] Since every citizen—through the mechanisms of volunteering, the lot, and pay—had an equal chance of being able to serve, but no special access to a position, and any citizen could challenge a decision or an action, legitimacy did not depend on universal participation.

The participatory process itself, as the sophist Protagoras suggested and later commentators like John Stuart Mill recognized, broadened the citizen's perspective beyond his own particular interests, to consideration of how those interests related to the concerns of the polis as a whole. According to Aristotle the exercise of citizenship through taking turns in office, discussing alternatives, and reaching decisions involved "considering the interest of others" (*Politics* 1275b, 1279a; see discussion in Mansbridge 1999). I would go further and suggest that the operation of the democratic system inculcated civic virtues and attitudes even among those citizens who did not themselves step forward, but who knew that they could. The point is not that the Athenians were inherently more disposed to think about shared concerns or a common good; indeed, perhaps precisely because they did not believe that this attitude came naturally to human beings who differed in wealth, education, intelligence, and a host of other characteristics, they created institutions of democratic governance to instill this broader perspective.

Leadership

In the modern state, leadership is the crucial factor: leaders frame issues and take actions, while citizens pass judgment only infrequently and retrospectively (Schumpeter 1942; Rosenstone and Hansen 1996). And indeed, many citizens do not even bother to do that. It is sometimes claimed that the Athenians made no room for leadership (Schumpeter 1942). Yet in fact they reserved election, seen quite clearly as an "aristocratic" procedure, for certain roles for which experience and talent were deemed particularly important, such as generals and treasurers. These elected officials, like those chosen by lot, were subject to preliminary scrutiny (*dokimasia*), votes of no confidence, prosecutions, and an accounting for their performance at the end of their tenure (*euthuna*). Other, self-appointed, and unofficial leaders could make their case in the assembly or the council or the law courts.

Because of the various forms of scrutiny and oversight, the principle of rotation, and the need to persuade and to be accountable to the assembly, a self-selected elite of talent can influence but not dominate.

TAKING DEMOCRACY SERIOUSLY

To some professional critics of advanced industrial democracies, as well as to some citizens, procedural democracy has come to seem rather hollow: necessary, but not sufficient.[32] The divisions that exist in modern pluralist societies may not be bridgeable through procedures alone. Benign inattention to difference may deteriorate into fragmentation, segregation, and conflict. The current interest in "deliberative democracy"—shorthand for participation by ordinary citizens in deliberation about matters that affect them—has been prompted by concerns of this kind. They include (1) the belief that the traditional liberal conception of democracy does not deliver real equality of opportunity, accountability, or an equal say in decision making, in part because liberal proceduralism permits economic power to rule; and (2) the recognition that procedural democracy ignores—or resolves by judicial fiat—disagreements that are rooted in the values and commitments that matter most to citizens.[33]

Yet it is striking that even deliberative democracy, designed to remedy the problem of liberal overabstraction from the realities of inequality and difference, reflects uneasiness with the idea of popular political control. Many of the theorists of deliberative democracy want to bring the people back into popular government; they also want to ensure that what emerges from participation is freedom and justice, and are unwilling to rely on political institutions to achieve this (discussion in Macedo 1999; Bohman and Rehg 1997). In these formulations, the "deliberative" component of the equation carries much of the burden of constraining the free exercise of power. "Deliberative" may be construed to mean "rational," which can be given content of various kinds. Or deliberation may be defined as "giving reasons that fellow citizens can be expected to regard as reasons for them," for example, not pure assertions of self-interest. Deliberation is meant to embody reciprocity, which imposes a prior constraint on the content of the argument: it must be moral (i.e., universalizable, not self-regarding) in form (see introductions in Macedo 1999; Elster 1998).

Theories of deliberative democracy seek to construct democratic institutions on assumptions about the reasoned deliberation of individuals who have no purely personal stake in the outcome. For Jürgen Habermas, the very conditions of deliberative exchange (the construction of an ideal speech situation) ensure this kind of disinterestedness and reciprocity.[34] Some theorists see consensus as the goal of deliberation.[35] Under this scenario, the arena of political engagement becomes essentially nonpolitical:

issues of power and competing interests are not joined (Shapiro, Walzer in Macedo 1999). Others are braver and assert that all principles, even those they regard as fundamental, must be put to the deliberative test, at least as a thought experiment if not in reality.[36] Yet the deliberative test itself is still fundamentally moral in structure: it depends on constraints on what individuals can appropriately say.[37]

Moreover, although part of the aim of the deliberative democrats is to give more substance to the idea of equality, in fact many of them acknowledge that deliberation may well only reinforce existing power relationships unless relevant kinds of equality are fostered.[38] Yet one important mechanism for promoting greater deliberative equality—namely, making it possible for all citizens to participate freely in a sovereign process of deliberation—is regarded as too risky to other values unless it is constrained in ways that are unrealistic and that undermine its educative and equalizing power. The great conundrum of modern liberal democracy is that the people themselves, if they are to be construed as autonomous and truly free, must be seen to be actually determining what procedures will govern democratic decision-making, yet the procedures themselves must also genuinely constrain what the people may do and decide, on the basis of some principle of rightness or justice.[39] And indeed, all free and democratic (as opposed to anarchic) societies must impose rules on themselves. But if they are truly democratic, they must also continually reassess whether their guiding principles and institutions are "justice-tending," and thereby call into question the very procedures that were thought to underlie the rightness of their collective judgments (Michelman 1997). If autonomous self-government is to be real, and not merely, in Benjamin Constant's words, an "abstract presumption," then this nettle must be grasped, and institutions created that keep popular power alive and preserve the genuine possibility of questioning and reform of current practices, while also securing the overall stability and reliability and perceived legitimacy of the prevailing system of lawmaking.[40] I suggest that although there were some notable lapses, the institutions of Athenian democracy, as developed and refined over the course of the late sixth, fifth, and fourth centuries, by and large succeeded in this aim.

The uniqueness of Athens consisted not merely in the emergence of democratic self-consciousness, not just in the extension of political power to the propertyless thetes, but also in the interlocking and mutually reinforcing institutional mechanisms the Athenians created to make this diverse and dynamic polity work. It is striking that none of the contributors to this volume discusses in any detail the institutional features that underlie the distinctiveness of the Athenian democracy and its significance for us: the use of the lot, rotation, pay for office, and the principle of *ho boulomenos*. These Athenian institutions sought to build the "public" view into each citizen, without denying individual difference or constraining individual freedom or imposing external controls on the collective exercise of power.[41] The Athenians removed the extrinsic reasons for not participating (via pay), established certain minimal qualifications to be met before entry into office and procedures for accountability (through scrutiny) during and afterwards, addressed barriers to acquiring a sense of competence (through, for example, exposure to debates in the assembly), and stymied the will to dominate (which lot and rotation and the authority of the assembly and the courts rule out); the motivation that survives this filtration is the essence of civic virtue. This motivation could never be assumed. Indeed, Athenian drama, philosophy, and history reveal that the Athenians were acutely aware of the risks inherent in the attempt to combine freedom and order, and for this very reason civic virtue was actively promoted. Every citizen was free and eligible to put himself to this test. The kind of participation made possible by the institutions of democracy expressed the power and freedom of the people and in the process sought to cultivate the reciprocity, reflectiveness, experience, and public-mindedness that others have sought to impose through external constraints on popular power.

LIVING DEMOCRACY

What might all this mean for us, if anything? What if we were to take seriously both the fundamental principles of Athenian democracy and the way in which the Athenians sought to realize them? What if we tried to deal with our disquiet about popular power by creating institutions that strengthen democracy rather than constrain it? The emergence and evolution of the Athenian system offers clues to how we, inhabitants of a very different world, might better realize the full potential of democracy.

Since we—unlike the archaic Athenians—already endorse the concept of equality among citizens, one might think that it would be easier for us than it was for them to make the people, in Ober's words, a "grammatical subject rather than an object of someone else's verb." On the contrary, it seems: our commitment to one kind of equality—individual rights and human potential—gets in the way of our ability to achieve another—political capacity and access to power. Our understanding of equality has enabled us to span large differences while preserving order and retaining citizen loyalty. But will the belief that every citizen has an equal stake in the polity survive the growing awareness of inequalities generated and reinforced by the differential exercise of mobility and choice, the increasingly entrenched power of those with wealth and education, and the actions of governments ever more detached and remote from the will and self-understanding of citizens?[42]

The Athenian reworking of concepts of equality may be useful here. Solon extended citizenship status and protections to all residents of

Attica—even those without property—who met certain specified criteria. Shared citizenship was later supplemented by a more demanding kind of civic equality. At the heart of the arguments of both Ober and Raaflaub rests the claim that the triumph of democracy meant a fundamental change in the very nature of the relationship between political status, on the one hand, and social or economic status, on the other. In response to a threat to the integrity of the polis from Spartans allied with certain aristocrats (Ober), the Athenians mobilized as a polis and forged a shared political identity that explicitly transcended (though it by no means eliminated) their social and economic differences. In part because of their reliance on the lower (rowing) classes to vanquish the Persians (Raaflaub), the Athenians later proceeded to institute further changes in the political structure that reflected the commitment to inclusiveness and equal sovereignty and cultivated the capacity for self-rule.

Those who seek to democratize modern liberal republics start—as reformers will—by extending existing methods or offering specific proposals for institutional change, often on the assumption that these will engender a different construal of political power and equality. Some point to the recent increase in ballot initiatives, recall procedures, and referenda, and even the growing reliance on opinion polls, as signs of a democratic renaissance. However, without the opportunity for collective discussion and deliberation, such procedures are neither demanding nor civic-minded; they simply aggregate the preferences of individual consumers.[43] Other modern commentators have suggested, in the words of one, the creation of a genuine "popular branch" of the American government at the national level, using random selection, deliberation in small groups, payment, and, in some instances, mandated participation.[44] This proposal is intended to supplement, not displace, representative government and the judiciary. The government of the Canadian province of British Columbia recently empanelled a random sample of citizens to hold hearings on electoral reform and participation and draft a referendum on the issue.[45] These Athens-like contrivances are well worth taking seriously. They could add a genuinely popular voice to decision making.

However, if our primary concern is the ability of political institutions to mobilize and empower capable democratic citizens, then the local level is the most appropriate context for implementing the lessons gleaned from Athens. These lessons fall under two headings: (1) increasing the power of political status and (2) forging a sense of mutual connectedness and responsibility while preserving individual freedom. In the modern context, institutional change is needed to build citizen capacity through the political process.[46] Perhaps, if fully institutionalized and frequent, and with provisions for continued involvement by participants in other contexts after the end of their term, some of the proposed national mechanisms could begin to alter the citizens' understanding of their role and responsibilities. But this kind of transformation is most likely to be achieved at the local level.[47]

Some degree of similarity across the population and some limitations on size are probably essential if citizens are to have an equal and genuine opportunity to make decisions. The Athenian example suggests that political institutions can themselves create and sustain such a system in a community of substantial size (not face to face) and significant diversity.[48] The point of democratic citizenship as understood by the Athenians was precisely to make political equality possible for a large and diverse population. How then, in the world as it now is, might one go about creating a boundary at the local level that effectively institutionalizes exposure to difference, collective identification, and civic participation for both the elite and the masses and those in between? The boundary need not coincide with an entity currently considered a political unit or, still less, an existing "community." Part of the challenge is to create a form of community through political processes. Collective identification, equal power, citizen competence, and accountability could be promoted through the institutionalization of mechanisms of deliberative democracy in which every citizen of a local area has an equal chance to participate. Because it matters that these citizens can come to see themselves as connected, and not primarily as transients for whom exit is an easy option, the local unit should have a plausible claim to being a functional boundary (ideally, both economic and political).

Consider the following possible scenario.[49] Each year, a randomly selected group of citizens is invited to participate in deliberation about a significant policy question.[50] They decide whether or not to come.[51] They are paid (equally) for their time. They are given materials that present balanced, often competing, views, on the question at issue. They meet in small heterogeneous groups. Moderators help to ensure that everyone has an opportunity to make his or her views known.[52] There is no constraint on what they may say except the demands of civility. Participants are not required to reach consensus but explore each other's views. Public officials are asked to attend these discussions. They meet with participants afterwards and are asked how they will attempt to pursue the ideas generated by citizens and take into account the priorities identified in the deliberation. Participating citizens are invited to contribute to the implementation process in appropriate ways.

Throughout the year, the media are encouraged to cover the activities of participants and officials. Participants for one year are not permitted to participate in the deliberation the following year so that over time significant numbers of formerly uninvolved citizens are exposed to the views of their neighbors and make their own voices heard. This kind of sustained public consultation at the local level is still a far cry from formal empowerment but could contribute to the gradual development of institutions of popular decision-making.[53] The actual experience of giving first influence then power to the people may, for us as for the Athenians, help to assuage the fear—apparently confirmed by empirical evidence—that the masses are incompetent to rule.[54]

One implication of this volume is that these ambitious experiments in democracy may be premature: that to be transformative they must be given formal authority, and that this can never occur without a prior and powerful collective recognition of the interdependence and competence of all citizens. What gave the Athenians the confidence to depart from *their* deeply ingrained assumptions? According to Ober, the threat posed by Sparta's alliance with Isagoras motivated spontaneous action by the full citizen body to defend the integrity of the city and then to act on Cleisthenes' revolutionary proposals. According to Raaflaub, the recognition that they could trust the thetes—as rowers of the ships sent out against the Persians—emboldened the Athenians to support Ephialtes' radical reforms. Ideological "ruptures" and tectonic shifts cannot be deliberately instigated, only exploited. Perhaps transformative change in political structures can occur only in response to a powerful external threat coupled with a perceived risk of crippling internal disunity. As experiments in democracy acquire traction, it may be worth inquiring of ourselves, as this volume inquires of ancient Athens, whether a galvanizing challenge may already be in play.[55]

NOTES

1. The most frequent grounds for dismissing the ancient example is the fact that even the Athenian democracy excluded slaves and women from (full) citizenship rights. Yet the American republic excluded the former until the third quarter of the nineteenth century, and the latter until the early twentieth century. The power of the Athenian revolution lay precisely in an unprecedented expansion of citizenship to include individuals without property or social status. A second oft-cited reason for describing our democracy as entirely different in kind from the ancient version is the Athenians' alleged belief in the "priority of the polis over the individual" and related disregard for human rights (see, for example, Holmes 1979, with Hansen 1999: 79–81). It is certainly true that for the Athenians freedom was a political achievement, not a quality inherent in every human being. But the impression that this entailed subjection of citizens to the state derives from paying too much attention to the philosophers and not enough to the practices. (Cartledge offers pertinent thoughts on the lack of a "state" in the modern sense.) References to other chapters in this volume are given by name only.

2. Attributed to Bruce Ackerman in Leib 2002.

3. In Raaflaub's words, the "decisive characteristics" of *dēmokratia* were "that political equality among all citizens was realized to the fullest extent possible, and in the assembly and related institutions the demos not only made final decisions but was fully sovereign, representing the actual government of the polis and controlling

the entire political process." See Dunn 2005: 37 on the "fierce directness" of Athenian democracy.

4. Raaflaub points to the violence that followed Ephialtes' reforms—but not Cleisthenes'—as a sign that Ephialtes' were the truly revolutionary initiatives. However, violent opposition did attend the Cleisthenic reforms: the expulsion of Isagoras and Cleomenes. The leading opponents of the Ephialtic proposals were away from Athens at the time they were passed.

5. Or to give them the opportunity to ostracize a leader considered to be too powerful (as discussed by Ober)? Note that one purpose of this volume is to explain the unprecedented and peculiar emergence of full democracy at Athens. This peculiarity is often ascribed to the creation of a naval empire, because the thetes therefore became critical to the survival of the polis. However, the peculiarity began decades earlier, when Athens created new "tribes."

6. See Arist. *Ath. Pol.* 21.4; as Raaflaub suggests, Cleisthenes' reforms did alter participation dramatically but were not seen as threatening.

7. Did the offices rotate? It seems clear that councillors served for only one year and could serve only two terms, but could they be reelected for the second term? See Rhodes 1972: 3–4. Manin (1997: 31) discusses the logical incompatibility of election and rotation, since election implies unrestricted choice.

8. Cleisthenes did create an elected board of generals to perform a specific function; but it was only after the use of the lot diminished the role of the archons as political leaders that the elected *stratēgoi* came into their own as the most powerful magistrates; so this fact need not affect our construal of Cleisthenes' intentions in enhancing the power of the council and the assembly. See *Ath. Pol.* 28.3, with Hansen 1999: 233.

9. So Raaflaub 1983 and Eder 1998.

10. Note Raaflaub on the significance of paying the rowers in the fleet as precursor to payment for political participation. After about 460, hoplites were also paid a per diem. (I owe this last point to Paul Cartledge.) In 403/2, the restored assembly considered proposals both to introduce a property qualification and to make citizens of the slaves who had fought for the democracy. It rejected both. This may be one indication that military service was not thought sufficient reason to award full citizenship rights (the American treatment of black combatants after the Civil War may be comparable). However, it is true that reliance on the thetes was necessarily more systematic and sustained than dependence on loyal slaves during the oligarchic revolts.

11. I am of course not suggesting that Wallace (this volume) and Eder (1998) do not recognize the differences, only that it is the similarities that appear to be most salient in their determination of when Athens became a democracy. I have not here given Wallace's careful comparative argument the attention it deserves: because I am discussing the implications of the birth of democracy for our own time, I have limited myself to his characterization of the Solonian achievement. He argues that the full demos could have exerted its power (through the assembly and the courts) at any time after Solon's reforms, and did so on a few occasions, including when the people welcomed the tyrant Peisistratus. This seems to me to underestimate the significance of continued elite dominance and hierarchical assumptions in all the Solonian institutions (the people chose a tyrant, not democracy, over the squabbling

aristocrats). According to Wallace, the people—despite an egalitarian and self-confident frame of mind—chose not to take the reins of power because they were too busy with farming, and there seemed little benefit in participation. But if it was not necessary to break the hold of aristocratic elites clustered in different regions, why, then, were the Cleisthenic reforms required? Like Ober and Raaflaub, Wallace acknowledges that "fully active, day-to-day democracy at Athens followed the establishment of the Delian League."

12. See Eder 1998 for the first interpretation; Hansen 1999, Ostwald 1986, and Strauss 1991 for the second.

13. Note, for example, Pericles in Thuc. 2.37.3: *agraphoi nomoi*.

14. *Ath. Pol.* 29.3, 31.1, 34. See Finley 1971, reprinted with revisions in Finley 1975 and 1986; Hansen 1999, 296–300.

15. *Contra:* e.g., Ostwald 1986; Wolin 1994; Hansen 1999: 154–55, 301–3.

16. As Hansen has observed, an assembly-democracy became a people's court–democracy (Hansen 1999: 154–55, 303). The *nomothetai* were chosen by lot from among the six thousand citizens who had been selected (also by lot) to serve as jurors. Juries, unlike the assembly before 403, were paid. Laws passed by the *nomothetai* could be challenged and referred to a group of jurors assembled as *dikastai*, with ordinary citizens arguing the case on either side.

17. Note that these are often seen as largely overlapping, if not identical, by Montesquieu and the American Federalists, for example. See analysis of election as an aristocratic principle in Manin 1997: chaps. 2–4.

18. See Farrar 1988; cf. Rousseau's analysis of the rule of law, as described in Pateman 1972: 23: "An even better formulation of the role of participation is that men are to be ruled by the logic of the operation of the political situation that they had themselves created and that this situation was such that the possibility of the rule of individual men was 'automatically' precluded."

19. Michelman 1997. Michelman offers the notion of "validity" as a way to preserve appearances when we decide to treat as binding laws that we recognize to be less than just but are prepared to regard as "defensibly justice-seeking."

20. *Contra* Wolin 1994, who seems to adopt the view of the theorists he criticizes, i.e., that democracy is lawlessness. We seem to be offered a choice between a constricting form (i.e., any institutionalization or constitution) that violates democratic principles, or no form at all.

21. As Paul Cartledge has reminded me, Thucydides (8.66) observes that the antidemocratic conspiracy of 411 succeeded in part because "the size of the city made it impossible for people to know each other."

22. For the distinction between *homoiotēs* and *isotēs*, see Cartledge 1996a.

23. Cf. Skinner 1990 on the similar views of the Italian republican theorists (especially Machiavelli, in the *Discorsi*). By contrast with these theorists, however, Athenians did not recommend "coercion" to enforce the performance of civic duty, though they often asserted that participation was expected and prized (e.g., Thuc. 2.40) and they structured institutions and culture to promote participation.

24. See Protagoras's account of democratic socialization in Pl. *Prt.* 320d–328d, with Farrar 1988: 77–78.

25. In support of this claim, Stephen Holmes quotes M. I. Finley: "Classical Greeks and Republican Romans possessed a considerable measure of freedom, in

speech, in political debate, in their business activities and even in religion. However, they lacked, and would have been appalled by, inalienable rights. There were no theoretical limits to the power of the state, no activity, no sphere of human behaviour, in which the state could not legitimately intervene provided the decision was properly taken for any reason that was held to be valid by a legitimate authority" (Holmes 1979: 119, citing Finley 1973: 154–55). Compare Finley 1976, where the same point is followed by the sentence "Freedom meant the rule of law and participation in the decision-making process, not the possession of inalienable rights." Robert Dahl (1989) suggests that the notion of rights can be seen as an alternative to full participation, now that the latter is in his view no longer feasible. Benjamin Constant, in his essay comparing the liberties of the ancients and the moderns (1819), portrays Athens as the ancient state where the people wielded the greatest power and enjoyed the most individual freedom. Note that modern constitutional democracies intervene in many spheres of human behavior when it is deemed warranted for reasons of public good or security and "held to be valid by a legitimate authority." See Finley 1973: 74; Hansen 1999: 80–81. Compare Ostwald (1996), who construes Athenian citizenship in terms of "sharing in or being part of a community" that defines the individual's identity.

26. See Montesquieu's observations about the importance of self-selection as a way to prevent rule by incompetents: "People without ability must have been very reluctant to put their names forward for selection by lot" (*Spirit of the Laws*, Book II, chap. 2, discussed by Manin 1997: 70–74). An anonymous reviewer notes that the Pnyx acted as another filter: its small size relative to the total citizen population limited the number who participated in the all-important assembly. However, this constraint filters only quantitatively, not qualitatively.

27. Schumpeter 1942, with Manin 1997: 161–62. The increasing use of opinion polls and apparent deference by elected officials to the wishes of the electorate may be thought to have altered this situation. See further below.

28. Sartori (1987), the political scientist cited most frequently by Eder (1998), belongs in this Schumpeterian tradition. See Manin 1997: 161 with nn. 1 and 2.

29. Pl. *Prt.*, with Farrar 1988: chap. 3. The ascription to the people of consent to political society (for example, by Hume and Hobbes) is based on an analysis of man's basic need for security and protection. They construe man as a presocial being with essentially fixed tendencies and characteristics; see Farrar 1998: 89–93.

30. It is unclear why they established six thousand as the quorum. Cartledge (personal communication) suggests several reasons: that it was the same figure as for ostracisms, established by the 480s at the latest; that roughly this number tended to show up; and that as approximately one fifth of the total citizen body, it was considered a sufficiently large proportion to be relatively representative. It is, however, interesting that the ancient sources do not discuss the issue. See Hansen 1999: 130–32: the new Pnyx was adapted to the required size of the assembly (not vice versa) and thus made it easy to tell if a quorum was present.

31. Cartledge argues that the fact that "only a small proportion of the total citizen body was present and voting" in the assembly at any one time was unproblematic and in no way compromised the "transparency" and "face-to-face-ness" of the system of governance. It is interesting and rarely noted that the Athenians enforced rota-

tion for "offices" (including being on the council), but not for participation in the assembly or the juries. And self-selection was the only criterion for participation in the assembly. Their comfort with the idea that one citizen (or six thousand) could "stand in" for the rest is not attributable to "face-to-face-ness"—at least not in the sense that everyone knew everyone else, because they did not—but to a system designed to promote a sense of civic continuity and reciprocity and a shared and equal stake in the well-being of the city. It is, however, doubtless the case, as Cartledge observes, that the experience of "being in full view" of fellow decision-makers reinforced this sense of mutuality and unity or continuity amidst difference. See the analysis by Manin 1997: 29–30. Cf. Carl Schmitt's definition of democracy as based on identity between ruler and ruled, with discussion by Manin, 150–53.

32. However, it cannot be said often enough that in many parts of the world procedural democracy would be a major achievement.

33. See, for example, Gutmann and Thomson 1996; Macedo 1999; Bohman and Rehg 1997; Elster 1998.

34. E.g., Habermas 1982; cf. Elster 1997; Cohen 1997.

35. See, for example, Gutman and Thompson 1996; Barber 1984; and Mansbridge's account of unitary democracy (1983) and of the need to retain mechanisms to deal with conflict (1999).

36. See Gutmann and Thompson 1999: the core principles are not defined by actual deliberations. Cf. Finley 1973: 26, 102.

37. See Michelman 1997 on how popular sovereignty fits with the requirement of equal respect. See critiques of deliberative democracy by Sanders 1997; Dryzek 2000.

38. Mendelberg 2002; Sanders 1997; Knight and Johnson 1997; Shapiro 1999.

39. See Michelman 1997. And see Finley (1973: 74), who refers to the dilemma faced by modern states as well as Athens: i.e., the need to balance various claims, such as freedom of speech and security. The dilemma, he observes, "will be found wherever the final sanction for political decisions and actions lies within the community itself, not in some higher authority."

40. Constant 1819. See Dryzek (2000), who argues for a deliberative democracy that is critical of existing power structures and institutions.

41. Although Wolin (1994) argues that institutionalization inevitably saps democratic sovereignty, and did so in Athens, he also recognizes the lot and rotation (which persisted throughout) as "institutions that subvert institutionalization" (43).

42. See the literature on disengagement and distrust, including Putnam 2000; Rosenstone and Hansen 1996; Norris 2002. And see "Vox Populi," a project of the Center for Policy Attitudes, which in 1999 ascertained through surveys that the American public thinks a random sample of the population would make better decisions than the Congress (www.vox-populi.org). The entrenchment of social and economic inequality is most powerfully visible, in the United States, in the extent of spatial differentiation and segregation by income and race that results from choices made by those with resources to live in communities that effectively exclude poorer citizens; see Rae 1999; Oliver 2001; Shapiro 1999. Local democracy will depend on giving residents of a particular area a stake in their collective civic identity. This modern boundary must acknowledge the mobility and respect for individual choice that

now characterizes Western capitalist democracies. That is, means must be found to root people in a community in ways that inhibit without preventing the choice to leave; see Farrar 1996.

43. The rationality of the outcomes achieved through aggregation has been challenged by Riker (1982) and others. There is evidence that deliberation shortcircuits the probability of cycles in majority preferences (which result in meaningless majority decisions) and results in agreement on criteria. See List 2002; Dryzek and List 2003; Farrar, Fishkin, Green et al. forthcoming.

44. Leib 2002; see also Gastil 2000; Burnheim 1985; cf. Crosby 1995; Threlkeld 1998; Dahl 1970 on the idea of a minipopulus. And note the proposal for a national Deliberation Day: Fishkin and Ackerman 2004. Cf. Hibbing and Theiss-Morse 2002; Mansbridge 1999; Mendelberg 2002; Carson and Martin 1999: chap. 6 regarding lack of evidence on the effects of deliberation.

45. The Citizens Assembly on Democratic Reform (www.citizensassembly.bc.ca).

46. Cf. Knight and Johnson 1997; Mansbridge 1999. Cf. the literature on social capital, which assumes that creating social capital in other contexts increases citizen capacity to participate in democracy: Putnam 2000, with Skocpol 1999 and Norris 2002.

47. See the recent book by Gary Hart (2002), which proposes creation of local wards along the lines originally outlined by Thomas Jefferson. *Contra:* Cohen 1997. And see Manin 1991 on dilution of power of rotation and lot in a large polity. See also Dahl 1989 on the significance of scale for the practices of democracy. Constant (1819) remarks on the relative political unimportance of the individual citizen in the modern nation-state.

48. Although the Athenian citizenry did not include different races or recent immigrants (or not many), the claim of autochthony, or local origin, was a civic myth, and the polis spanned substantial differences in wealth, breeding, and origins.

49. A scenario currently being implemented in the Greater New Haven region (Connecticut, USA) by the Community Foundation and the League of Women Voters, with Yale University's Institution for Social and Policy Studies and James Fishkin's Center for Deliberative Democracy at Stanford University. I am the project coordinator of the annual Citizens Forum. See Fishkin and Farrar 2005. See also the examples of public participation in civic governance at the local level assembled by the National League of Cities (www.nlc.org/Issues/Democracy_Governance/index.cfm), the Citizen Juries organized by the Jefferson Center (www.jefferson-center.org), and the budget discussions convened by Mayor Tony Williams of Washington, D.C., with the assistance of America Speaks (http://americaspeaks.org). Analyses of a number of these methods are included in Gastil and Levine 2005. In Europe, note the Planungstelle in Germany (e.g., www.havelland-flaeming.de/Links/frame_links.htm) and the Danish process presented in Flyvbjerg 1998. For examples from the developing world, see www.ids.ac.uk/logolink/newsletter/index.htm.

50. For an account of this mechanism, known as a Deliberative Poll©, which Fishkin invented and has implemented in a range of contexts, see Fishkin 1991 and 1997; McCombs and Reynolds 1999; Fishkin and Laslett 2003; Fishkin and Farrar 2005; and the websites of the Center for Deliberative Democracy at Stanford University (www.stanford.edu/cdd) and of the Yale Institution for Social and Policy Studies (www.yale.edu/isps).

51. Note the difference between this strategy and the Athenian: in the D.P. the lottery comes first, then *ho boulomenos,* or self-selection. The procedure of using the lottery first facilitates access to a broader group, who are recruited and only then make the decision about whether to come. This was perhaps not so important in Athens, where the system was well established and access to offices rotated among citizens.

52. Note that the Athenians "deliberated" in large groups: juries of 201 up to 2,501; assemblies of up to 6,000; the council of 500; the smallest, apart from groups of officials, were the 50-member tribal subsets of the council (with 17-member subsubsets serving as "executive committees," called prytanies). Small-group deliberation is necessary precisely because modern citizens are not regularly exposed to a variety of arguments and perspectives or given a chance to practice how to make themselves heard. By contrast, the Athenians could attend forty or more assemblies a year, participate in juries and the council, and serve as one of seven hundred magistrates.

53. A national initiative sponsored by MacNeil/Lehrer Productions, *By the People,* has been promoting the idea of local deliberations of this kind in communities around the country, on the issue of America's role in the world. Ten were held in January 2004; seventeen (including seven of the January ten) in October 2004; fifteen in 2005. For additional information, see www.pbs.org/newshour/btp/. I am coordinating these citizen deliberations. The aim is to develop a local infrastructure committed to carrying forward a process of civic problem-solving of the kind contemplated in New Haven—using the public broadcasting system as a scaffolding—and to give participants the sense that their voices are being heard not just locally, but nationally, and that they must consider the relationship between local concerns and national needs.

54. For empirical evidence of citizen incompetence, see, for example, Delli Carpini et al. 1996. But note the point made by Finley (1973: 70): it is absurd to exclude citizens from effective participation on the grounds that they will make extreme demands, and then to point to their extrademocratic actions as evidence that it was right to exclude them.

55. I am grateful to Paul Cartledge and Kurt Raaflaub for their very helpful comments on earlier drafts. Conversations with John Dunn over many years have shaped my understanding of why Athenian democracy still matters. See most recently Dunn 2005.

BIBLIOGRAPHY

Ackerman, Bruce, and James Fishkin. 2004. *Deliberation Day*. New Haven.

Adkins, Arthur W. H. 1960. *Merit and Responsibility: A Study in Greek Values*. Oxford. Repr., Chicago, 1975.

———. 1972. *Moral Values and Political Behavior in Ancient Greece*. New York.

Amit, Moshe. 1965. *Athens and the Sea: A Study in Athenian Sea-Power*. Brussels.

Anderson, Greg. 2003. *The Athenian Experiment: Building an Imagined Political Community in Ancient Attica, 508–490 B.C.* Ann Arbor.

———. 2006. "Why the Athenians Forgot Cleisthenes: Literacy and the Politics of Remembrance in Ancient Athens." In *The Politics of Orality*, edited by Craig Cooper. Leiden.

Anderson, J. K. 1970. *Military Theory and Practice in the Age of Xenophon*. Berkeley.

Andrewes, Antony. 1981. "The Hoplite *Katalogos*." In *Classical Contributions: Studies . . . M. F. McGregor*, edited by G. S. Shrimpton and D. J. McCargar, 1–3. Locust Valley, NJ.

———. 1982a. "The Growth of the Athenian State." *CAH* III.3²: 360–91.

———. 1982b. "The Tyranny of Pisistratus." *CAH* III.3²: 392–416.

Anhalt, Emily K. 1993. *Solon the Singer: Politics and Poetics*. Lanham, MD.

Arendt, Hannah. 1958. *The Human Condition*. Chicago.

———. 1963. *On Revolution*. New York.

Asheri, David. 1966. *Distribuzione di terre nell'antica Grecia*. Memorie dell'Accademia delle Scienze di Torino, Cl. di Scienze Morali, Storiche e Filologiche, ser. 4, 10. Turin.

———. 1975. "Osservazioni sulle origini dell'urbanistica ippodamea." *Rivista storica italiana* 87: 5–16.

———, ed. and comm. 1988. *Erodoto, Le storie, libro I: La Lidia e la Persia*. Milan.

Badian, Ernst. 1971. "Archons and Strategoi." *Antichthon* 5: 1–34.

———. 1993. "Toward a Chronology of the Pentecontaetia down to the Renewal of the Peace of Callias." In *From Plataea to Potidaea: Studies in the History and Historiography of the Pentecontaetia*, 73–107. Baltimore.

———. 1995. "The Ghost of Empire: Reflections on Athenian Foreign Policy in the Fourth Century B.C." In Eder 1995b: 79–106.

———. 2000. "Back to Kleisthenic Chronology." In *Polis and Politics: Studies in Ancient Greek History Presented to M. H. Hansen,* edited by P. Flensted-Jensen, T. H. Nielsen, and L. Rubinstein, 447–64. Copenhagen.

Bakewell, Geoffrey W. 1997. "*Metoikia* in the *Supplices* of Aeschylus." *Classical Antiquity* 16: 209–28.

Bakker, Egbert, Irene J. F. de Jong, and Hans van Wees, eds. 2002. *Brill's Companion to Herodotus.* Leiden.

Balcer, Jack M. 1976. "Imperial Magistrates in the Athenian Empire." *Historia* 25: 257–87.

Barber, Benjamin. 1984. *Strong Democracy.* Berkeley and Los Angeles.

———. 2002. *Fear's Empire: War, Terrorism, and Democracy.* New York.

Barker, Ernest, ed. and trans. 1946. *The Politics of Aristotle.* Oxford.

Bekker-Nielsen, Tønnes, and Lise Hannestad, eds. 2001. *War as a Cultural and Social Force: Essays on Warfare in Antiquity.* Copenhagen.

Beloch, Julius. 1886. *Die Bevölkerung der griechisch-römischen Welt.* Leipzig. Repr., Rome, 1968.

———. 1922. *Griechische Geschichte,* II.2². Berlin and Leipzig. Repr., 1931.

Berent, M. 1994. "The Stateless Polis: Towards a Re-Evaluation of the Classical Greek Political Community." PhD diss., Cambridge University.

———. 1996. "Hobbes and the 'Greek Tongues.'" *History of Political Thought* 17: 36–59.

———. 2004. "In Search of the Greek State: A Rejoinder to M. H. Hansen." *Polis* 21.1–2: 107–46.

Berger, Shlomo. 1992. *Revolution and Society in Greek Sicily and Southern Italy.* Stuttgart.

Bers, Victor. 1985. "Dikastic *thorubos.*" In Cartledge and Harvey 1985: 1–15.

Berve, Helmut. 1967. *Die Tyrannis bei den Griechen.* 2 vols. Munich.

Bleicken, Jochen. 1987. "Die Einheit der athenischen Demokratie in klassischer Zeit." *Hermes* 115: 257–83.

———. 1994. *Die athenische Demokratie.* 2d ed. Paderborn.

Bloedow, E. F. 1992. "Pericles and Ephialtes in the Reforms of 462 B.C." *Scholia: Natal Studies in Classical Antiquity* 1: 85–101.

Blok, Josine, and André Lardinois, eds. 2006. *Solon: New Historical and Philological Perspectives.* Leiden.

Boedeker, Deborah. 2001. "Paths to Heroization at Plataea." In *The New Simonides: Contexts of Praise and Desire,* edited by Deborah Boedeker and David Sider, 148–63. Oxford.

———. 2007. "Athenian Religion in the Age of Pericles." In Samons 2007: 46–69.

Boedeker, Deborah, and Kurt A. Raaflaub, eds. 1998. *Democracy, Empire, and the Arts in Fifth-Century Athens.* Cambridge, MA.

Boegehold, Alan L. 1994. "Perikles' Citizenship Law of 451/0 B.C." In Boegehold and Scafuro 1994: 57–66.

———. 1995. *The Lawcourts at Athens: Sites, Buildings, Equipment, Procedure, and Testimonia.* The Athenian Agora, vol. 28. Princeton.

Boegehold, Alan L., and Adele C. Scafuro, eds. 1994. *Athenian Identity and Civic Ideology.* Baltimore.

Boersma, J. S. 1970. *Athenian Building Policy from 561/0 to 405/4 B.C.* Groningen.

Bohman, James, and William Rehg, eds. 1997. *Deliberative Democracy: Essays on Reason and Politics.* Cambridge, MA.

Bordes, J. 1982. *Politeia dans la pensée grecque jusqu'à Aristote.* Paris.

Braun, Maximilian. 1998. *Die "Eumeniden" des Aischylos und der Areopag.* Tübingen.

Breuil, Jean-Luc. 1995. "De *kratos* à *dēmokratiē:* Une famille de mots chez Hérodote." *Ktema* 20: 71–84.

Broadhead, H. D. 1960. *The Persae of Aeschylus.* Cambridge.

Brock, Roger. 1991. "The Emergence of Democratic Ideology." *Historia* 40: 160–69.

Brunt, P. A. 1988. *The Fall of the Roman Republic and Related Essays.* Oxford.

———. 1993. *Studies in Greek History and Thought.* Oxford.

Buck, Carl D. 1955. *The Greek Dialects: Grammar, Selected Inscriptions, Glossary.* Chicago.

Buitron-Oliver, Diana, ed. 1992. *The Greek Miracle: Classical Sculpture from the Dawn of Democracy: The Fifth Century B.C.* Washington, D.C.

Burckhardt, Leonhard A. 1996. *Bürger und Soldaten: Aspekte der politischen und militärischen Rolle athenischer Bürger im Kriegswesen des 4. Jh. v. Chr.* Stuttgart.

Burn, Lucilla. 1989. "The Art of the State in Fifth-Century Athens." In *Images of Authority: Papers Presented to Joyce Reynolds,* edited by M. M. Mackenzie and C. Roueché, 62–81. *Proceedings of the Cambridge Philological Society,* supp. 16. Cambridge.

Burnheim, John. 1985. *Is Democracy Possible? The Alternative to Electoral Politics.* Berkeley and Los Angeles.

Buxton, R. G. A. 1982. *Persuasion in Greek Tragedy: A Study of Peitho.* Cambridge.

Camp, John M. 1992. *The Athenian Agora.* 2d ed. London and New York.

Campbell, David A., ed. and trans. 1982. *Greek Lyric.* Vol. 1: *Sappho, Alcaeus.* LCL 142. Cambridge, MA.

———. 1991. *Greek Lyric.* Vol. 3. LCL 476. Cambridge, MA.

Carena, Carlo, Mario Manfredini, and Luigi Piccirilli, eds. and comms. 1990. *Plutarco, Le vite di Cimone e di Lucullo.* Milan.

Carlier, Pierre. 1998. "Observations sur la décision politique en Grèce, de l'époque mycénienne à l'époque archaïque." In Schuller 1998: 1–18.

Carson, Lyn, and Brian Martin. 1999. *Random Selection in Politics.* Westport, CT.

Cartledge, Paul. 1977. "Hoplites and Heroes: Sparta's Contribution to the Technique of Ancient Warfare." *Journal of Hellenic Studies* 97: 11–27.

———. 1979. *Sparta and Lakonia: A Regional History, 1300–362 B.C.* London. 2d ed.: Cartledge, 2001c.

———. 1987. *Agesilaos and the Crisis of Sparta.* London.

———. 1991. "Richard Talbert's Revision of the Spartan-Helot Struggle: A Reply." *Historia* 38: 379–81.

———. 1996a. "Comparatively Equal: A Spartan Approach." In Ober and Hedrick 1996: 175–85.

———. 1996b. "La nascita degli opliti e l'organizzazione militare." In Settis 1996–2002: 2.1. 681–714.

———. 1997. " 'Deep Plays': Theatre as Process in Greek Civic Life." In Easterling 1997: 3–35.

———. 1998. "Writing the History of Archaic Greek Political Thought." In Fisher and van Wees 1998: 379–99.

————. 2000a. "Democratic Politics Ancient and Modern: From Cleisthenes to Mary Robinson." *Hermathena* 166: 5–29.

————. 2000b. "The Historical Context." In Rowe and Schofield 2000: 11–22.

————. 2001a. "The Birth of the Hoplite: Sparta's Contribution to Early Greek Military Organization." In Cartledge 2001d: 153–66, 225–28.

————. 2001b. "The Peculiar Position of Sparta in the Development of the Greek City-State." In Cartledge 2001d: 21–38, 194–97.

————. 2001c. *Sparta and Lakonia: A Regional History 1300–362 B.C.* 2d ed. London.

————. 2001d. *Spartan Reflections.* London; Berkeley and Los Angeles.

————. 2002. *The Greeks. A Portrait of Self and Others.* 2d ed. Oxford.

Cartledge, Paul, and F. D. Harvey, eds. 1985. *Crux: Essays in Greek History Presented to G. E. M. de Ste. Croix.* Exeter and London.

Cartledge, Paul, Paul Millett, and Sitta von Reden, eds. 1998. *KOSMOS: Essays in Order, Conflict, and Community in Classical Athens.* Cambridge.

Cartledge, Paul, Paul Millett, and Stephen Todd, eds. 1990. *NOMOS: Essays in Athenian Law, Society, and Politics.* Cambridge.

Castriota, David. 1992. *Myth, Ethos, and Actuality: Official Art in Fifth-Century B.C. Athens.* Madison, WI.

————. 1998. "Democracy and Art in Late-Sixth- and Fifth-Century-B.C. Athens." In Morris and Raaflaub 1998: 197–216.

Cawkwell, G. L. 1988. "Nomophylakia and the Areopagus." *Journal of Hellenic Studies* 108: 1–12.

Ceccarelli, Paola. 1993. "Sans thalassocratie, pas de démocratie? Le rapport entre thalassocratie et démocratie à Athènes dans la discussion du Vᵉ et IVᵉ siècle av. J. C." *Historia* 42: 444–70.

Chadwick, John. 1976. *The Mycenaean World.* Cambridge.

Chambers, Mortimer, trans. and comm. 1990. *Aristoteles, Staat der Athener.* Berlin.

Chwe, Michael. 2001. *Rational Ritual: Culture, Coordination, and Common Knowledge.* Princeton.

Cohen, David. 1986. "The Theodicy of Aeschylus: Justice and Tyranny in the *Oresteia.*" *Greece and Rome* 33: 129–41.

————. 1991. "New Legal History." *Rechtshistorisches Journal* 10: 7–40.

Cohen, Joshua. 1997. "Procedure and Substance in Deliberative Democracy." In Bohman and Rehg 1997: 407–38.

Connor, W. Robert. 1971. *The New Politicians of Fifth-Century Athens.* Princeton. Repr. with new introduction, Indianapolis, 1992.

————. 1977. "Tyrannis Polis." In *Ancient and Modern: Essays in Honor of Gerald F. Else,* edited by John D'Arms and John W. Eady, 95–109. Ann Arbor.

————. 1988. "Early Greek Land Warfare as Symbolic Expression." *Past and Present* 119: 3–28.

————. 1989. "City Dionysia and Athenian Democracy." *Classica et Mediaevalia* 40: 7–32. Repr. in Connor et al. 1990: 7–32.

————. 1996a. "Civil Society, Dionysiac Festival, and Athenian Democracy." In Ober and Hedrick 1996: 217–26.

————. 1996b. "Festival and Democracy." In Sakellariou 1996: 79–89.

Connor, W. Robert, M. H. Hansen, K. A. Raaflaub, and B. S. Strauss. 1990. *Aspects of Athenian Democracy.* Copenhagen.

Constant, Benjamin. 1819. "The Liberty of the Ancients Compared with that of the Moderns." In *Constant, Political Writings*, edited and translated by Biancamaria Fontana, 307–28. Cambridge, 1988.

Cornell, T. J. 1995. *The Beginnings of Rome: Italy and Rome from the Bronze Age to the Punic Wars (c. 1000–264 B.C.).* London.

Crane, Gregory. 1992a. "The Fear and Pursuit of Risk: Corinth on Athens, Sparta, and the Peloponnesians (Thucydides 1.68–71, 120–121)." *Transactions of the American Philological Association* 122: 227–56.

———. 1992b. "Power, Prestige, and the Corcyrean Affair in Thucydides 1." *Classical Antiquity* 11: 1–27.

———. 1998. *Thucydides and the Ancient Simplicity: The Limits of Political Realism.* Berkeley and Los Angeles.

Crick, Bernard. 2002. *Democracy: A Very Short Introduction.* Oxford.

Crosby, Ned. 1995. "Citizen Juries: One Solution for Difficult Environmental Questions." In *Fairness and Competence in Citizen Participation: Evaluating Models for Environmental Discourse*, edited by Ortwin Renn, Thomas Webler, and Peter Wiedemann, 157–74. Dordrecht, Netherlands.

Dahl, Robert A. 1956. *A Preface to Democratic Theory.* New Haven.

———. 1970. *After the Revolution: Authority in a Good Society.* New Haven.

———. 1989. *Democracy and Its Critics.* New Haven.

Davies, J. K. 1992. "Greece after the Persian Wars," "Society and Economy." *CAH* V²: 15–33, 287–305. Cambridge.

———. 1993. *Democracy and Classical Greece.* 2d ed. Cambridge, MA.

———. 1995. "The Fourth-Century Crisis. What Crisis?" In Eder 1995b: 29–36.

———. 1996. "Strutture e suddivisioni delle *poleis* arcaiche: Le ripartizioni minori." In Settis 1996–2002: 2.1. 599–652.

———. 2003. "Democracy Without Theory." In *Herodotus and His World*, edited by Peter Derow and Robert Parker, 319–35. Oxford.

Day, J. H., and M. H. Chambers. 1962. *Aristotle's History of Athenian Democracy.* Berkeley and Los Angeles.

Debrunner, Albert. 1947. "Demokratia." In *Festschrift für Edouard Tièche*, 11–24. Bern. Repr. in Kinzl 1995b: 55–69.

Deger-Jalkotzy, Sigrid. 1995. "Mykenische Herrschaftsformen ohne Paläste und die griechische Polis." In Niemeier and Laffineur 1995: 363–77.

Delli Carpini, Michael X., and Scott Keeter. 1996. *What Americans Know about Politics and Why It Matters.* New Haven.

Demont, P. 2003. "Le *klērōtērion* ("machine à tirer au sort") et la démocratie athénienne." *Bulletin de l'Association Guillaume Budé* 2003.1: 26–52.

Derow, Peter, and Robert Parker, eds. 2003. *Herodotus and His World.* Oxford.

Detienne, Marcel. 1965. "En Grèce archaïque: Géométrie, politique et société." *Annales ESC* 20: 425–41.

Dewey, John. 1954. *The Public and Its Problems.* Denver.

Dickinson, Oliver. 1994. *The Aegean Bronze Age.* Cambridge.

Dillon, Matthew. 2002. *Girls and Women in Classical Greek Religion.* London.

Dolezal, Joseph P. 1974. *Aristoteles und die Demokratie.* Frankfurt am Main.

Donlan, Walter. 1970. "Changes and Shifts in the Meaning of Demos in the Literature of the Archaic Period." *La parola del passato* 25: 381–95.

————. 1999. *The Aristocratic Ideal and Selected Papers.* Wauconda, IL.

Dougherty, Carol, and Leslie Kurke, eds. 1993. *Cultural Poetics in Archaic Greece: Cult, Performance, Politics.* Cambridge.

Dreher, Martin. 1983. *Sophistik und Polisentwicklung.* Frankfurt am Main.

Dryzek, John S. 2000. *Deliberative Democracy and Beyond: Liberals, Critics, Contestations.* Oxford.

Dryzek, John S., and Christian List. 2003. "Social Choice Theory and Deliberative Democracy: A Reconciliation." *British Journal of Political Science* 33: 1–28.

Ducat, Jean. 1990. *Les hilotes. Bulletin de Correspondance Hellénique,* supp. 20. Athens and Paris.

Dunn, John, ed. 1992. *Democracy: The Unfinished Journey, 508 B.C. to A.D. 1993.* Oxford.

————. 1993. *Western Political Theory in the Face of the Future.* 2d ed. Cambridge.

————. 2005. *Setting the People Free: The Story of Democracy.* London.

Easterling, P. E., ed. 1997. *The Cambridge Companion to Greek Tragedy.* Cambridge.

Eder, Walter. 1988. "Political Self-Confidence and Resistance: The Role of Demos and Plebs after the Expulsion of the Tyrant in Athens and the King in Rome." In *Forms of Control and Subordination in Antiquity,* edited by Toro Yuge and Masaoki Doi, 465–75. Leiden.

————. 1991. "Who Rules? Power and Participation in Athens and Rome." In Molho et al. 1991: 169–96.

————. 1992. "Polis und Politai: Die Auflösung des Adelsstaates und die Entwicklung des Polisbürgers." In Heilmeyer and Wehgartner 1992: 24–38.

————. 1995a. "Die athenische Demokratie im 4. Jahrhundert v. Chr.: Krise oder Vollendung?" In Eder 1995b: 11–28.

————, ed. 1995b. *Die athenische Demokratie im 4. Jahrhundert v. Chr.: Vollendung oder Verfall einer Verfassungsform?* Stuttgart.

————. 1998. "Aristocrats and the Coming of Athenian Democracy." In Morris and Raaflaub 1998: 105–40.

————. 2000. "Demokratie und Größenwahn: Die Paradoxien der athenischen Demokratie." In *Genie und Wahnsinn: Konzepte psychischer 'Normalität' und 'Abnormität' im Altertum,* edited by Bernhard Effe and R. F. Glei, 83–95. Trier.

————. 2005. "The Political Significance of the Codification of Law in Archaic Societies: An Unconventional Hypothesis." In Raaflaub 2005b: 239–67.

Edwards, Mark W. 1991. *The Iliad: A Commentary.* Vol. V: *Books 17–20.* Cambridge.

Effenterre, Henri van. 1976. "Clisthène et les mesures de mobilisation." *Revue des études grecques* 89: 1–17.

————. 1985. *La cité grecque: Des origines à la défaite de Marathon.* Paris.

Effenterre, Henri van, and Françoise Ruzé, eds. 1994–95. *Nomima: Recueil d'inscriptions politiques et juridiques de l'archaïsme grec.* 2 vols. Rome.

Ehrenberg, Victor. 1937. "When Did the Polis Rise?" *Journal of Hellenic Studies* 57: 147–59. Repr. in Ehrenberg 1965: 83–97.

————. 1943. "An Early Source of Polis-Constitution." *Classical Quarterly* 37: 14–18. Repr. in Ehrenberg 1965: 98–104.

————. 1950. "Origins of Democracy." *Historia* 1: 515–48. Repr. in Ehrenberg 1965: 264–97.

————. 1965. *Polis und Imperium: Beiträge zur Alten Geschichte.* Zurich.

————. 1969. *The Greek State.* 2d ed. London.

————.1973. *From Solon to Socrates: Greek History and Civilization during the Sixth and Fifth Centuries* B.C. 2d ed. London.

Elster, Jon. 1997. "The Market and the Forum: Three Varieties of Political Theory." In Bohman and Rehg 1997: 3–34.

————, ed. 1998. *Deliberative Democracy*. Cambridge.

Euben, J. Peter, John R. Wallach, and Josiah Ober, eds. 1994. *Athenian Political Thought and the Reconstruction of American Democracy*. Ithaca, NY.

Faraguna, M. 2005. "La figura dell'aisymnetes tra realtà storica e teoria politica." In Wallace and Gagarin 2005: 321–38.

Farrar, Cynthia. 1988. *The Origins of Democratic Thinking: The Invention of Politics in Classical Athens*. Cambridge.

————. 1992. "Ancient Greek Political Theory as a Response to Democracy." In Dunn 1992: 17–39.

————. 1996. "Gyges' Ring: Reflections on the Boundaries of Democratic Citizenship." In Sakellariou 1996: 109–36.

Farrar, Cynthia, James Fishkin, Donald Green, et al. Forthcoming. "Experimenting with Deliberative Democracy: Effects on Policy Preferences and Social Choice."

Fehr, Burkhard. 1971. *Orientalische und griechische Gelage*. Bonn.

Ferrill, Arther. 1997. *The Origins of War from the Stone Age to Alexander the Great*. Boulder, CO.

Figueira, T. J. 1985. "Chronological Table: Archaic Megara, 800–500 B.C." In Figueira and Nagy 1985: 261–303.

————. 1991. *Athens and Aigina in the Age of Imperial Colonization*. Baltimore.

Figueira, T. J., and Gregory Nagy, eds. 1985. *Theognis of Megara: Poetry and the Polis*. Baltimore.

Finley, M. I. 1971. *The Ancestral Constitution*. Cambridge. Repr. in Finley 1986.

————. 1976. "The Freedom of the Citizen in the Greek World." *Talanta* 7: 1–23. Repr. in Finley 1982: chap. 5.

————. 1977. *The World of Odysseus*. 2d ed. New York. New ed., introduction by Simon Hornblower, London, 2002.

————. 1982. *Economy and Society in Ancient Greece*. Edited by Brent Shaw and Richard Saller. New York.

————. 1983. *Politics in the Ancient World*. Cambridge.

————. 1985. *Democracy Ancient and Modern*. 2d ed. London.

————. 1986. *The Use and Abuse of History*. 2d ed. London.

Fisher, Nick. 1990. "The Law of *hubris* in Athens." In Cartledge et al. 1990: 123–45.

Fisher, Nick, and Hans van Wees, eds. 1998. *Archaic Greece: New Approaches and New Evidence*. London.

Fishkin, James S. 1991. *Democracy and Deliberation: New Directions for Democratic Reform*. New Haven.

————. 1997. *The Voice of the People: Public Opinion and Democracy*. Expanded paperback ed. New Haven.

Fishkin, James S., and Cynthia Farrar. 2005. "Deliberative Polling: From Experiment to Community Resource." In Gastil and Levine 2005: 68–79.

Fishkin, James S., and Peter Laslett, eds. 2003. *Debating Deliberative Democracy*. Oxford.

Fishkin, James S., and Robert C. Luskin. 1999. "Bringing Deliberation to the Democratic Dialogue: The NIC and Beyond." In McCombs and Reynolds 1999: 3–38.

Flaig, Egon. 1993. "Die spartanische Abstimmung nach der Lautstärke: Überlegungen zu Thukydides 1,87." *Historia* 42: 139–60.

———. 2004. "Der verlorene Gründungsmythos der athenischen Demokratie: Wie der Volksaufstand von 507 v. Chr. vergessen wurde." *Historische Zeitschrift* 279: 35–61.

Fleming, Daniel E. 2004. *Democracy's Ancient Ancestors: Mari and Early Collective Governance.* Cambridge.

Flyvbjerg, Bent. 1998. *Rationality and Power: Democracy in Practice.* Translated by Steven Sampson. Chicago.

Fornara, Charles W. 1966. "The Hoplite Achievement at Psyttaleia." *Journal of Hellenic Studies* 86: 51–54.

———, ed. and trans. 1983. *Archaic Times to the End of the Peloponnesian War.* Translated Documents of Greece and Rome 1. 2d ed. Cambridge.

Fornara, Charles W., and L. J. Samons II. 1991. *Athens from Cleisthenes to Pericles.* Berkeley and Los Angeles.

Forrest, W. G. 1966. *The Emergence of Greek Democracy, 800–400 B.C.* New York.

Forsdyke, Sara. 2000. "Exile, Ostracism, and the Athenian Democracy." *Classical Antiquity* 19: 232–63.

———. 2005. *Exile, Ostracism, and Democracy: The Politics of Expulsion.* Princeton.

Forsythe, Gary. 2005. *A Critical History of Early Rome from Prehistory to the First Punic War.* Berkeley.

Foxhall, Lin. 1997. "A View from the Top: Evaluating the Solonian Property Classes." In Mitchell and Rhodes 1997: 113–36.

Frankel, M. 1878. "Der Attische Heliasteneid." *Hermes* 13: 452–66.

Frost, F. J. 1976. "Tribal Politics and the Civic State." *American Journal of Ancient History* 1: 66–75.

———. 1984. "The Athenian Military before Cleisthenes." *Historia* 33: 283–94.

Fuks, Alexander. 1953. *The Ancestral Constitution: Four Studies in Athenian Party Politics at the End of the 5th Cent. B.C.* Cambridge.

———. 1984. *Social Conflict in Ancient Greece.* Jerusalem and Leiden.

Gabba, Emilio. 1976. *Republican Rome, the Army, and the Allies.* Berkeley and Los Angeles.

Gabrielsen, Vincent. 1994. *Financing the Athenian Fleet: Public Taxation and Social Relations.* Baltimore.

———. 2001. "Naval Warfare: Its Economic and Social Impact on Ancient Greek Cities." In Bekker-Nielsen and Hannestad 2001: 72–89.

Gagarin, Michael. 1986. *Early Greek Law.* Berkeley and Los Angeles.

Galaty, M. L., and W. A. Parkinson, eds. 1999. *Rethinking Mycenaean Palaces.* Los Angeles.

Garland, Robert. 1987. *The Piraeus from the Fifth to the First Century B.C.* Ithaca, NY. Repr. (with some add.), Bristol, 2001.

Gastil, John. 2000. *By Popular Demand: Revitalizing Representative Democracy through Deliberative Elections.* Berkeley and Los Angeles.

Gastil, John, and Peter Levine, eds. 2005. *The Deliberative Democracy Handbook: Strategies for Effective Civic Engagement in the Twenty-First Century.* San Francisco.

Gehrke, Hans-Joachim. 1985. *Stasis: Untersuchungen zu den inneren Kriegen in den griechischen Staaten des 5. und 4. Jh.s v. Chr.* Munich.

————. 1993. "Konflikt und Gesetz: Überlegungen zur frühen Polis." In *Colloquium aus Anlass des 80. Geburtstages von Alfred Heuss*, edited by Jochen Bleicken, 49–67. Kallmünz.

————. 2000. "Verschriftung und Verschriftlichung sozialer Normen im archaischen und klassischen Griechenland." In *La codification des lois dans l'antiquité*, edited by Edmond Lévy, 141–59. Strasbourg.

Georges, Pericles. 1993. "Athenian Democracy and Athenian Empire: Review Article." *International History Review* 15: 84–105.

————. 1994. *Barbarian Asia and the Greek Experience: From the Archaic Period to the Age of Xenophon*. Baltimore.

Giuliani, Luca. 1991. "Euphronios: Ein Maler im Wandel." In *Euphronios der Maler: Exhibition Catalogue, Berlin*, 14–24. Milan.

Gomme, A. W. 1951. "The Working of the Athenian Democracy." *History* 36: 12–28. Repr. in *More Essays in Greek History and Literature*, 177–93. Oxford, 1962. Repr., New York, 1987.

Gomme, A. W., A. Andrewes, and K. J. Dover. 1945–81. *A Historical Commentary on Thucydides*. 5 vols. Oxford.

Gouldner, A. W. 1965. *Enter Plato: Classical Greece and the Origins of Social Theory*. London.

Griffin, Audrey. 1982. *Sikyon*. Oxford.

Griffith, G. T. 1966. "Isegoria in the Assembly at Athens." In *Ancient Society and Institutions: Studies . . . Victor Ehrenberg*, edited by Ernst Badian, 115–38. Oxford.

Griffith, Mark. 1998. "The King and Eye: The Rule of the Father in Greek Tragedy." *Proceedings of the Cambridge Philological Society* 44: 20–84.

Griffiths, Alan. 1989. "Was Kleomenes Mad?" In *Classical Sparta: Techniques behind Her Success*, edited by Anton Powell, 51–78. London.

Gschnitzer, Fritz, ed. 1969. *Zur griechischen Staatskunde*. Wege der Forschung 96. Darmstadt.

————. 1981. *Griechische Sozialgeschichte von der mykenischen Zeit bis zum Ausgang der klassischen Zeit*. Wiesbaden.

————. 1983. "Der Rat in der Volksversammlung: Ein Beitrag des homerischen Epos zur griechischen Verfassungsgeschichte." In *Festschrift R. Muth*, edited by P. Händel and W. Meid, 151–63. Innsbruck.

Gutmann, Amy, and Dennis Thompson. 1996. *Democracy and Disagreement*. Cambridge, MA.

————. 1999. "A Reply to Our Critics." In Macedo 1999: 243–81.

Haas, C. J. 1985. "Athenian Naval Power before Themistokles." *Historia* 34: 29–46.

Habermas, Jürgen. 1990. "Discourse Ethics: Notes on a Program of Philosophical Justification." In *Moral Consciousness and Communicative Action*, translated by Christian Lenhardt and S. W. Nicholsen, 43–115. Cambridge, MA.

Hall, Jonathan. 2000. "Sparta, Lakedaimon, and the Nature of Perioikic Dependency." In *Further Studies in the Ancient Greek Polis*, edited by Pernille Flensted-Jensen et al., 73–80. *Historia* Einzelschriften 138. Stuttgart.

Hall, L. J. H. 1990. "Ephialtes, the Areopagus, and the Thirty." *Classical Quarterly* 40: 319–28.

Hansen, Mogens H. 1980. "Seven Hundred Archai in Classical Athens." *Greek, Roman, and Byzantine Studies* 21: 151–73.

——. 1981. "The Number of Athenian Hoplites in 431." *Symbolae Osloenses* 56: 19–32.

——. 1983a. *The Athenian Ecclesia: A Collection of Articles, 1976–83.* Copenhagen.

——. 1983b. "The Athenian 'Politicians,' 403–322." *Greek, Roman, and Byzantine Studies* 24: 33–55. Repr. in Hansen 1989a: 1–24.

——. 1985. *Demography and Democracy: The Number of Athenian Citizens in the Fourth Century* B.C. Herning, Denmark.

——. 1986. "The Origin of the Term *Demokratia*." *Liverpool Classical Monthly* 11: 35–36.

——. 1987. *The Athenian Assembly in the Age of Demosthenes.* Oxford.

——. 1988. "Athenian Population Losses 431–403 B.C. and the Number of Athenian Citizens in 431 B.C." In *Three Studies in Athenian Demography*, 14–28. Historisk-filosofiske Meddelelser 56. Copenhagen.

——. 1989a. *The Athenian Ecclesia* II: *A Collection of Articles, 1983–89.* Copenhagen.

——. 1989b. "The Athenian Heliaia from Solon to Aristotle." In Hansen 1989a: 219–61.

——. 1989c. "On the Importance of Institutions in an Analysis of Athenian Democracy." In Hansen 1989a: 263–69.

——. 1989d. "Solonian Democracy in Fourth-Century Athens." *Classica et Mediaevalia* 40: 71–99. Repr. in Connor et al. 1990: 71–99.

——. 1989e. *Was Athens a Democracy? Popular Rule, Liberty, and Equality in Ancient and Modern Political Thought.* The Royal Danish Academy of Sciences and Letters, Historisk-filosofiske Meddelelser 59. Copenhagen.

——. 1990. "The Political Powers of the People's Court in Fourth-Century Athens." In *The Greek City from Homer to Alexander*, edited by Oswyn Murray and Simon Price, 215–43. Oxford.

——, ed. 1993. *The Ancient Greek City-State.* Copenhagen.

——. 1994. "The 2500th Anniversary of Cleisthenes' Reforms and the Tradition of Athenian Democracy." In Osborne and Hornblower 1994: 25–37.

——, ed. 1997. *The Polis as an Urban Centre and as a Political Community.* Copenhagen.

——. 1999. *The Athenian Democracy in the Age of Demosthenes.* New, augmented ed. Bristol and Norman, OK.

——. 2002. "Was the Polis a State or a Stateless Society?" In *Even More Studies in the Ancient Greek Polis*, edited by T. H. Nielsen, 17–48. *Historia* Einzelschriften 162. Stuttgart.

——. 2005. *The Tradition of Ancient Greek Democracy and Its Importance for Modern Democracy.* Copenhagen.

Hanson, Victor D., ed. 1991. *Hoplites: The Classical Greek Battle Experience.* London.

——. 1995. *The Other Greeks: The Family Farm and the Agrarian Roots of Western Civilization.* New York.

——. 1996. "Hoplites into Democrats: The Changing Ideology of Athenian Infantry." In Ober and Hedrick 1996: 289–312.

——. 2000. *The Western Way of War: Infantry Battle in Classical Greece.* 2d ed. Berkeley.

——. 2001. "Democratic Warfare, Ancient and Modern." In *War and Democracy: A Comparative Study of the Korean War and the Peloponnesian War*, edited by D. R. McCann and B. S. Strauss, 3–33. Armonk, NY.

Harding, Philip, ed. and trans. 1985. *From the End of the Peloponnesian War to the Battle of Ipsus.* Translated Documents of Greece and Rome 2. Cambridge.

Harris, W. V. 1979. *War and Imperialism in Republican Rome, 327–70 B.C.* Oxford. Paperback repr. with new preface, 1984.

Hart, Gary. 2002. *The Restoration of the Republic.* Oxford.

Harvey, F. D. 1990. "The Sykophant and Sykophancy: Vexatious Redefinition?" In Cartledge et al. 1990: 103–21.

Haubold, Johannes. 2000. *Homer's People: Epic Poetry and Social Formation.* Cambridge.

Havelock, E. A. 1978. *The Greek Concept of Justice: From Its Shadow in Homer to Its Substance in Plato.* Cambridge, MA.

Headlam, James W. 1933. *Election by Lot at Athens.* 2d ed., rev. by D. C. Macgregor. Cambridge.

Hedrick, Charles W., Jr. 1994. "Writing, Reading, and Democracy." In Osborne and Hornblower 1994: 157–74.

———. 1999. "Democracy and the Athenian Epigraphical Habit." *Hesperia* 68: 387–439.

Heilmeyer, W.-D., and Irma Wehgartner, eds. 1992. *Euphronios und seine Zeit.* Berlin.

Herman, Gabriel. 1995. "Honour, Revenge, and the State in Fourth-Century Athens." In Eder 1995b: 43–66.

Herzog, Roman. 1971. *Allgemeine Staatslehre.* Frankfurt am Main.

Hesk, J. P. 2000. *Deception and Democracy in Classical Athens.* Cambridge.

Heubeck, Alfred, Stephanie West, and J. B. Hainsworth. 1988. *A Commentary on Homer's Odyssey.* Vol. I: *Introduction and Books i–viii.* Oxford.

Hibbing, John, and Elizabeth Theiss-Morse. 2002. *Stealth Democracy.* Cambridge.

Hignett, Charles. 1952. *A History of the Athenian Constitution to the End of the Fifth Century B.C.* Oxford.

Hodkinson, Stephen. 1983. "Social Order and the Conflict of Values in Classical Sparta." *Chiron* 13: 239–81.

———. 1993. "Warfare, Wealth, and the Crisis of Spartiate Society." In Rich and Shipley 1993: 146–76.

———. 1997. "The Development of Spartan Society and Institutions in the Archaic Period." In Mitchell and Rhodes 1997: 83–102.

———. 2000. *Property and Wealth in Classical Sparta.* London.

Hoepfner, Wolfram, and Ernst-Ludwig Schwandner. 1994. *Haus und Stadt im klassischen Griechenland.* 2d ed. Munich.

Hölkeskamp, K.-J. 1992. "Written Law in Archaic Greece." *Proceedings of the Cambridge Philological Society* 38: 87–117.

———. 1998. "Parteiungen und politische Willensbildung im demokratischen Athen: Perikles und Thukydides, Sohn des Melesias." *Historische Zeitschrift* 267: 1–27.

———. 1999. *Schiedsrichter, Gesetzgeber und Gesetzgebung im archaischen Griechenland. Historia* Einzelschriften 131. Stuttgart.

Holmes, Stephen. 1979. "Aristippus in and out of Athens." *American Political Science Review* 73: 113–28.

Hornblower, Simon. 1987. *Thucydides.* Baltimore.

———. 1991. *A Commentary on Thucydides.* Vol. I: *Books I–III.* Oxford. New ed. with additions and corrections, 1997.

———. 1992. "Creation and Development of Democratic Institutions in Ancient Greece." In Dunn 1992: 1–16.

———. 1996. *A Commentary on Thucydides*. Vol. II: *Books IV–V.24*. Oxford. Repr. with additions and corrections, 2004.

Humphreys, S. C. 1977/78. "Public and Private Interests in Classical Athens." *Classical Journal* 73: 97–103. Repr. in Humphreys 1993: chap. 2, and in Rhodes 2004: chap. 9.

———. 1978. *Anthropology and the Greeks*. London.

———. 1991. "A Historical Approach to Draco's Law on Homicide." In *Symposion 1990: Vorträge zur griechischen und hellenistischen Rechtsgeschichte*, edited by Michael Gagarin, 17–45. Cologne and Vienna.

———. 1993. *The Family, Women, and Death*. 2d ed. Ann Arbor.

Hunt, Peter. 1997. "Helots at the Battle of Plataea." *Historia* 46: 129–44.

———. 1998. *Slaves, Warfare, and Ideology in the Greek Historians*. Cambridge.

———. 2001. "The Slaves and the Generals of Arginusae." *American Journal of Philology* 122: 359–80.

Hunter, Virginia J. 1994. *Policing Athens: Social Control in the Attic Lawsuits, 420–320 B.C.* Princeton.

Jackson, A. H. 1969. "The Original Purpose of the Delian League." *Historia* 18: 12–15.

Jacobsen, Thorkild. 1970. *Toward the Image of Tammuz*. Cambridge.

Jameson, Michael H. 1998. "Religion in the Athenian Democracy." In Morris and Raaflaub 1998: 171–95.

Jenkins, I. 1994. *The Parthenon Frieze*. London and Austin, TX.

Jones, A. H. M. 1957. *Athenian Democracy*. Oxford. Repr., Baltimore, 1986.

Jones, L. A. 1987. "The Role of Ephialtes in the Rise of Athenian Democracy." *Classical Antiquity* 6: 53–76.

Kallet (-Marx), Lisa. 1993a. *Money, Expense, and Naval Power in Thucydides' History 1–5.24*. Berkeley and Los Angeles.

———. 1993b. "Thucydides 2.45.2 and the Status of War Widows in Periclean Athens." In *Nomodeiktes: Studies Presented to Martin Ostwald*, edited by Ralph Rosen and Joseph Farrell, 133–43. Ann Arbor.

———. 1994a. "Institutions, Ideology, and Political Consciousness in Ancient Greece: Some Recent Books on Athenian Democracy." *Journal of the History of Ideas* 55: 307–35.

———. 1994b. "Money Talks: Rhetor, Demos, and the Resources of the Athenian Empire." In Osborne and Hornblower 1994: 227–51.

———. 1998. "Accounting for Culture in Fifth-Century Athens." In Boedeker and Raaflaub 1998: 43–58, 357–64.

———. 2001. *Money and the Corrosion of Power in Thucydides: The Sicilian Expedition and Its Aftermath*. Berkeley and Los Angeles.

Kapparis, Konstantinos. 1998. "The Law on the Age of the Speakers in the Athenian Assembly." *Rheinisches Museum* 141: 255–59.

Kassel, Rudolf, and Colin Austin, eds. 1984. *Poetae Comici Graeci*. Vol. III.2: *Aristophanes, Testimonia et Fragmenta*. Berlin.

Keane, J. 2003. *Global Civil Society?* Cambridge.

Keaney, John J. 1992. *The Composition of Aristotle's Athenaion Politeia: Observation and Explanation*. New York.

Keaveney, Arthur. 1987. *Rome and the Unification of Italy.* Totowa, NJ.

Kennell, Nigel M. 1995. *The Gymnasium of Virtue: Education and Culture in Ancient Sparta.* Chapel Hill, NC.

Keppie, Lawrence. 1984. *The Making of the Roman Army: From Republic to Empire.* London.

Kilian, Klaus. 1988. "Mycenaeans Up to Date: Trends and Changes in Recent Research." In *Problems in Greek Prehistory,* edited by E. B. French and K. A. Wardle, 115–52. Bristol.

Kinzl, Konrad H. 1977. "Athens: Between Tyranny and Democracy." In *Greece and the Eastern Mediterranean in Ancient History and Prehistory,* edited by Konrad H. Kinzl, 199–223. Berlin.

———. 1978. "Demokratia: Studien zur Frühgeschichte des Begriffs." *Gymnasium* 85: 117–27, 312–26.

———. 1995a. "Athen: Zwischen Tyrannis und Demokratie." Translation of Kinzl 1977. In Kinzl 1995b: 213–47.

———, ed. 1995b. *Demokratia: Der Weg der Griechen zur Demokratie.* Wege der Forschung 657. Darmstadt.

Knight, Jack, and James Johnson. 1997. "What Sort of Equality Does Deliberative Democracy Require?" In Bohman and Rehg 1997: 279–320.

Koenigsberger, H., ed. 1988. *Republiken und Republikanismus im Europa der Frühen Neuzeit.* Munich.

Krentz, Peter. 2002. "Fighting by the Rules: The Invention of the Hoplite Agōn." *Hesperia* 71: 23–39.

Kuran, Timur. 1991. "Now Out of Never: The Element of Surprise in the East European Revolution of 1989." *World Politics* 44: 7–48.

Kurke, Leslie. 1998. "The Cultural Impact of (on) Democracy: Decentering Tragedy." In Morris and Raaflaub 1998: 155–69.

Labarbe, Jules. 1957. *La loi navale de Thémistocle.* Paris.

Laffineur, Robert, and Wolf-Dietrich Niemeier, eds. 1995. *Politeia: Society and State in the Aegean Bronze Age.* Brussels and Austin, TX.

Larsen, J. A. O. 1949. "The Origin and Significance of the Counting of Votes." *Classical Philology* 44: 164–81. Repr. (in German) in Gschnitzer 1969: 184–218.

———. 1966. *Representative Government in Greek and Roman History.* Berkeley and Los Angeles.

Lateiner, Donald. 1989. *The Historical Method of Herodotus.* Toronto.

Lattimore, Richmond. 1951. *The Iliad of Homer, Translated and with an Introduction.* Chicago.

Lavelle, Brian M. 1993. *The Sorrow and the Pity: A Prolegomenon to a History of Athens under the Peisistratids, c. 560–510 B.C. Historia* Einzelschriften 80. Stuttgart.

———. 2000. "Herodotus and the 'Parties' of Attika." *Classica et Mediaevalia* 51: 51–102.

———. 2005. *Fame, Money, and Power: The Rise of Peisistratos and "Democratic" Tyranny of Athens.* Ann Arbor.

Lazenby, J. F. 1996. *The First Punic War.* Stanford.

Legon, R. P. 1981. *Megara: The Political History of a Greek City-State to 336 B.C.* Ithaca, NY.

Lehmann, Gustav Adolf. 1995. "Überlegungen zu den oligarchischen Machtergreifungen im Athen des 4. Jahrhunderts v. Chr." In Eder 1995b: 139–50.

Leib, Ethan J. 2002. "Towards a Practice of Deliberative Democracy: A Proposal for a Popular Branch." *Rutgers Law Journal* 33: 359–455.

Lendon, J. E. 2001. "Voting by Shouting in Sparta." In *Essays in Honor of Gordon Williams*, edited by E. Tylawski and C. Weiss, 169–75. New Haven.

Leppin, Hartmut. 1999. *Thukydides und die Verfassung der Polis: Ein Beitrag zur politischen Ideengeschichte des 5. Jahrhunderts v. Chr.* Berlin.

Lepore, Ettore. 1973. "Problemi dell'organizzazione della chora coloniale." In *Problèmes de la terre en Grèce ancienne*, edited by M. I. Finley, 15–47. Paris and The Hague.

Lévêque, Pierre, and Pierre Vidal-Naquet. 1996. *Cleisthenes the Athenian: An Essay on the Representation of Space and Time in Greek Political Thought from the End of the Sixth Century to the Death of Plato.* Translated by David Ames Curtis. Atlantic Highlands, NJ. Orig. French ed., Paris, 1964.

Lévy, Edmond. 1980. "Cité et citoyen dans la Politique d'Aristote." *Ktema* 5: 223–48.

Lewis, D. M. 1963. "Cleisthenes and Attica." *Historia* 12: 22–40.

———. 1988. "The Tyranny of the Pisistratidae." *CAH* IV²: 287–302.

Lewis, J. D. 1971. "Isegoria at Athens: When Did It Begin?" *Historia* 20: 129–40.

Link, Stefan. 1991. *Landverteilung und sozialer Frieden im archaischen Griechenland. Historia* Einzelschriften 69. Stuttgart.

———. 2000. *Das frühe Sparta: Untersuchungen zur spartanischen Staatsbildung im 7. und 6. Jahrhundert v. Chr.* St. Katharinen.

———. 2003. "Eunomie im Schoss der Rhetra? Zum Verhältnis von Tyrt. Frgm. 14 W und Plut. Lyk. 6,2 und 8." *Göttinger Forum für Altertumswissenschaft* (www.gfa.d-r.de) 6: 141–50.

Lintott, Andrew. 1999. *The Constitution of the Roman Republic.* Oxford.

Lissarrague, François. 1990. *L'autre guerrier: Archers, peltastes, cavaliers dans l'imagerie attique.* Paris and Rome.

List, Christian. 2002. "Two Concepts of Agreement." *PEGS: The Good Society* 11.1: 72–79.

Lohmann, Hans. 1992. "Agriculture and Country Life in Classical Athens." In *Agriculture in Ancient Greece*, edited by Berit Wells, 29–57. Stockholm.

———. 1993. *Atēnē: Forschungen zur Siedlungs- und Wirtschaftsstruktur des klassischen Attika.* Cologne and Vienna.

Lombardo, Stanley, trans. 1997. *Homer, Iliad.* Introduction by Sheila Murnaghan. Indianapolis.

Loraux, Nicole. 1987. "Le lien de la division." *Le Cahier du Collège International de Philosophie* 4: 101–24. Repr. in Loraux 1997: chap. 4.

———. 1991. "Reflections of the Greek City on Unity and Division." In Molho et al. 1991: 33–51.

———. 1997. *La cité divisée.* Paris. English translation, New York, 2002.

Lord, Carnes, and David K. O'Connor, eds. 1991. *Essays on the Foundations of Aristotelian Political Science.* Berkeley and Los Angeles.

Lotze, Detlev. 1990. "Die sogenannte Polis." *Archaeologischer Anzeiger* 33: 237–42.

Luraghi, Nino. 2001a. "Der Erdbebenaufstand und die Entstehung der messenischen Identität." In *Gab es das griechische Wunder? Griechenland zwischen dem Ende des 6. und der Mitte des 5. Jahrhunderts v. Chr.*, edited by Dietrich Papenfuss and Volker M. Strocka, 279–301. Mainz.

————, ed. 2001b. *The Historian's Craft in the Age of Herodotus*. Oxford.

————. 2002. "Helotic Slavery Reconsidered." In *Sparta: Beyond the Mirage*, edited by Anton Powell and Stephen Hodkinson, 227–48. London.

Luraghi, Nino, and Susan Alcock, eds. 2003. *Helots and Their Masters in Laconia and Messenia: Histories, Ideologies, Structures*. Washington, D.C.

Macedo, Stephen, ed. 1999. *Deliberative Politics: Essays on Democracy and Disagreement*. Oxford.

Madison, James. 1788. "Number X." In *The Federalist, or The New Constitution*, edited by Max Beloff, 41–48. Oxford, 1948.

Malkin, Irad. 1987. *Religion and Colonization in Ancient Greece*. Leiden.

————. 1994. "Inside and Outside: Colonisation and the Formation of the Mother City." *Annali di archeologia e storia antica* n.s. 1: 1–9.

Manfredini, Mario, and Luigi Piccirilli, eds. and comms. 1977. *Plutarco, La vita di Solone*. Milan.

Manin, Bernard. 1997. *The Principles of Representative Government*. Cambridge.

Mansbridge, Jane. 1983. *Beyond Adversary Democracy*. Chicago.

————. 1999. "On the Idea That Participation Makes Better Citizens." In *Citizen Competence and Democratic Institutions*, edited by S. Elkin and K. E. Soltan, 219–325. University Park, PA.

Manville, P. Brook. 1990. *The Origins of Citizenship in Ancient Athens*. Princeton.

Manville, P. Brook, and Josiah Ober. 2003a. "Beyond Empowerment: Building a Company of Citizens." *Harvard Business Review* 81.1: 2–7.

————. 2003b. *A Company of Citizens: What the World's First Democracy Teaches Leaders about Creating Great Organizations*. Boston.

Markle, M. M. 1985. "Jury Pay and Assembly Pay at Athens." In Cartledge and Harvey 1985: 265–97. Repr. in Rhodes 2004: chap. 4.

Marr, J. L. 1993. "Ephialtes the Moderate?" *Greece and Rome* 40: 11–19.

Marshall, Thomas H. 1964. "Citizenship and Social Class." In *Class, Citizenship, and Social Development*, 65–122. New York. Repr. from *Citizenship and Social Class, and Other Essays*, 71–134. Cambridge, 1950.

Martin, Jochen. 1974. "Von Kleisthenes zu Ephialtes." *Chiron* 4: 5–42.

McCargar, David J. 1974. "Isagoras, Son of Teisandros, and Isagoras, Eponymous Archon of 508/7: A Case of Mistaken Identity." *Phoenix* 28: 275–81.

McCombs, Maxwell, and Amy Reinolds, eds. 1999. *A Poll with a Human Face: The National Issues Convention Experiment in Political Communication*. New York.

McGlew, J. F. 1993. *Tyranny and Political Culture in Ancient Greece*. Ithaca, NY.

————. 2003. *Citizens on Stage: Comedy and Political Culture in the Athenian Democracy*. Ann Arbor.

Meier, Christian. 1968. "Drei Bemerkungen zur Vor- und Frühgeschichte des Begriffs Demokratie." In *Discordia Concors: Festgabe für Edgar Bonjour*, edited by Marc Sieber, 1: 3–29. Basel and Stuttgart. Repr. in Kinzl 1995b: 125–59.

————. 1970. *Entstehung des Begriffs "Demokratie."* Frankfurt am Main.

————. 1987. "Der Umbruch zur Demokratie in Athen 462/61 v. Chr." In *Epochenschwelle und Epochenbewusstsein*, edited by R. Herzog and R. Koselleck, 353–80. Poetik und Hermeneutik 12. Munich.

————. 1988. *Die politische Kunst der griechischen Tragödie*. Munich. English translation: Meier 1993.

———. 1990. *The Greek Discovery of Politics*. Translated by David McLintock. Cambridge, MA. German ed., Frankfurt am Main, 1980.

———. 1993. *The Political Art of Greek Tragedy*. Translated by Andrew Webber. Baltimore.

———. 1995. "Entstehung und Besonderheit der griechischen Demokratie." In Kinzl 1995b: 248–301.

Meier, Mischa. 1998. *Aristokraten und Damoden: Untersuchungen zur inneren Entwicklung Spartas im 7. Jh. v. Chr. und zur politischen Funktion der Dichtung des Tyrtaios*. Stuttgart.

———. 2002. "Tyrtaios fr. 1^B G/P bzw. fr. 14 G/P (= fr. 4 W) und die grosse Rhetra—kein Zusammenhang?" *Göttinger Forum für Altertumswissenschaft* (www.gfa.d-r.de) 5: 65–87.

Meiggs, Russell. 1972. *The Athenian Empire*. Oxford.

Meiggs, Russell, and David Lewis, eds. 1988. *A Selection of Greek Historical Inscriptions to the End of the Fifth Century B.C.* Rev. ed. Oxford.

Mendelberg, Tali. 2002. "The Deliberative Citizen: Theory and Evidence." In *Political Decision Making, Deliberation, and Participation: Research in Micropolitics*, vol. 6, edited by Michael X. Delli Carpini, Leonie Huddy, and Robert Y. Shapiro, 151–93. Boston.

Meritt, Benjamin D., H. T. Wade-Gery, and Malcolm F. McGregor. 1950. *The Athenian Tribute Lists*. Vol. III. Princeton.

Michelman, Frank. 1997. "How Can the People Ever Make the Laws? A Critique of Deliberative Democracy." In Bohman and Rehg 1997: 145–72.

Millender, Ellen G. 2002. "*Nomos despotēs:* Spartan Obedience and Athenian Lawfulness in Fifth-Century Thought." In *Oikistes: Studies in Constitutions, Colonies, and Military Power in the Ancient World, Offered in Honor of A. J. Graham*, edited by Vanessa B. Gorman and Eric W. Robinson, 33–59. Leiden.

Miller, A. M. 1996. *Greek Lyric: An Anthology in Translation*. Indianapolis.

Millett, Paul. 1984. "Hesiod and His World." *Proceedings of the Cambridge Philological Society* n.s. 30: 84–115.

———. 1989. "Patronage and Its Avoidance in Classical Athens." In *Patronage in Ancient Society*, edited by Andrew Wallace-Hadrill, 15–48. London.

———. 1993. "Warfare, Economy, and Democracy in Classical Athens." In Rich and Shipley 1993: 177–96.

Mills, Sophie. 1997. *Theseus, Tragedy, and the Athenian Empire*. Oxford.

Mitchell, Lynette G., and P. J. Rhodes, eds. 1997. *The Development of the Polis in Archaic Greece*. London.

Mitchell, Stephen. 1996. "Hoplite Warfare in Ancient Greece." In *Battle in Antiquity*, edited by Alan B. Lloyd, 87–105. London and Swansea.

Molho, Anthony, Kurt Raaflaub, and Julia Emlen, eds. 1991. *Athens and Rome, Florence and Venice: City-States in Classical Antiquity and Medieval Italy*. Stuttgart and Ann Arbor.

Molyneux, J. H., ed. 1993. *Literary Responses to Civil Discord*. Nottingham.

Momigliano, Arnaldo. 1973. "Freedom of Speech in Antiquity." In *Dictionary of the History of Ideas*, edited by P. P. Wiener, 2: 252–63. New York.

Moore, J. M. 1975. *Aristotle and Xenophon on Democracy and Oligarchy: Translations with Introductions and Commentary*. Berkeley and Los Angeles. 2d ed., 1983.

Morris, Ian. 1986. "The Use and Abuse of Homer." *Classical Antiquity* 5: 81–138.

———. 1987. *Burial and Ancient Society: The Rise of the Greek City-State.* Cambridge.

———. 1996. "The Strong Principle of Equality and the Archaic Origins of Greek Democracy." In Ober and Hedrick 1996: 19–48.

———. 1997. "Homer and the Iron Age." In Morris and Powell 1997: 535–59.

———. 1998. "Beyond Democracy and Empire: Athenian Art in Context." In Boedeker and Raaflaub 1998: 59–86, 365–71.

———. 2000. *Archaeology as Cultural History: Words and Things in Iron Age Greece.* Malden, MA, and Oxford.

Morris, Ian, and Barry Powell, eds. 1997. *A New Companion to Homer.* Leiden.

Morris, Ian, and Kurt A. Raaflaub, eds. 1998. *Democracy 2500? Questions and Challenges.* Archaeological Institute of America, Colloquia and Conference Papers 2. Dubuque, IA.

Mulgan, R. G. 1991. "Aristotle's Analysis of Oligarchy and Democracy." In *A Companion to Aristotle's Politics,* edited by D. Keyt and F. D. Miller, Jr., 307–22. Oxford.

Murray, Oswyn. 1993. *Early Greece.* 2d ed. Cambridge, MA.

Musti, Domenico. 1985. "Pubblico e privato nella democrazia periclea." *Quaderni urbinati di cultura classica* 49 (n.s. 20.2): 7–17.

Nafissi, Massimo. 1991. *La nascita del kosmos: Studi sulla storia e la società di Sparta.* Naples.

Nagy, Gregory. 1979. *The Best of the Achaeans: Concepts of the Hero in Archaic Greek Poetry.* Baltimore.

———. 1990. *Greek Mythology and Poetics.* Ithaca, NY.

Neils, Jennifer. 2002. *The Parthenon Frieze.* Cambridge.

Niemeier, W.-D., and R. Laffineur, eds. 1995. *Politeia: Society and State in the Aegean Bronze Age.* Aegaeum 12. Liège.

Nippel, Wilfried. 1988. "Bürgerideal und Oligarchie: 'Klassischer Republikanismus' aus althistorischer Sicht." In Koenigsberger 1988: 1–18.

———. 1993. "Macht, Machtkontrolle und Machtentgrenzung: Zu einigen Konzeptionen und ihrer Rezeption in der frühen Neuzeit." In *Bürgerschaft und Herrschaft: Zum Verhältnis von Macht und Demokratie im antiken und neuzeitlichen politischen Denken,* edited by J. Gebhardt and H. Münkler, 58–78. Baden-Baden.

———. 1994. "Ancient & Modern Republicanism." In *The Invention of the Modern Republic,* edited by B. Fontana, 6–26. Cambridge.

Norris, Pippa. 2002. *Democratic Phoenix.* Cambridge.

Nowag, Werner. 1983. *Raub und Beute in der archaischen Zeit der Griechen.* Frankfurt am Main.

Ober, Josiah. 1989. *Mass and Elite in Democratic Athens: Rhetoric, Ideology, and the Power of the People.* Princeton.

———. 1993. "The Athenian Revolution of 508/7 B.C.E.: Violence, Authority, and the Origins of Democracy." In Dougherty and Kurke 1993: 215–32. Repr. in Ober 1996: 32–52.

———. 1996. *The Athenian Revolution: Essays on Ancient Greek Democracy and Political Theory.* Princeton.

———. 1998a. *Political Dissent in Democratic Athens: Intellectual Critics of Popular Rule.* Princeton.

———. 1998b. "Revolution Matters: Democracy as Demotic Action." In Morris and Raaflaub 1998: 67–85.

——. 2004. "Classical Athenian Democracy and Democracy Today: Culture, Knowledge, Power." In *The Promotion of Knowledge: Essays to Mark the Centenary of the British Academy, 1902–2002*, edited by John Morrill, 145–61. London. Repr. in Ober, *Athenian Legacies: Essays on the Politics of Going On Together*, 27–42. Princeton, 2005.

Ober, Josiah, and Charles Hedrick, eds. 1993. *The Birth of Democracy: An Exhibition Celebrating the 2500th Anniversary of Democracy*. Princeton.

——. 1996. *Dēmokratia: A Conversation on Democracies, Ancient and Modern*. Princeton.

Ogilvie, R. M. 1965. *A Commentary on Livy Books 1–5*. Oxford.

Oliva, Pavel. 1971. *Sparta and Her Social Problems*. Amsterdam and Prague.

Oliver, J. Eric. 2001. *Democracy and Suburbia*. Princeton.

O'Neil, James L. 1995. *The Origins and Development of Ancient Greek Democracy*. Lanham, MD.

Orsi, D. P., and Silvana Cagnazzi. 1980. "Lessico politico: Dēmokratia." *Quaderni di storia* 11: 267–314.

Osborne, Robin. 1989. "A Crisis in Archaeological History? The Seventh Century B.C. in Attica." *Annual of the British School at Athens* 84: 297–322.

——. 1996. *Greece in the Making, 1200–479 B.C.* London.

——. 1997. Review of Lohmann 1993. *Gnomon* 69: 243–47.

——. 2007. "When Was the Athenian Democratic Revolution?" In *Rethinking Revolution through Ancient Greece*, edited by Simon Goldhill and Robin Osborne. Cambridge.

Osborne, Robin, and Simon Hornblower, eds. 1994. *Ritual, Finance, Politics: Athenian Democratic Accounts Presented to David Lewis*. Oxford.

Ostwald, Martin. 1969. *Nomos and the Beginnings of the Athenian Democracy*. Oxford.

——. 1986. *From Popular Sovereignty to the Rule of Law*. Berkeley and Los Angeles.

——. 1988. "The Reform of the Athenian State by Cleisthenes." *CAH* IV²: 303–46. Cambridge.

——. 1993. "The Areopagus in the Athenaion Politeia." In Piérart 1993: 139–53.

——. 1996. "Shares and Rights: 'Citizenship' Greek Style and American Style." In Ober and Hedrick 1996: 49–61.

——. 2000. *Oligarchia: The Development of a Constitutional Form in Ancient Greece. Historia* Einzelschriften 144. Stuttgart.

Parker, Victor. 1998. "*Tyrannos:* The Semantics of a Political Concept from Archilochus to Aristotle." *Hermes* 126: 145–72.

——. Forthcoming. "Local Administration in the Kingdom of Pylos and the Classical Polis." In *Acts of the 11th Colloquium Mycenaeum*.

Pateman, Carole. 1970. *Participation in Democratic Theory*. Cambridge.

Patterson, Cynthia. 1981. *Pericles' Citizenship Law of 451–50 B.C.* New York.

Perlman, Shalom. 1967. "Political Leadership in Athens in the Fourth Century B.C." *La parola del passato* 22: 161–76.

Piérart, Marcel, ed. 1993. *Aristote et Athènes*. Paris.

——. 1995. "Du règne des philosophes à la souveraineté des lois." In Eder 1995b: 249–68.

Poliakoff, Michael B. 1987. *Combat Sports in the Ancient World: Competition, Violence, and Culture*. New Haven.

Powis, Jonathan. 1984. *Aristocracy*. New York.

Pritchard, David. 1994. "From Hoplite Republic to Thetic Democracy: The Social Context of the Reforms of Ephialtes." *Ancient History: Resources for Teachers* 24: 111–39.

——. 1999. "The Fractured Imaginary: Popular Thinking on Citizen Soldiers and Warfare in Fifth-Century Athens." PhD diss., Macquarie University, Sydney.

Putnam, Robert D. 2000. *Bowling Alone: The Collapse and Revival of American Community*. New York.

Putnam, Robert D., Robert Leonardi, et al. 1993. *Making Democracy Work: Civic Traditions in Modern Italy*. Princeton.

Raaflaub, Kurt A. 1983. "Democracy, Oligarchy, and the Concept of the 'Free Citizen' in Late Fifth-Century Athens." *Political Theory* 11: 517–44.

——. 1985. *Die Entdeckung der Freiheit*. Vestigia 37. Munich. English ed.: Raaflaub 2004.

——. 1987. "Die Militärreformen des Augustus und die politische Problematik des frühen Prinzipats." In *Saeculum Augustum*, vol. I: *Herrschaft und Gesellschaft*, edited by Gerhard Binder, 246–307. Darmstadt.

——. 1988a. "Athenische Geschichte und mündliche Überlieferung." In *Vergangenheit in mündlicher Überlieferung*, edited by Jürgen von Ungern-Sternberg and Hansjörg Reinau, 197–225. Stuttgart.

——. 1988b. "Politisches Denken im Zeitalter Athens." In *Pipers Handbuch der politischen Ideen*, edited by Iring Fetscher and Herfried Münkler, 1: 273–368. Munich.

——. 1989a. "Die Anfänge des politischen Denkens bei den Griechen." *Historische Zeitschrift* 248: 1–32.

——. 1989b. "Contemporary Perceptions of Democracy in Fifth-Century Athens." *Classica et Mediaevalia* 40: 33–70. Repr. in Connor et al. 1990: 33–70.

——. 1990/91. "I greci scoprono la libertà." *Opus* 9–10: 7–27.

——. 1992. "Politisches Denken und Krise der Polis: Athen im Verfassungskonflikt des späten 5. Jahrhunderts v. Chr." *Historische Zeitschrift* 255: 1–60.

——, ed. 1993a. *Anfänge politischen Denkens in der Antike: Die nahöstlichen Kulturen und die Griechen*. Munich.

——. 1993b. "Homer to Solon: The Rise of the Polis." In Hansen 1993: 41–105.

——. 1994. "Democracy, Power, and Imperialism in Fifth-Century Athens." In Euben et al. 1994: 103–46.

——. 1995. "Einleitung und Bilanz: Kleisthenes, Ephialtes und die Begründung der Demokratie." In Kinzl 1995b: 1–54.

——. 1996a. "Born to be Wolves: Origins of Roman Imperialism." In *Transitions to Empire: Essays in Greco-Roman History, 360–146 B.C., in Honor of E. Badian*, edited by Robert W. Wallace and Edward M. Harris, 273–314. Norman, OK.

——. 1996b. "Equalities and Inequalities in Athenian Democracy." In Ober and Hedrick 1996: 139–74.

——. 1996c. "Solone, la nuova Atene e l'emergere della politica." In Settis 1996–2002: 2.1. 1035–81.

——. 1997a. "Homeric Society." In Morris and Powell 1997: 625–49.

——. 1997b. "Politics and Interstate Relations among Early Greek Poleis: Homer and Beyond." *Antichthon* 31: 1–27.

216   BIBLIOGRAPHY

———. 1997c. "Soldiers, Citizens, and the Evolution of the Greek Polis." In Mitchell and Rhodes 1997: 49–59.

———. 1998a. "A Historian's Headache: How to Read 'Homeric Society'?" In Fisher and van Wees 1998: 169–93.

———. 1998b. "Power in the Hands of the People: Foundations of Athenian Democracy"; "The Thetes and Democracy (A Response to Josiah Ober)." In Morris and Raaflaub 1998: 31–66, 87–103.

———. 1998c. "The Transformation of Athens in the Fifth Century." In Boedeker and Raaflaub 1998: 15–41, 348–57.

———. 1999. "Archaic and Classical Greece." In *War and Society in the Ancient and Medieval Worlds,* edited by Kurt A. Raaflaub and Nathan Rosenstein, 129–61. Washington, D.C.

———. 2000. "Poets, Lawgivers, and the Beginnings of Political Reflection in Archaic Greece." In Rowe and Schofield 2000: 23–59.

———. 2001. "Political Thought, Civic Responsibility, and the Greek Polis." In *Agon, Logos, Polis: The Greek Achievement and Its Aftermath,* edited by Johann P. Arnason and Peter Murphy, 72–117. Stuttgart.

———. 2003. "Stick and Glue: The Function of Tyranny in Fifth-Century Athenian Democracy." In *Popular Tyranny: Sovereignty and Its Discontents in Ancient Greece,* edited by Kathryn A. Morgan, 59–93. Austin, TX.

———. 2004. *The Discovery of Freedom in Ancient Greece.* Translated by Renate Franciscono. Rev. and updated ed. Chicago.

———. 2005a. "Homerische Krieger, Proto-Hopliten und die Polis: Schritte zur Lösung alter Probleme." In *Krieg, Gesellschaft, Institutionen: Beiträge zu einer vergleichenden Kriegsgeschichte,* edited by Burkhard Meissner et al., 229–66. Berlin.

———. 2005b. *Social Struggles in Archaic Rome: New Perspectives on the Conflict of the Orders.* Expanded and updated edition. Malden, MA, and Oxford.

———. 2006. "Athenian and Spartan *eunomia,* or What to Do with Solon's Timocracy?" In Blok and Lardinois 2006: 390–428.

———. 2007. "Warfare and Athenian Society." In Samons 2007: 96–124.

Rae, Douglas. 1999. "Democratic Liberty and Tyrannies of Place." In *Democracy's Edges,* edited by Ian Shapiro and Casiano Hacker-Cordón, 165–92. New Haven.

Raubitschek, A. E., ed. 1949. *Dedications from the Athenian Acropolis.* Cambridge, MA.

Rawson, Elizabeth. 1969. *The Spartan Tradition in European Thought.* Oxford. Repr., 1991.

Redfield, James M. 1994. *Nature and Culture in the Iliad: The Tragedy of Hector.* Expanded ed. Durham, NC.

Rhodes, P. J. 1972. *The Athenian Boule.* Oxford. Repr. with additions and corrections, 1985.

———. 1980. "Athenian Democracy after 403 B.C." *Classical Journal* 75: 305–23.

———. 1981. *A Commentary on the Aristotelian Athenaion Politeia.* Oxford. Repr. with additions and corrections, 1993.

———. 1984. *Aristotle, The Athenian Constitution, Translated with Introduction and Notes.* Harmondsworth.

———. 1985. "Nomothesia in Fourth-Century Athens." *Classical Quarterly* 35: 55–60.

———. 1986. "Political Activity in Classical Athens." *Journal of Hellenic Studies* 106: 132–44. Repr. in Rhodes 2004: chap. 7.

———. 1991. "The Athenian Code of Law, 410–399 B.C." *Journal of Hellenic Studies* 111: 87–100.

———. 1992. "The Delian League to 449 B.C.," "The Athenian Revolution." *CAH* V²: 34–61, 62–95. Cambridge.

———. 1993. "'Alles eitel Gold?' The Sixth and Fifth Centuries in Fourth-Century Athens." In Piérart 1993: 53–64.

———. 1994a. "The Ostracism of Hyperbolos." In Osborne and Hornblower 1994: 85–98.

———. 1994b. "The Polis and the Alternatives." In *CAH* VI²: 565–91. Cambridge.

———. 1998. "How to Study Athenian Democracy." *Polis* 15: 75–82.

———. 2003a. *Ancient Democracy and Modern Ideology.* London.

———. 2003b. "Nothing to Do with Democracy: Athenian Drama and the *polis.*" *Journal of Hellenic Studies* 123: 104–19.

———, ed. 2004. *Athenian Democracy.* Edinburgh.

Rhodes, P. J., and Robin Osborne, eds. 2003. *Greek Historical Inscriptions, 404–323 B.C.* Oxford.

Rich, John, and Graham Shipley, eds. 1993. *War and Society in the Greek World.* London.

Richard, Carl J. 1994. *The Founders and the Classics: Greece, Rome, and the American Enlightenment.* Cambridge, MA.

Richer, Nicolas. 1998. *Les éphores: Etude sur l'histoire et sur l'image de Sparte (VIIIᵉ–IIIᵉ siècle av. J.-C.).* Paris.

Rihll, T. E. 1991. "Ektēmoroi: Partners in Crime?" *Journal of Hellenic Studies* 111: 101–27.

Rijksbaron, A. 1984. *The Syntax and Semantics of the Verb in Classical Greek.* Amsterdam.

Riker, William H. 1982. *Liberalism against Populism.* San Francisco.

Roberts, J. T. 1994. *Athens on Trial: The Anti-Democratic Tradition in Western Thought.* Princeton.

Robinson, Eric W. 1997. *The First Democracies: Early Popular Government outside Athens. Historia* Einzelschriften 107. Stuttgart.

———, ed. 2004. *Ancient Greek Democracy: Readings and Sources.* Cambridge, MA.

———. Forthcoming. *Classical Democracy beyond Athens.*

Roisman, Joseph. 1993. *The General Demosthenes and His Use of Military Surprise.* Stuttgart.

Rorty, Richard. 1982. *Consequences of Pragmatism: Essays, 1972–1980.* Minneapolis.

Rosenbloom, David. 1995. "Myth, History, and Hegemony in Aeschylus." In *History, Tragedy, Theory: Dialogues on Athenian Drama,* edited by Barbara Goff, 91–130. Austin, TX.

Rosenstone, Steven J., and Mark Hansen. 1996. *Mobilization, Participation, and Democracy in America.* New York.

Rosivach, V. J. 1985. "Manning the Athenian Fleet, 433–426 B.C." *American Journal of Ancient History* 10: 41–66.

Roussel, Denis. 1976. *Tribu et cité: Etudes sur les groupes sociaux dans les cités grecques aux époques archaïque et classique.* Paris.

Rowe, Christopher, and Malcolm Schofield, eds. 2000. *The Cambridge History of Greek and Roman Political Thought.* Cambridge.

Rubinstein, Lene. 1998. "The Athenian Political Perception of the *idiōtēs.*" In Cartledge et al. 1998: 125–43.

Ruschenbusch, Eberhard. 1958. "Patrios Politeia: Theseus, Drakon, Solon, und Kleisthenes in Publizistik und Geschichtsschreibung des 5. und 4 Jh. v. Chr." *Historia* 7: 398–424.

———. 1966a. "Ephialtes." *Historia* 15: 369–76.

———. 1966b. *SOLONOS NOMOI: Die Fragmente des solonischen Gesetzeswerkes mit einer Text- und Überlieferungsgeschichte.* Wiesbaden.

———. 1978. *Untersuchungen zu Staat und Politik in Griechenland vom 7.-4. Jh. v. Chr.* Bamberg.

———. 1979. *Athenische Innenpolitik im 5. Jahrhundert v. Chr.: Ideologie oder Pragmatismus?* Bamberg.

———. 1995. "Zur Verfassungsgeschichte Griechenlands." In Kinzl 1995b: 432–45.

Russo, Joseph, Manuel Fernandez-Galiano, and Alfred Heubeck. 1992. *A Commentary on Homer's Odyssey.* Vol. III: *Books xvii–xxiv.* Oxford.

Ruzé, Françoise. 1997. *Délibération et pouvoir dans la cité grecque de Nestor à Socrate.* Paris.

Ryan, F. X. 1994a. "Areopagite Domination and Prytanies." *L'antiquité classique* 63: 251–52.

———. 1994b. "The Original Date of the *demos plethyon* Provisions of *IG* I³ 105." *Journal of Hellenic Studies* 114: 120–34.

———. 2002. "Die Zeugiten und das Archontat." *Revue des études anciennes* 104: 5–9.

Sagan, Eli. 1991. *The Honey and the Hemlock: Democracy and Paranoia in Ancient Athens and Modern America.* New York.

Saïd, Suzanne. 1993. "Le mythe de l'Aréopage avant la Constitution d'Athènes." In Piérart 1993: 155–84.

Ste. Croix, G. E. M. de. 1981. *The Class Struggle in the Ancient Greek World.* Ithaca, NY.

———. 2004. *Athenian Democratic Origins and Other Essays.* Edited by David Harvey and Robert Parker. Oxford.

Sakellariou, Michael B. 1993. "L'idée du juste dans la pensée de Solon." *Comptes-rendus del' Acad. Inscript. & Belles Lettres,* Avril-Juin 1993: 589–601.

———, ed. 1996. *Colloque international: Démocratie athénienne et culture.* Athens.

———. 1998. "Comments on Innovation in the Legislative Procedures of the Athenian Democracy around and after 400 B.C." In *Praktika of the Academy at Athens* (Meeting of Jan. 15, 1998), 67–88. Athens.

Salmon, John. 1997. "Lopping off the Heads? Tyrants, Politics, and the *Polis.*" In Mitchell and Rhodes 1997: 60–73.

Samons, L. J. II. 1998. "Mass, Elite, and Hoplite-Farmer in Greek History." *Arion* 3d ser. 5.3: 100–123.

———. 2000. *Empire of the Owl: Athenian Imperial Finance. Historia* Einzelschriften 142. Stuttgart.

———. 2004. *What's Wrong with Democracy? From Athenian Practice to American Worship.* Berkeley.

———, ed. 2007. *Cambridge Companion to the Age of Pericles.* Cambridge.

Sanders, Lynn. 1997. "Against Deliberation." *Political Theory* 25.3: 347–76.

Sartori, Giovanni. 1987. *The Theory of Democracy Revisited.* Chatham, NJ.

Schemeil, Yves. 1999. *La politique dans l'ancien orient.* Paris.

Schmitt-Pantel, Pauline. 1990. "Sacrificial Meal and Symposion: Two Models of

Civic Institutions in the Archaic City?" In *Sympotica: A Symposium on the Symposion*, edited by Oswyn Murray, 14–33. Oxford.

Schmitz, Winfried. 1988. *Wirtschaftliche Prosperität, soziale Integation und die Seebundpolitik Athens*. Munich.

———. 1999. "Nachbarschaft und Dorfgemeinschaft im archaischen und klassischen Griechenland." *Historische Zeitschrift* 268: 561–97.

———. 2004. *Nachbarschaft und Dorfgemeinschaft im archaischen und klassischen Griechenland*. Berlin.

Schuller, Wolfgang. 1984. "Wirkungen des Ersten Attischen Seebunds auf die Herausbildung der athenischen Demokratie." In J. M. Balcer et al., *Studien zum Attischen Seebund*. Xenia 8, 87–101. Konstanz.

———, ed. 1998. *Politische Theorie und Praxis im Altertum*. Darmstadt.

Schuller, Wolfgang, Wolfram Hoepfner, and Ernst-Ludwig Schwandner, eds. 1989. *Demokratie und Architektur*. Munich.

Schumpeter, Joseph. 1942. *Capitalism, Socialism, and Democracy*. 3d ed., New York, 1957.

Scott-Kilvert, Ian, trans. 1960. *Plutarch, The Rise and Fall of Athens*. Harmondsworth.

Sealey, Raphael. 1974. "The Origins of *demokratia*." *California Studies in Classical Antiquity* 6: 253–94.

———. 1976. *A History of the Greek City States, 700–338 B.C.* Berkeley and Los Angeles.

———. 1987. *The Athenian Republic: Democracy or the Rule of Law?* University Park, PA.

Settis, Salvatore, ed. 1996–2002. *I Greci*. 4 vols. Turin.

Shapiro, H. Alan. 1989. *Art and Cult under the Tyrants in Athens*. Mainz. With a supplement, Mainz, 1995.

Shapiro, Ian. 1999. "Enough of Deliberation: Politics Is about Interests and Power." In Macedo 1999: 28–39.

Shear, T. L., Jr. 1994. "*Isonomous t'Athēnas epoiēsatēn:* The Agora and the Democracy." In *The Archaeology of Athens and Attica under the Democracy*, edited by W. D. E. Coulson et al., 225–48. Oxbow Monograph 37. Oxford.

Shipley, Graham. 1997. "'The Other Lakedaimonians': The Dependent Perioikic *Poleis* of Laconia and Messenia." In Hansen 1997: 189–281. Copenhagen.

Siewert, P. 1982. *Die Trittyen Attikas und die Heeresreform des Kleisthenes*. Vestigia 33. Munich.

Sinclair, T. A., and Trevor J. Saunders, trans. 1981. *Aristotle, The Politics*. Revised ed. Harmondsworth.

Skinner, Quentin. 1990. "The Republican Ideal of Political Liberty." In *Machiavelli and Republicanism*, edited by Gisela Bock, Quentin Skinner, and Maurizio Viroli, 293–308. Cambridge.

Skocpol, Theda. 1999. "How Americans Became Civic"; "Advocates without Members." In *Civic Engagement in American Democracy*, edited by Theda Skocpol and Morris Fiorina, 27–80, 461–510. Washington, D.C.

———. 2003. *Diminished Democracy: From Membership to Management in American Civic Life*. Norman, OK.

Small, David B. 1998. "An Archaeology of Democracy?" In Morris and Raaflaub 1998: 217–27, 241–46.

Snodgrass, Anthony. 1964. *Early Greek Armour and Weapons from the End of the Bronze Age to 600 B.C.* Edinburgh.

———. 1965. "The Hoplite Reform and History." *Journal of Hellenic Studies* 85: 110–22.

———. 1967. *Arms and Armour of the Greeks*. London and Ithaca, NY. New ed., Baltimore 1999.

———. 1971. *The Dark Age of Greece*. Edinburgh. 2d ed., 2000.

———. 1980. *Archaic Greece: The Age of Experiment*. Berkeley and Los Angeles.

———. 1993. "The Hoplite Reform Revisited." *Dialogues d'histoire ancienne* 19: 47–61.

Spahn, Peter. 1990. "Kritik und Legitimation politischer Institutionen in der Sophistik." In *Politische Institutionen im gesellschaftlichen Umbruch*, edited by G. Köhler, K. Lemk, H. Münkler, and M. Walther, 26–40. Opladen.

Stadter, P. A. 1989. *A Commentary on Plutarch's Pericles*. Chapel Hill, NC.

Stahl, Michael. 1987. *Aristokraten und Tyrannen im archaischen Athen*. Stuttgart.

Stanton, Greg R. 1984. "The Tribal Reform of Kleisthenes the Alkmeonid." *Chiron* 14: 1–41.

———. 1990. *Athenian Politics, c. 800–500 B.C.: A Sourcebook*. London.

Starr, Chester G. 1970. *Athenian Coinage, 480–449 B.C.* Oxford.

———. 1977. *The Economic and Social Growth of Early Greece, 800–500 B.C.* Oxford.

Staveley, E. S. 1972. *Greek and Roman Voting and Elections*. London.

Stein-Hölkeskamp, Elke. 1989. *Adelskultur und Polisgesellschaft: Studien zum griechischen Adel in archaischer und klassischer Zeit*. Stuttgart.

———. 1992. "Lebensstil als Selbstdarstellung: Aristokraten beim Symposium." In Heilmeyer and Wehgartner 1992: 39–48.

———. 1996. "Tirannidi e ricerca dell'*eunomia*." In Settis 1996–2002: 2.1. 653–79.

Stokes, Susan. 1998. "Pathologies of Deliberation." In Elster 1998: 123–39.

Strasburger, Hermann. 1954. "Der Einzelne und die Gemeinschaft im Denken der Griechen." *Historische Zeitschrift* 177: 227–48. Repr. in Gschnitzer 1969: 97–122.

Strauss, Barry S. 1986. *Athens after the Peloponnesian War: Class, Faction, and Policy 403–386 B.C.* Ithaca, NY.

———. 1989. "Oikos/Polis: Towards a Theory of Athenian Paternal Ideology, 450–399 B.C." *Classica et Mediaevalia* 40: 101–27. Repr. in Connor et al. 1990: 101–27.

———. 1991. "On Aristotle's Critique of Athenian Democracy." In Lord and O'Connor 1991: 212–33.

———. 1996. "The Athenian Trireme: School of Democracy." In Ober and Hedrick 1996: 313–25.

———. 1998. "Genealogy, Ideology, and Society in Democratic Athens." In Morris and Raaflaub 1998: 141–54.

Stroud, Ronald S. 1968. *Draco's Law on Homicide*. Berkeley and Los Angeles.

———. 1978. "State Documents in Archaic Athens." In *Athens Comes of Age: From Solon to Salamis*, edited by W. A. P. Childs, 20–42. Princeton.

———. 1979. *The Axones and Kyrbeis of Drakon and Solon*. Berkeley and Los Angeles.

Szegedy-Maszak, Andrew. 1978. "Legends of the Greek Lawgivers." *Greek, Roman, and Byzantine Studies* 19: 199–209.

Talbert, Richard. 1988. *Plutarch on Sparta, Translated with Introduction and Notes*. Harmondsworth. 2d expanded ed., 2005.

———. 1989. "The Role of the Helots in the Class Struggle at Sparta." *Historia* 38: 22–40.

Taylor, Lily R. 1966. *Roman Voting Assemblies from the Hannibalic War to the Dictatorship of Caesar.* Ann Arbor.

Thalmann, William G. 1988. "Thersites: Comedy, Scapegoats, and Heroic Ideology in the *Iliad.*" *Transactions of the American Philological Association* 118: 1–28.

Thomas, Carol G. 1995. "The Components of Political Identity in Mycenaean Greece." In Laffineur and Niemeier 1995: 349–64.

Thomas, Carol G., and Craig Conant. 1999. *Citadel to City-State: The Transformation of Greece, 1200–700 B.C.E.* Bloomington and Indianapolis.

Thomas, Rosalind. 1989. *Oral Tradition and Written Record in Classical Athens.* Cambridge.

Thommen, Lukas. 1996. *Lakedaimonion politeia: Die Entstehung der spartanischen Verfassung. Historia* Einzelschriften 103. Stuttgart.

Threlkeld, Simon. 1998. "A Blueprint for Democratic Law-Making: Give Citizen Juries the Final Say." *Social Policy* 28.4: 5–9.

Todd, S. C. 1993. *The Shape of Athenian Law.* Oxford.

Traill, J. S. 1975. *The Political Organization of Attica: A Study of the Demes, Trittyes, and Phylai, and Their Representation in the Athenian Council.* Hesperia Supp. 14. Princeton.

———. 1986. *Demos and Trittys: Epigraphical and Topographical Studies in the Organization of Attica.* Toronto.

Urbinati, Nadia. 2002. *Mill on Democracy: From the Athenian Polis to Representative Government.* Chicago.

Vallet, Georges. 1968. "La cité et son territoire dans les colonies grecques d'occident." In *Atti del VII convegno di studi sulla Magna Grecia,* 67–142. Taranto.

Vellacott, Philip, trans. 1961. *Aeschylus, Prometheus Bound and Other Plays.* Harmondsworth.

Vernant, Jean-Pierre. 1974. "Travail et nature dans la Grèce ancienne." In *Mythe et pensée chez les Grecs,* II: 16–36. Paris.

———. 1982. *The Origins of Greek Thought.* Ithaca, NY. Original French ed., 1962.

———. 1985. "Espace et organisation politique en Grèce ancienne." In *Mythe et pensée chez les Grecs,* 238–60. 3d ed. Paris.

———. 1991. "The Individual within the City-State." In *Mortals and Immortals: Collected Essays,* edited by Froma I. Zeitlin, 318–33. Princeton.

Versnel, Hendrik S. 1995. "Religion and Democracy." In Eder 1995b: 367–87.

Vickery, Kenneth P. 1974. "'Herrenvolk,' Democracy, and Egalitarianism." In *South Africa and the U.S. South. Comparative Studies in Society and History* 16: 309–28.

Vlastos, Gregory. 1953. "Isonomia." *American Journal of Philology* 74: 337–66.

———. 1964. "*Isonomia politikē.*" In *Isonomia: Studien zur Gleichheitsvorstellung im griechischen Denken,* edited by J. Mau and E. G. Schmidt, 1–35. Berlin.

Voutsaki, Sophia, and John Killen, eds. 2001. *Economy and Politics in the Mycenaean Palace States.* Cambridge.

Wade-Gery, H. T. 1933. "Studies in the Structure of Athenian Society: II. The Laws of Kleisthenes." *Classical Quarterly* 27: 17–29.

Wallace, Robert W. 1989. *The Areopagos Council to 307 B.C.* Baltimore.

———. 1998. "Solonian Democracy." In Morris and Raaflaub 1998: 11–29.

———. 1999. "The Structure of Aristotle's Athenaion Politeia." In *Text and Tradition:*

Studies in Greek History and Historiography in Honor of Mortimer Chambers, edited by Ronald Mellor and Lawrence Tritle, 239–56. Claremont, CA.

———. 2005. "'Listening to' the *Archai* in Democratic Athens." In Wallace and Gagarin 2005: 147–57.

———. 2007. "Tyrants, Lawgivers, Sages." In *The Blackwell Companion to the Archaic Greek World,* edited by Kurt A. Raaflaub and Hans van Wees. Malden, MA, and Oxford.

Wallace, Robert W., and Michael Gagarin, eds. 2005. *Symposion 2001: Vorträge zur griechischen und hellenistischen Rechtsgeschichte.* Vienna.

Wallinga, Herman T. 1993. *Ships and Sea-Power before the Great Persian War: The Ancestry of the Ancient Trireme.* Leiden.

Walter, Uwe. 1993. *An der Polis teilhaben: Bürgerstaat und Zugehörigkeit im archaischen Griechenland. Historia* Einzelschriften 82. Stuttgart.

Walzer, Michael. 1999. "Deliberation—and What Else?" In Macedo 1999: 58–69.

Warner, Rex, trans. 1954. *Thucydides, History of the Peloponnesian War.* Harmondsworth. Repr. with introduction and appendices by M. I. Finley, 1972.

Wees, Hans van. 1992. *Status Warriors: War, Violence, and Society in Homer and History.* Amsterdam.

———. 1994. "The Homeric Way of War: The *Iliad* and the Hoplite Phalanx." *Greece and Rome* 41: 1–18, 131–55.

———. 1995. "Politics and the Battlefield: Ideology in Greek Warfare." In *The Greek World,* edited by Anton Powell, 153–78. London.

———. 1997. "Homeric Warfare." In Morris and Powell 1997: 668–93.

———. 1998. "Greeks Bearing Arms: The State, the Leisure Class, and the Display of Weapons in Archaic Greece." In Fisher and van Wees 1998: 333–78.

———. 1999a. "The Mafia of Early Greece: Violent Exploitation in the Seventh and Sixth Centuries B.C." In *Organized Crime in Antiquity,* edited by Keith Hopwood, 1–51. London and Swansea.

———. 1999b. "Tyrtaeus' *Eunomia:* Nothing to Do with the Great Rhetra." In *Sparta: New Perspectives,* edited by Stephen Hodkinson and Anton Powell, 1–41. London and Swansea.

———. 2000. "The Development of the Hoplite Phalanx: Iconography and Reality in the Seventh Century." In *War and Violence in Ancient Greece,* edited by Hans van Wees, 125–66. London and Swansea.

———. 2001. "The Myth of the Middle-Class Army: Military and Social Status in Ancient Athens." In Bekker-Nielsen and Hannestad 2001: 45–71.

———. 2002. "Gute Ordnung ohne Grosse Rhetra—Noch einmal zu Tyrtaios' *Eunomia. Göttinger Forum für Altertumswissenschaft* (www.gfa.d-r.de) 5: 89–103.

———. 2004. *Greek Warfare: Myths and Realities.* London.

———. 2006. "Mass and Elite in Solon's Athens." In Blok and Lardinois 2006: 357–89.

Welwei, K.-W. 1974. *Unfreie im antiken Kriegsdienst.* Vol. I: *Athen und Sparta.* Wiesbaden.

———. 1992. *Athen: Vom neolithischen Siedlungsplatz zur archaischen Grosspolis.* Darmstadt.

———. 1997. "Apella oder Ekklesia? Zur Bezeichnung der spartanischen Volksversammlung." *Rheinisches Museum* 140: 243–49. Repr. in Welwei 2000: 172–79.

————. 2000. *Polis und Arché: Kleine Schriften zu Gesellschafts- und Herrschaftsstrukturen in der griechischen Welt*, edited by Mischa Meier. Stuttgart.

West, Cornel. 1989. *The American Evasion of Philosophy: A Genealogy of Pragmatism.* Madison, WI.

West, M. L. 1974. *Studies in Greek Elegy and Iambus.* Berlin and New York.

————, ed. 1992. *Iambi et elegi Graeci ante Alexandrum cantati.* Vol. II. 2d ed. Oxford.

————. 1993. *Greek Lyric Poetry, Translated with Introduction and Notes.* Oxford.

Whibley, L. 1896. *Greek Oligarchies: Their Character and Organization.* London. Repr., Chicago, 1975.

Whitehead, David. 1977. *The Ideology of the Athenian Metic. Proceedings of the Cambridge Philological Society*, supp. 4. Cambridge.

————. 1981. "The Archaic Athenian *zeugitai*." *Classical Quarterly* 31: 282–86.

————. 1986. *The Demes of Attica, 508/7—ca. 250 B.C.* Princeton.

————. 1991. "Norms of Citizenship in Ancient Greece." In Molho et al. 1991: 135–41.

————. 1993. "[*Ath. Pol.*] 1–41, 42–69: A Tale of Two Polities." In Piérart 1993: 25–38.

Willetts, R. F. 1955. *Aristocratic Society in Ancient Crete.* London.

Wolin, Sheldon. 1994. "Norm and Form: The Constitutionalizing of Democracy." In Euben et al. 1994: 29–59.

————. 1996. "Transgression, Equality, and Voice." In Ober and Hedrick 1996: 63–90.

Wood, E. M. 1994. "Democracy: An Idea of Ambiguous Ancestry." In Euben et al. 1994: 59–80.

————. 1995. "The Demos versus 'We, the People': From Ancient to Modern Conceptions of Citizenship." In Wood, *Democracy against Capitalism: Renewing Historical Materialism*, 204–37. Cambridge.

Woodhead, A. G. 1967. "Isegoria and the Council of 500." *Historia* 16: 129–40.

Woodruff, Paul. 2005. *First Democracy: The Challenge of an Ancient Idea.* New York.

Yunis, Harvey. 1988. "Law, Politics, and the *Graphe Paranomon* in Fourth-Century Athens." *Greek, Roman, and Byzantine Studies* 29: 361–82.

————. 1991. "How Do the People Decide? Thucydides on Periclean Rhetoric and Civic Instruction." *American Journal of Philology* 112: 170–200.

————. 1997. *Taming Democracy: Models of Political Rhetoric in Classical Athens.* Ithaca, NY.

Zelnick-Abramowitz, Rachel. 2000. "Did Patronage Exist in Classical Athens?" *L'antiquité classique* 69: 65–80.

INDEX OF PRIMARY SOURCES

GENERAL INDEX

Morris, Ian, 2, 32, 44, 120
Murray, Oswyn, 39, 61, 71, 78
Mycenae, Mycenaean, 24
Myrmidons, 25–26
Mytilene, 42, 54

navy, 5, 10, 17, 78, 80, 99–101, 117–19,
    121–27, 131–39, 147–48. *See also*
    democracy, naval power and; pay, for
    service in the navy; pentekonter; rowers;
    thetes, militarization of; trireme
Naxos, 43
nomos, 4, 17, 41, 66–67. *See also* law
nomothetēs, nomothetai, 4, 17, 54, 58, 176–77,
    191n16

Ober, Josiah, vii–viii, 2–3, 13–14, 16–18,
    65, 77–78, 137–38, 142, 145–46, 148,
    155, 158, 160, 164, 168n20, 171–73,
    175, 186–87, 189, 190–1n11
Odysseus, 26, 28–33, 47n6, 47n10, 51,
    81n6
officials. *see* public office, officials
oikistēs, 44
oikos, oikoi, 33
"Old Oligarch" (Pseudo-Xenophon), 12,
    20n6, 80, 95, 108, 122, 151–2n18, 162
oligarchy, oligarchs, 10, 15, 43, 50, 52, 54,
    56–57, 60, 64, 67–68, 77, 82n17,
    82n22, 95, 100, 106, 111, 121, 124, 126,
    127, 137, 156, 168–9n21, 176–77, 181,
    190n10. *See also* Four Hundred; Thirty
    Tyrants
Olympia, 42
Olympic games, 36, 49, 51
oral tradition. *See* sources, deriving from oral
    tradition
Orestes, 116
Orsilochos, 26
Orthagoras, 51–52
Osborne, Robin, 14, 16
ostracism, 79, 85, 98–99, 110, 114–15, 140,
    162, 174, 190n5, 192n30
Ostwald, Martin, 61
Otanes, 158–59, 162–63

panhellenic, 22, 24, 32–33, 43, 49, 55
Paros, 78, 135
parrhēsia, 66
Parthenon, 131
participation in government, 3, 5, 11, 18,

22, 24, 32, 41, 43, 80, 89, 119–20, 148,
    150, 161, 165, 166, 179–80, 183, 186–
    88, 190n6, 190–91n11, 191n18,
    191n23, 191–92n25, 192–93n31,
    195nn53–54; based on birth, 14, 35,
    60–61, 63, 66, 119, 141, 144, 178; based
    on social status, 35, 60, 119, 148, 189n1;
    based on wealth, 14, 23–24, 35, 60–61,
    68, 97, 128, 129–31, 140–41, 144, 178;
    by all citizens, 14, 17, 41, 43, 60–61, 63,
    69, 71, 86, 97, 112, 113, 115, 117, 138,
    140–41, 143–46, 148–49, 160–61,
    174–76, 184–85; by commoners, 17, 63,
    160, 184; by the *dēmos*, 22, 71–72, 143,
    145–6; by hoplites, 121; by lower classes,
    140, 144–45, 178; by poor, 115, 117,
    177, 187; by thetes, 61, 63, 73, 77, 80,
    106, 115, 121–22, 131, 132, 136–37,
    139, 140, 143, 147–49, 171, 173–75,
    178; military service and, 23–24, 40–41,
    61–62, 68, 80, 119–36, 139, 143, 144,
    148, 151n14, 190n10; property
    qualification for, 36–7, 43, 61, 106,
    119–20, 128–29, 141, 144, 148, 177,
    189n1, 190n10. *See also* pay, for
    participation in government
patricians, 126
patriotism, patriotic, 90, 98, 145
Patroclus, 25–6
patronage, 33–34, 46, 87, 91, 101n2
Pausanias, 8
pay, for attending the assembly, 17, 177,
    191n16; for attending the council, 140;
    for hoplites, 190n10; for jurors, 80, 109–
    10, 140, 165, 177, 191n16; for participa-
    tion in government, 115, 122, 140, 175,
    179–81, 186–88, 190n10; for public
    officials, 177, 185
for service in the navy, 80, 117–18, 122,
    124, 175, 190n10
for state service, 17, 61, 110, 183, 186
peasants. *See* farming, farms, farmers,
    peasant
Peisistratids, 7, 16, 79, 84, 89, 102n9
Peisistratus, 16, 63, 65, 67, 75–77, 86,
    103n20, 164, 190–91n11
pelatai, 50, 59–60, 63, 72
Peloponnese, Peloponnesians, 99, 125
Peloponnesian War, 5, 6, 17–18, 75, 124,
    133–34, 153n33, 177
penestai, 34

Text   10/12 Baskerville

Display   Baskerville

Compositor   BookMatters, Berkeley